HOUSE OF MOURNING

House of Mourning

A Biocultural History of the Mountain Meadows Massacre

SHANNON A. NOVAK

The University of Utah Press
Salt Lake City

The Defiance House Man colophon is a registered trademark of the University of Utah Press. It is based upon a four-foot-tall, Ancient Puebloan pictograph (late PIII) near Glen Canyon, Utah.

LIBRARY OF CONGRESS CATALOGING-IN-PUBLICATION DATA

Novak, Shannon A.
House of mourning : a biocultural history of the Mountain Meadows Massacre / Shannon A. Novak.
p. cm.
Includes bibliographical references and index.
ISBN 978-1-60781-169-5 (paperback : alk.paper) 1. Mountain Meadows Massacre, Utah, 1857. 2. Mormon pioneers—Utah—Mountain Meadow—Biography. 3. Murder victims—Utah—Mountain Meadow—Biography. 4. Mormon pioneers—Arkansas—Biography. 5. Oral history—Utah—Mountain Meadow. 6. Human remains (Archaeology)—Utah—Mountain Meadow. 7. Historic sites—Utah—Mountain Meadow. 8. Excavations (Archaeology)—Utah—Mountain Meadow. 9. Mountain Meadow (Utah)—Antiquities. I. Title.
F826.N685 2008
979.2'48—dc22 2007047485

It is better to go to the house of mourning,
than to go to the house of feasting:
for that is the end of all men;
and the living will lay it to his heart.

— ECCLESIASTES 7:2

Let sanguine healthy-mindedness do its best with its strange power
of living in the moment and ignoring and forgetting,
still the evil background is really there to be thought of,
and the skull will grin in at the banquet.

— WILLIAM JAMES, *VARIETIES OF RELIGIOUS EXPERIENCE*, 1902

CONTENTS

LIST OF FIGURES

LIST OF TABLES

PREFACE

In the summer of 1999 I had just finished my doctoral dissertation at the University of Utah. What I was working on at the time had nothing to do with the American West, the Ozarks, or the 1850s; in fact, I was writing about a mass grave from a medieval battle in northern England. In early August, however, I got a call from the state archaeologist, Kevin Jones. He said that some human remains had been unearthed in southern Utah and hoped I might analyze them, especially their injury patterns. He paused. "They're from the Mountain Meadows massacre," he said, as if this would explain everything. But the words meant little to me at the time, and I had no idea why Kevin was using hushed tones. Though I had grown up in Utah, I had never been especially interested in the history of the state—only its *pre*history, as reconstructed from the archaeological record and the skeletal remains of its native peoples.

Grave sites in southern Utah, where the dry air and soil can preserve bones for centuries, had been my training grounds. During the 1990s, however, one field project after another had drawn me far away, and always to the east. First, while working at the Smithsonian Museum of Natural History, I studied an antebellum cemetery in the Tidewater region of Virginia. In 1996 I moved to England and undertook the analysis of some forty skeletons from the Battle of Towton (1461), a major engagement in the War of the Roses. From England I went to Croatia with a team of Smithsonian scientists led by Douglas Owsley. Here we excavated mass graves in rural areas that had been recently occupied by Serbian forces. At the same time, we analyzed older remains from the so-called Bleiburg Incident, the execution of thousands of soldiers and civilians by Tito's partisans in the final days of World War II. In what was left of Yugoslavia, I had seen how human remains could be used to rewrite history according to the latest political agenda. By the time I returned to Salt Lake City, however, I thought I had left such "dead-body politics" behind.

Yet the Mountain Meadows massacre would prove to be as complex, compelling, and potentially divisive as any battlefield atrocity or act of ethnic cleansing. Moreover, it involved the kind of religious conflict that Americans tend to associate with the Middle East or the Middle Ages. To this day, people are fighting over what *really* happened at Mountain Meadows. Each major version of the story has tended to attract a distinct following, more or less formally organized, with its own meetings, commemorations, sacred places, and historical narratives. But because these narratives are both emotionally charged and open to interpretation, they are ripe for manipulation by historical "entrepreneurs" (Novak and Rodseth 2006). Such entrepreneurs are eager to discover and control almost any trace of evidence that might favor "their" narrative over rival accounts.

The most powerful kind of evidence tends to be both material and personal—something enduring that vividly reminds us of specific individuals who are gone. Human bones, in particular, constitute this kind of evidence. They can be used to challenge historical accounts, including "official" or scholarly versions as well as the popular variants that circulate in families and communities. What Michel-Rolph Trouillot (1995) calls "credibility testing" requires individuals and factions to reflect on their own versions of history and to confront alternatives held by others. This can be a painful and confusing process, as familiar and comforting assumptions are called into question and a new consensus may be impossible to achieve. Yet physical evidence, to some extent, *bounds* the process, preventing an endless proliferation of competing accounts: "What happened leaves traces, some of which are quite concrete—buildings, dead bodies, censuses, monuments, diaries, political boundaries—that limit the range and significance of any historical narrative" (Trouillot 1995:29). Because dead bodies, furthermore, are not artifacts or texts (at least not in the sense that monuments and diaries are), they appear to be beyond politics and thus capable of closing off debate.

In the case of Mountain Meadows, this significance was suggested to me many times, especially by descendants of the massacre victims. Robert Paul Wilson, for example, a grandson of one of the few surviving children, put it this way: "I held those remains before they were buried. I saw the bullet holes in the bones. Until that point, it was just what people had told you about the massacre, but when you saw the bodies it became real and undeniable." With this kind of power, human bodies are prone to lead "posthumous political lives," reinforcing morality, sanctifying space, even redefining the social order (Verdery 1999:127). One of their most important political functions, as Katherine Verdery suggests, is "to line people up with alternative ancestors and thereby reconfigure the communities" in which people participate.

This process continues to unfold in Utah, in Arkansas, and across the country. Although the bones cannot settle the matter of what *really* happened at Mountain Meadows, or who is to blame, or what is to be done, they are a powerful catalyst for the ongoing process of forming and reforming communities on the basis of historical evidence. Indeed, my own scientific findings, as they circulated in a preliminary report and by word of mouth, were quickly recruited to the task. A bit astonished by this at first, I have come to accept that my efforts, for better or worse, are now part of the story. Perhaps this book will provide people new ways to line up with their ancestors and each other.

Thus what began as a routine project became an extraordinary experience that engaged issues of social identity, history, and power. Perhaps the best way to convey this experience is to acknowledge and thank the many people who made it possible. First and foremost, I express my gratitude to Lars Rodseth. His name appears a number of times in this book, as he has been my partner and collaborator for the past seven years. Lars and I conducted interviews, sifted through archives, and attended meetings, memorials, and family reunions. We tramped through brush to old graveyards and abandoned homesteads and logged hundreds of miles in and around the Boston Mountains. Most important, we learned that it is not necessary to travel to exotic lands to gain anthropological insights. It helps, however, to have countless hours of discussion and debate with a fellow anthropologist and a kindred spirit. This book would be very different, and incomplete, without him.

The initial analysis of the skeletal remains was aided by a dedicated and talented intern, Derinna Kopp. I thank Shane Baker and the students at the Museum of Peoples and Cultures, Brigham Young University, for washing and sorting the bones. Shane graciously provided space and support at the museum for our early work, before the remains were transported to the University of Utah. At Utah, the Department of Anthropology provided lab space, as well as a safe haven when things started to get rough. During the final frantic hours before reinterment, Laurel Casjens of the Utah Museum of Natural History stepped in to take photographs while we performed a kind of analytical triage. The images of bone that you see in this book are the result of Laurel's expert skills as a photographer, even under duress.

The subsequent phase of this research was supported in part by the University Research Council at the University of Utah and the Social Science and Humanities Council at Idaho State University. As an American Fellow of the American Association of University Women, I was given a precious year to devote my undivided attention to archival research, interviews, and writing.

The archival research was facilitated by the staff at Special Collections and Manuscripts, Marriott Library, and at the Family and Church History Department of the Church of Jesus Christ of Latter-day Saints; and by Janet Seegmiller, Special Collections, Gerald R. Sherratt Library, Southern Utah University. In Arkansas I owe special thanks to James Redman, Shirley Pyron at the Carroll County Historical Society, Marilyn Smith at the Boone County Historical Society, and Debra Blackard at the Johnson County Historical Society.

One enjoyable aspect of the research was my interaction with descendant groups who shared family texts, histories, and lore. For their perspectives on southern Utah pioneers and militiamen, provided through correspondence and discussions, I thank Colten Bracken, Robert Briggs, Ralph Hafen, Vern R. Lee, and LeRoy Lee. For perspectives from the Utah Native American community, I am grateful to Lora Tom, chairwoman of the Paiute Indian Tribe of Utah; Forrest S. Cuch, director of the Utah Division of Indian Affairs; Gary Tom, and Nikki Borchardt. I also thank Logan Hebner and Michael Plyler for sharing their experiences in southern Utah and for their photo documentary on the Southern Paiutes.

To descendants of the Arkansans on the 1857 train, I express my fondest thanks and wishes for the future: Garrick Bailey; Charles Rodney Baker; Cherry Baker; Roy Baker Jr.; Joan Bell and the Collins family; James, Jerry, and Phil Bollinger; Burr (Doc) and Ada Fancher; Lynne-Marie Fancher; J. K. Jr. and Genevieve Fancher; Harley and Diann Fancher; Robert Fancher; Scott, Karen, Jake, and Rachel Fancher; Judy Farris; Larry Frye; Francis Gardner; Cheryl Gremaux; Karin Heymer; Charlotte Lucas; Jewell and Shirley Pyron; Elisa Rawlinson; Robert Paul and Elaine Wilson. For providing a home away from home, I thank Burr and Ada Fancher, Scott and Karen Fancher, Harley and Diann Fancher, and Robert Paul and Elaine Wilson. I owe special thanks to Harley for allowing me to use the photograph of his kin on the book cover. Many of you will recognize your contribution to this manuscript, some will not agree with my interpretations, and others will find it curious that the conversations we had do not seem to relate to this book. As you read this, Lars and I will be working on the next one.

I thank the boards and members of the Mountain Meadows Association (MMA), the Mountain Meadows Massacre Descendants (MMMD), and the Mountain Meadows Monument Foundation (MMMF). All these organizations extended their hospitality, but the MMMF has been especially supportive of my research. I should also divulge that I am a member of this foundation and endorse the group's charter to secure federal stewardship of the massacre site.

My thinking was guided by lively discussions at a number of colloquia and conferences. For their prodigious organizational abilities, I thank David Knowlton (American Anthropological Association), Holly Campbell (Tanner Humanities Center at the University of Utah), Melissa Brown (Stanford University), Douglas Seefeldt (Western History Association), and Robert Wall (Society for Historical Archaeology).

For sharing their independent research and incomparable insights, I thank Abbey Burnett (on mortuary practices in the Ozarks), Hugh Stocks (on the publishing history of the Book of Mormon), and Garrick Bailey (on Cherokee history in general and to the Baker family in particular). I owe special thanks to Will Bagley, who generously shared his unpublished manuscripts, archival findings, and extraordinary knowledge of Utah history and the American West.

Portions of the book were previously published in the *Journal of Historical Archaeology* and the *Journal of Anthropological Research*. Critiques of these articles by Douglas Scott, Melissa Connor, and anonymous reviewers contributed to work on this book. I thank all who read and reviewed the manuscript in one form or another: Will Bagley, Everett Bassett, Kelly Dixon, Meredith Ellis, George Gill, Mallorie Hatch, Scott M. Matheson Jr., David Schwendiman, and Gerald Smith. My editors at the University of Utah Press, Jeff Grathwohl, Peter DeLafosse, and Glenda Cotter, were patient and supportive. In addition, Kim Vivier provided valuable editorial assistance. In Arkansas, Rachael Fancher and Kris Hollingsworth were kind enough to take some last-minute photographs of the Carleton Monument replica at the Carrollton Lodge.

At Syracuse University I have been welcomed, encouraged, and inspired by a wonderful group of colleagues: Douglas Armstrong, Hans Buechler, John Burdick, Peter Castro, Christopher DeCorse, Michael Freedman, William Kelleher, Deborah Pellow, Robert Rubinstein, Maureen Schwartz, Theresa Singleton, John Townsend, Cecilia Van Hollen, and Susan Wadley. Their collegiality and support provided the haven in which I finished this book. Also at Syracuse, David Broda prepared the black-and-white photographs for publication, and Joseph W. Stall produced the figures and maps.

Finally, to my own kith and kin—Charles E. Puff; Andrea, Lance, and Jordan Newberry; Sherry and Ian Burton; Gerald Smith; and Everett and Maeve Bassett—I extend my deepest gratitude for your love and patience. My mother, Nancy Smith Puff, passed away before the book was finished, but she encouraged and supported me throughout this often tumultuous project. In the end, she urged me to tell the truth as best I could. I hope she would be pleased.

HOUSE OF MOURNING

INTRODUCTION:

PERSPECTIVES

Horror and fatality have been stalking abroad in all ages.
Why then give a date to this story I have to tell?

— Edgar Allan Poe, "Metzengerstein," 1832

It is precisely through the process of making a power situation appear a fact
in the nature of the world that traditional authority works.

— Maurice Bloch, "Symbols, Song, Dance, and Features of Articulation," 1974

Right off U.S. Highway 412, in Carroll County, Arkansas, is the old county seat of Carrollton (Figure I.1). Now just a crossroads in the southern Ozarks, the town is about equidistant from Branson, Missouri (dinner-theater mecca for families and retirees) and Bentonville, Arkansas (the world headquarters of Wal-Mart). Most of Carrollton burned in the Civil War and was never rebuilt. Aside from some overgrown foundations, the only Victorian structure for miles around is the Carrollton Lodge. Even this is not the original building, known as the "old Yell Lodge," but a post–Civil War replica. Having served as a Masonic temple and the headquarters of the VFW, it now houses a small museum as well. The lodge is set off from the road, and through the treetops you might glimpse a little white bell tower. If you slow down, though, and turn up the hill, you'll see the building: a clapboard hall with seventeen windows, meticulously restored, overlooking a perfect country graveyard (Figure I.2).

Most of the graves are marked with simple headstones, some with Masonic symbols or military insignia. The family names are English, Scottish,

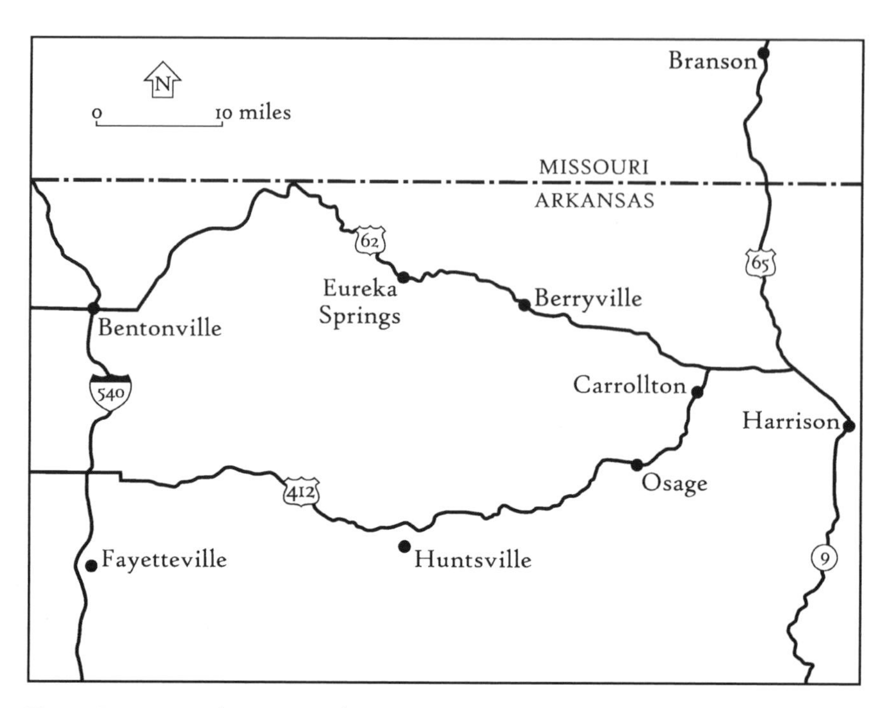

Figure I.1. ◆ Northwestern Arkansas, c. 2000.

Figure I.2. ◆ Restored Carrollton Lodge, Carrollton, Arkansas. Photo by Shannon A. Novak.

or Scotch-Irish, with a few French or German derivatives. Occasionally, a small Confederate flag is posted in the grass.

And then there is the cross.

Between the lodge and the graveyard, anchored in a mound of stones, is a massive cedar cross, standing sixteen feet high (Figure I.3). Although a roadside cross is hardly an unusual sight in the South, this one is different. Unpainted and hand-hewn, the iron-red surface bears an inscription of nine cryptic words:

VENGEANCE IS MINE: I WILL REPAY, SAITH THE LORD

The New Testament phrase, Romans 12:19, hovers in the air. (The following verse reads: "Therefore if your enemy hungers, feed him; if he thirsts, give him a drink; for in so doing you will heap coals of fire on his head.") The cross faces west. A few feet away a large cedar-slat sign provides the interpretation:

THE MOUNTAIN MEADOWS MASSACRE

IN EARLY 1857 A LARGE WAGON TRAIN KNOWN AS THE FANCHER-BAKER TRAIN LEFT CARAVAN SPRING (SOUTH OF HARRISON) AND HEADED FOR CALIFORNIA. THEY CAMPED AT THIS SITE ENROUTE TO INTERCEPT THE CHEROKEE TRAIL AT THE GRAND SALINE IN INDIAN TERRITORY. MONTHS LATER, THE WAGON TRAIN CAME UNDER SIEGE BY THE MORMONS AND INDIANS IN SOUTHWEST UTAH AT A PLACE CALLED MOUNTAIN MEADOWS. ON SEPTEMBER 11, 1857 THE MORMONS BRUTALLY MURDERED 121 MEN, WOMEN, AND CHILDREN AFTER ASSURING THEIR PROTECTION. ONLY 17 SMALL CHILDREN WERE SPARED FROM THE MASSACRE.

THE DEAD WERE LEFT EXPOSED TO THE ELEMENTS UNTIL 18 MONTHS LATER, WHEN U.S. ARMY TROOPS LED BY MAJOR JAMES H. CARLETON BURIED THE REMAINS IN SEVERAL MASS GRAVES. A CROSS AND STONE WERE PLACED OVER ONE SUCH GRAVESITE CONTAINING 34 OF THE VICTIMS. THIS IS A SCALED REPLICA OF CARLETON'S ORIGINAL CAIRN.

THE SURVIVING CHILDREN WERE BROUGHT BACK TO ARKANSAS AND SPENT THEIR FIRST NIGHT AT THE SITE OF THE OLD YELL LODGE. ON SEPTEMBER 25, 1859, THE ORPHANED CHILDREN WERE REUNITED WITH RELATIVES IN THE CARROLLTON TOWN SQUARE.

IN 1861, BRIGHAM YOUNG AND HIS ENTOURAGE VISITED THE UTAH GRAVESITE. HE READ THE WORDS ON THE CROSS AND SAID, "VENGEANCE IS MINE AND I HAVE TAKEN A LITTLE." THEN YOUNG RAISED HIS ARM IN THE DANITE SIGNAL OF THE SQUARE AND WITHIN MINUTES HIS FOLLOWERS COMPLETELY DESTROYED THE MONUMENT. PRESENTLY, THE LDS CHURCH OWNS THE GRAVE AT MOUNTAIN MEADOWS IN UTAH. THEY CONTROL THE INTERPRETATION OF THE MASSACRE. THIS REPLICA OF THE ORIGINAL GRAVE MARKER ALLOWS ARKANSAS RELATIVES TO MEMORIALIZE THE VICTIMS AND INTERPRET THE MASSACRE IN THEIR HOME STATE.

SPONSOR: MOUNTAIN MEADOWS MONUMENT FOUNDATION, INC.

Though clear and informative, the text remains enigmatic. Whatever light has been shed on the matter is eclipsed by one great mystery, the question of motive: why would "the Mormons" besiege and slaughter an apparently innocent company of men, women, and children? As members of the Church of Jesus Christ of Latter-day Saints (LDS)—a truly American religious tradition, founded in central New York in 1830—Mormons are famous for their temples and genealogy centers, their earnest young missionaries and conservative family values. So why would Mormons kill other Americans, especially in a brutal and treacherous manner?

The question has been asked many times since 1857, and a range of answers have been proposed in both popular and scholarly contexts. The most famous attempt at a comprehensive explanation is *The Mountain Meadows Massacre,* by Utah historian Juanita Brooks. Originally published in 1950, the book appeared in a new edition in 1962 and remained the standard source on the subject for forty years. Only in 2002, with the publication of Will Bagley's *Blood of the Prophets,* did a new generation of historians take up the study of Mountain Meadows. Bagley's book was quickly followed by three popular, journalistic accounts: *American Massacre* (Denton 2003), *Under the Banner of Heaven* (Krakauer 2003), and *Oh What a Slaughter* (McMurtry 2005). By now, it may seem as if there is little more to be said about this strange event.

Yet there is more—a great deal more—if we situate the massacre in a wider historical context and approach it not as a morality tale but as a busy intersection of social and cultural forces in antebellum America. If we are successful, we will avoid two closely related fallacies that crop up repeatedly in the Mountain Meadows literature. First, the story of the massacre almost inevitably supports a moral judgment that can be used to vilify (or

Figure I.3. ✦ Carleton cairn replica, Carrollton, Arkansas. Photo by Kris Hollingsworth.

to glorify) someone in the present. Second, and even more consistently, the story is artificially bounded by the western setting, as if the Arkansas emigrants first came into being when they entered the Utah Territory and took up their assigned role in Mormon history. Each of these fallacies deserves closer scrutiny.

For a century and a half, the massacre has been invoked to make a moral point in the present. What happened at Mountain Meadows is perennially cited as evidence of the perfidy or outright wickedness of the Mormon Church (e.g., Beadle 1870; Gibbs 1910; Tanner and Tanner 1987 [1964]; Wood 2004). At the same time, Mormon apologists have put their own spin on the story. These authors often take the opportunity to emphasize the suffering of the Saints, both before and after the massacre. Thus what happened at Mountain Meadows is explained, if not excused, in terms of the prior persecution of Mormons in Missouri and Illinois (e.g., Brooks 1962:57–58; Arrington and Bitton 1992:167; Alexander 2003:133). In the late nineteenth century one Utah history textbook went so far as to include the Mormons among the *victims* of Mountain Meadows: "That massacre was not only a crime against the Arkansas emigrants, but a crime against Utah, against the Latter-day Saints, who have borne for years the odium of a deed for which they were in no way responsible, and which they have never ceased to regard as a public calamity" (Whitney 1892:614–615).

This brings us to the second fallacy, the tendency to frame the story in narrow, parochial terms. In the existing literature, all eyes have focused on Utah. Invariably, what happened at Mountain Meadows is recounted from a western point of view; in the extreme case, the massacre is treated as little more than a footnote to Mormon history (e.g., Arrington and Bitton 1992: 167–168, Alexander 2003:129–134). The Utah perspective is shared by all the major works on the subject, even those that explicitly charge the Mormon leadership with a "monumental crime" (Wise 1976). Thus the very best historical studies (Bigler 1998; Bagley 2002) and the most provocative exposés (Denton 2003; Krakauer 2003) have this much in common: they tell us a great deal about the killers and rather little about those who were killed.

This book aims to redress the balance. It shifts attention from the question of motive to the question of loss. Who were the victims at Mountain Meadows? What might have been, had they lived and completed their journey? For once, the story of the massacre will begin in the South rather than the West; among Baptists and Methodists rather than Mormons; and with the rush to the goldfields rather than the exodus to Zion. Unlike other studies of Mountain Meadows, this one is mostly about unheralded lives in the hills rather than infamous deaths in the desert.

Unexpected Guests

The cross and cairn at the Carrollton Lodge were erected in summer 2005 and dedicated in mid-September. Among the participants in the somber ceremony were a Baptist minister, an Arkansas state representative, and several "down-the-line" descendants of the massacre victims. Taking notes on the periphery was a young employee of the LDS Church—a protégé, it was rumored, of the official church historians who were writing their own, "definitive" account of Mountain Meadows (Walker et al. in press). The dedication culminated in a simple but powerful ritual, a public reading of the names and stories of the seventeen massacre survivors. In honor of each survivor, a family representative approached the cross and placed a granite boulder on the cairn. The granite came not from the surrounding hills of the Boston Mountains but from the massacre site in southern Utah.

This site, it should be noted, has changed dramatically since 1857. What had been a lush, spring-fed meadow is now brambly and brown. Legend has it that after the massacre, nothing would grow there. In reality, Mountain Meadows has been overgrazed for generations. Torrential rains in the winter of 1861–1862 washed out the topsoil and cut deep ravines that disrupted the water table (Bagley 2002:250). At the same time, the land was apportioned into private farms and ranches, set off from one another by barbed-wire fences. In 1965 landowner Ezra Lytle transferred two and a half crucial acres to the LDS Church (Seefeldt 2001:304). This plot contained the Carleton gravesite and a small memorial that had been erected in 1932. The original and much grander cairn of 1859 was long gone, and the grave was dilapidated and overgrown.

In 1999 the church set out to renovate the site. Archaeologists from Brigham Young University (BYU) were commissioned to survey the area, monitor excavation, and prevent any disturbance of the suspected graves below (Baker et al. 2003). Despite these precautions, on August 3, 1999, a construction backhoe penetrated a mass grave and disinterred thousands of human bones. On August 6 Utah state archaeologist Kevin Jones issued a permit to excavate the historic site. The antiquities permit (U-99-0427f,p[e]) required scientific analysis of the human remains.

At the request of BYU and the state archaeologist, I initiated such analysis on August 10, 1999. Reinterment was originally scheduled for September 10, 1999, in conjunction with the dedication of the new grave site memorial. Sorting, reconstruction, and documentation of the cranial material proved to be extremely time-consuming. To allow more time for the analysis, Kevin Jones proposed a compromise, according to which most of the bones would be buried at the rededication while the skulls and cranial fragments would remain in the lab until the following spring. On September 8, however, this agreement was nullified. On the authority of Governor Mike Leavitt, the archaeological permit was rewritten so that the human remains could be reburied at once (Smith 2000). This new arrangement allowed just twenty-four hours to complete the analysis. On the morning of September 10, exactly one month after the study had begun, the remains were turned over to Brigham Young University and interred later that day beneath an impressive new monument at Mountain Meadows (Figure I.4).

Though it has been described as a re-creation of Carleton's 1859 cairn, this marker is rather obviously truncated. In particular, it omits "the inscribed cedar cross and the biblical quotation that provoked Brigham Young to destroy the original monument in 1861" (Bagley 2002:372). What is left is a simple but imposing cairn, some ten or twelve feet tall, on a sandstone platform enclosed by a wrought-iron fence. On entering the gate, visitors meet with the first of two engravings set into the cobbled wall:

Figure I.4. • Grave site memorial at Mountain Meadows, Utah. Photo by Shannon A. Novak.

MOUNTAIN MEADOWS MASSACRE GRAVE SITE MEMORIAL
Built and maintained by
The Church of Jesus Christ of Latter-day Saints
Out of respect for those who died and were buried here
and in the surrounding area
following the massacre of 1857.
Dedicated 11 September 1999

Circling to the back wall, one arrives at a much longer text. Here, under the heading "MEMORIALS," are six entries describing in some detail the historical markers that have been erected since 1859 in both Utah and Arkansas. This plaque is a "meta-marker," as Seefeldt puts it (2001:325)—a kind of memorial to memorials. Not surprisingly, the final entry is self-referential:

> 1999. Under the direction of President Gordon B. Hinckley and with the cooperation of the Mountain Meadows Association and others, The Church of Jesus Christ of Latter-day Saints replaced the 1932 wall and installed the present Grave Site Memorial. President Hinckley dedicated the memorial on 11 September 1999.

Below is a little blank space on the plaque, enough perhaps for two more lines of text. Was it left there deliberately, just in case another memorial might be added to the list? As it stands, however, the 1999 entry seems to have the final word on the subject, proclaiming this to be the definitive monument to Mountain Meadows.

Six years later, however, a load of Utah granite was transported to Arkansas and carefully placed on another cairn, back in the shadow of a cedar cross. The memorial at the Carrollton Lodge was established by and for "Arkansas relatives," who were thus enabled "to memorialize the victims and interpret the massacre in their home state." At the same time, the grave site in Utah has been effectively relinquished to the LDS Church. Thus while the bones of the victims have been sealed within a memorial to memorials, the most accurate replica of the original tomb is entirely devoid of human remains.

Fragmentary Records

Any historical account of Mountain Meadows must rely heavily on some rather dubious sources: the testimony of known killers,[1] the reconstructed memories of seventeen young children, and reams of propaganda that have been generated by Mormon apologists and their often fanatical opponents. No journals or logs are known to have been recovered from the wagon train (though rumors persist that Alexander Fancher's diary was stolen by the killers and perhaps secretly stored in the LDS archives). Yet a great many public records, including census and mortality schedules, legal documents, and family histories, provide evidence of the victims' lives both in the Ozarks and on the trail.

In writing this book, I drew on many sources, including the sample of human remains unearthed in 1999. If all the lines of evidence could be followed out and woven together, a detailed picture would emerge of each of the victims at Mountain Meadows. We would know, for example, how a young mother had died—and lived: how she had arrived at the Meadows, whom she had known and loved on the train, and the kind of community she had left behind. We would have some sense of her life in the Ozarks and of her ancestors' lives in the Appalachians or the Carolinas. We would know something of her dreams as well, and of what she had hoped for her children.

Yet such a picture was impossible to attain, even for a single individual. All the available sources had severe limitations and often provided only fragmentary clues about any given rider on the train. Some riders, especially the hired hands, were nearly impossible to track in the archival records; only through family histories was I able to learn anything about them. The easiest to follow were household heads with substantial holdings, especially those whose offspring had married and were resident on adjacent farms. As a result, eleven extended families, including yeoman farmers, a few prosperous slaveholders, and one self-described merchant, provide the bulk of the documentary evidence for this book. About 70 percent of the victims at Mountain Meadows were members (by birth or by marriage) of these eleven kin groups. Most of the remainder, at least thirty of the victims, seem to have been neighbors, employees, or distant kin of what I call the "core" families.

The mass grave contained an even smaller sample—twenty-eight men, women, and children, or about a quarter of those who died at Mountain Meadows. The skeletal remains were fragmented and commingled, presenting a jigsaw puzzle of more than 2,600 pieces (Novak and Kopp 2003:90). In the limited time available for the analysis, I was able to sort all the cranial remains and partially reconstruct eighteen skulls. The postcranial remains (those below the head) and most of the teeth were not sorted into individual skeletons but could be grouped only according to age and sex characteristics.[2]

Under these circumstances, the temptation is to divide the population into aggregate categories—young versus old, male versus female, diseased versus healthy—and abandon the effort to reconstruct individuals. In dealing with the skeletal sample, I have often used such categories for analytical purposes. At the same time, I have tried to remember that these bones were once inside bodies and that each of the bodies was shaped by a unique sequence of biographical events. As archaeologist Joanna Sofaer (2006:45) argues, "The body does not merely reflect life but was once life itself. Osteoarchaeology thus becomes a way of knowing about the body that allows for the life experiences of people by exploring the form, pattern and origin of osseous changes, understanding these in terms of the skeletal consequences of what people did and how they lived." The human skeleton, in short, "embodies the history of social relationships and is an artifact of those relationships" (Sofaer 2006:78). The victims at Mountain Meadows lived within specific families and communities, which were in turn embedded in a young and rapidly changing nation. At this level my analysis is concerned with the broad social and political ecology of antebellum America. This approach follows from the conviction that a case study, if it is well chosen, can shed light on a vast sociological landscape (Flyvbjerg 2001).

Thus the bodies that converged, and the corpses that were left, at Mountain Meadows may be rich with information, but only if the right questions are posed and vigorously pursued. What were the social and economic factors that brought this particular group together, first in the Ozarks and then on the overland trail? How was daily life managed on a highland farm or a wagon train by men, women, and their extended kin? How was it that their deaths—and bodies—became symbolic capital that was used locally and nationally in political debates? And ultimately, how were such social, political, and biological processes manifested in human bones?

STREAMS

What say you to a general move to a more southern latitude?
I want to go where I can make more money....
What say you to Florida, —or Kentuckie; or Tenesee; or Missouri?
I will go any where so that we may all settle together.

— Francis Eppes to Nicholas P. Trist, 1826

The streams of the Ozarks are distinctive.
Though they deeply entrench the plateau surface,
they follow meandering courses.

— Milton D. Rafferty, *The Ozarks*, 2001

First there were mountains, rivers, and valleys. Then came the frontiers, borders, and names. Because physical geography precedes and ultimately influences the social and political landscape, our discussion of the wagon train must begin with the Ozark Plateau, an area of some 40,000 square miles that spans parts of Missouri, Oklahoma, and Arkansas. The geopolitics of these states would come to shape the movement and settlement of peoples in their borders, but the physical environment would also profoundly condition the history of the region.

The Ozark Plateau is delineated by four major river systems: the Missouri to the north, the Black to the east, the Arkansas to the south, and the Grand to the west (Figure 1.1). The area within these boundaries is broadly characterized by good soils in the stream valleys; steep slopes with great relief; an extensive water network with many swiftly flowing streams; expanses of oak, hickory, and pine forests; a preponderance of dolomite and cherts; and an extensive array of sinkholes, caves, and springs (Rafferty 2001:1). Only two regions in the Ozarks can be considered mountainous: the St.

Figure 1.1. ◆ The Ozarks delineated by rivers. Adapted from Rafferty 2001.

Francois range in eastern Missouri and the Boston Mountains in northern Arkansas.

The Boston range lies on the southern edge of the Ozarks and contains some of the greatest relief and steepest topography in the region. Running roughly east to west, these mountains average 1,200 feet in elevation, with the highest peaks in the west. They are young in geological terms, composed of shale, sandstone, and limestone, with smooth wooded slopes and only a few patches of arable bottomland. The climate is technically known as

French Canadians set out for the Arkansas River or the post itself, they referred to their destination with the abbreviated name Aux-Arcs (Sauer 1920: 5 n. 1; Morrow 1996:5), from which derived the English name Ozarks. The location of the Arkansas Post tended to meander across the landscape, oftentimes disappearing completely along with the shifting floodplain of the Mississippi, Arkansas, and White rivers.

This region would be incorporated into "Louisiana," the vast colony claimed by the French in 1699 and taken over by Spain some seventy years later. In reality, however, Arkansas was too remote to be governed effectively by distant powers. For their security and well-being, the European residents found it necessary to forge alliances with local Native Americans (Whayne 2005). As a result, over the course of the eighteenth century the Arkansas Post became a focal point for European-Indian contact. Though the white settlers established forts and garrisons, they have been described as "immigrants rather than invaders" (Arnold 2002:62): "French and Spanish claims to sovereignty over Arkansas were basically hollow: The Indians did not consider themselves subjects, and the Europeans did not even pretend that they were. This was hegemony writ small." The French in particular intermarried with the Quapaw, and a symbiotic relationship, both cultural and economic, grew up within the settlement. The Spanish had less intimate ties with the Quapaw and hostile relations with the Osage, who harassed European hunters on the upper Arkansas River (Din 1995).

With the rise of Napoleon and the steep decline of Spanish power, a secret treaty signed in 1800 returned Louisiana to France. Three years later, however, the colony was sold to the United States as part of Napoleon's strategy to retain U.S. support against the British. Americans traveling to the Arkansas Post were startled to find that "most of its residents were of French-Indian blood or had very close collateral Indian kin" and that Europeans and natives had lived and worked together for nearly 120 years (Arnold 2002:56). Such a symbiotic relationship was often surprising to white Americans, and there was a growing call for Indians to be geographically separated from "civilization." The only question was where to draw the divide; the proposed boundary had shifted with the interests of the British Empire and now the American Republic (Meinig 1993:79). Having negotiated the Louisiana Purchase, Thomas Jefferson acknowledged in 1803 that this vast new territory might be the "means of tempting all our Indians on the East side of the Mississippi to remove to the West" (Jefferson 1984:249, see also Bolton 2005).

At the same time, Jefferson held out hope that whites and Native Americans might develop a symbiotic relationship and perhaps even hybridize through intermarriage. Addressing a contingent of northwestern chiefs in

1809, he proclaimed, "You will be as we are: you will become one people with us; your blood will mix with ours: and will spread with ours over this great island" (1984:234). Jefferson resisted the separatist position by encouraging a rapid accommodation of Indians to a rural American farming pattern. He argued that a government allotment of 640 acres per head of household, plus more acreage for each child, would provide each Indian family with a fair share of land to cultivate. This would reduce the need for large hunting territories, and the "excess" land now used by the Indians could be released to the growing number of white settlers in the East.

This strategy of appeasement was short-lived, however, as many of the prime farming and mining lands occupied by the Cherokee, Chickasaws, Choctaws, Creeks, and Seminoles were coveted by the emerging southern states. Brazen white settlers continued to stream west, disregarding treaty lines and occupying Indians lands. As confrontations became increasingly violent, calls grew for Indian removal, with the Mississippi River serving as the line of separation. Jefferson now supported relocation of the eastern tribes to the southern Ozarks, "the higher up the better," so as to avoid further confrontations (Sheehan 1973).

Relocation would have a devastating impact on the Osage, Quapaw, and other indigenous peoples who had settled the Arkansas plateau prior to European contact (Key 2005). The Osage, distant relatives of the Quapaw, claimed hunting rights in the highlands of northwest Arkansas and had a long history of aggressively defending this region against encroachment by other Native Americans, the French, the Spanish, and Anglo-Americans (Mathews 1961; Bailey 1973; Duval 2005). In an effort to pacify the region, the U.S. government established Fort Smith on the upper Arkansas River in 1817 (Whayne 2002:98).

By this time the Osage faced a new wave of settlers from the East—Cherokee farmers who had been forced out of their traditional homelands in Tennessee, North Carolina, and Georgia. Even before the Louisiana Purchase, Cherokee and other indigenous groups had begun to move west of the Mississippi. As early as 1803 some five hundred families "from the Delawares, Shawnese, Miamis, Chicasaws, Cherokees, [and] Piorias" were living on the St. Francis River (Carter 1948). More Shawnee would follow from Ohio and Missouri, briefly settling on the White River, only to move on to Texas and Kansas as a new wave of Cherokee pushed in from the east (Lankford 1999). This group included a large contingent of Lower Cherokee—traditionalists from South Carolina, Georgia, and Alabama—who settled along the Arkansas and White river valleys in hopes of escaping the "nocuous American influence" in the East (Lankford 1977:5).

By 1817 at least two thousand Cherokee were living on federal land delineated by the White River to the northeast and the Arkansas River to the southwest (McLoughlin 1986; Meinig 1993:85). Though the land had been set aside for the Cherokee, the two river corridors were already being scouted by white adventurers, who began to settle in the hills.

The White and the Arkansas

The White River originates on the shady north slopes of the Boston Mountains and is soon joined by the Kings, Buffalo, and other tributaries. Emerging from a thick undergrowth of ferns, mosses, and wildflowers, these waters meander through stands of oak, hickory, and red cedar (Bolton 1998; Rafferty 2001). The tributaries converge and flow north into Missouri but then bend south again, returning to Arkansas and ultimately emptying into the Mississippi. The White River had attracted some of the earliest European and American visitors, including Henry Rowe Schoolcraft, a young explorer from New York. In his journals from 1818, he complained that the hill country was "of unvaried sterility, consisting of a succession of lime-stone ridges, skirted with a feeble growth of oaks, with no depth of soil, often bare rocks upon the surface, and covered with coarse wild grass" (1996:95–96). In contrast, Schoolcraft was captivated by the waterways. Floating along the White River, he wrote that "our canoe often seemed as if suspended in the air, such is the remarkable transparency of the water" (1996:76).

The white settlers encountered by Schoolcraft had already occupied strategic points on the waterway, making them gatekeepers to the river trade (Blevins 2002:13). At the same time, they remained fearful of the Osage, who were defending their traditional hunting grounds against both white and Cherokee settlers. Between 1817 and 1825 the Osage and Cherokee would fight at least five wars. During Schoolcraft's journey along the Osage-Cherokee frontier, the only traces he found of native peoples were Osage hunting trails and abandoned camps. Such observations contrasted with warnings by the white settlers, who had advised Schoolcraft that his journey to the head of the White River was "extremely hazardous, on account of the Osage Indians...who never failed to rob white hunters and travelers who were so unfortunate as to fall in their way, and sometimes carried them into captivity" (Schoolcraft 1996:61). Emerging from the White River Hills, Schoolcraft headed west into the Springfield Plain and marveled at the rolling countryside, "covered by a coarse wild grass, which attains so great a height that it completely hides a man on horseback in riding through it" (1996:82).

Meanwhile, some two hundred miles to the south, another explorer was heading up the Arkansas River, collecting botanical specimens for his patrons in the East (Beidleman 1954). In January 1819 Thomas Nuttall arrived at the Arkansas Post, which at the time consisted of "about a score or so of scattered houses and several stores on two principal streets, Front and Main" (Graustein 1967:138). From here Nuttal traveled by skiff and trading boat up the Arkansas, all the way to what is now Oklahoma.

Nuttall's route traced the southern boundary of the Ozarks, skirting the foothills of the Boston Mountains. Unlike the northern slopes of these mountains, the southern are characterized by gradual change in the rocks, soils, and topography. A greater exposure to sunlight encourages evaporation and lessens the heavy undergrowth, making way for pure stands of oak and hickory. Furthermore, at an average elevation of 447 feet, the Arkansas Valley provides a more temperate climate than the Ozark Plateau. Warmer temperatures, more precipitation in the form of rain rather than snow, and slightly more sunny days extend the growing season on the southern slope (Rafferty 2001). A number of tributaries, including the Mulberry, Piney, Illinois, and Cadron, flow down into the Arkansas.

Camping on an island just below the Mulberry Creek outlet, Nuttall found that the surrounding spring vistas with their "rich alluvions were now clothed in youthful verdure, and backed in the distance by bluish and empurpled hills" (Nuttall 1821:138). A small settlement was also present at the mouth of Mulberry River, where some thirty families were subsisting largely on game, fish, and honey (Worley 1952:327–29). These early settlers exchanged bear, deer, and raccoon skins for fabric and dishware at the Arkansas Post and traded buffalo for flour at Fort Smith.

Many of the settlements Nuttall encountered along the riverbanks were Cherokee. These communities were bustling with activity and were often difficult to differentiate from white settlements. Nuttall was impressed with the "civilized" qualities of the Cherokee:

> Though their dress was a mixture of indigenous and European taste, yet in their houses, which are decently furnished, and in their farms, which are well fenced and stocked with cattle, we perceive a happy approach toward civilization. Their numerous families, also, well-fed and clothed, argue a propitious progress in their population. Their superior industry either as hunters or farmers proves the value of property among them, and they are no longer strangers to avarice and the distinctions created by wealth. Some of them are possessed of property to the amount of many thousands of dollars, and have houses handsomely and conveniently furnished, and their tables spread with our dainties and luxuries. (Mooney 1975:133)

Continuing upriver, Nuttall observed a change in vegetation and geography similar to that reported by Schoolcraft in the north. Nuttall noted that "the prairies or grassy plains begin to be prevalent, and the trees to decrease in number and magnitude," and that the thickly forested banks are now "bordered with groves of cottonwoods" (1821:40). Like the Springfield Plain, the fertile prairies along the upper Arkansas River would draw some of the earliest white settlers. By 1822, as reported in the Fort Smith *Gazette* on November 26, the "roads in that neighborhood [were] said to be literally swarming with emigrants."

Stream Migration

Who were these white Americans streaming into the Ozarks in the early decades of the nineteenth century? Most had been born on American soil, the grandchildren of immigrants from the British Isles. From the mid-eighteenth century a quarter of a million "Scotch-Irish" had moved from Ulster to the United States (Wolf 1982:363). A wave of Scottish Highlanders soon followed. At the same time, the new republic received a quarter of a million southwestern Germans fleeing the impoverished countryside of the Rhineland. Although such immigrants are usually classified according to their "homelands,"

> a large proportion of those who moved to America had already moved from their native localities. They had left the farms and villages of their youth and were living in or near one of the larger towns, seaports, or capital.... In our search for definition of the peoples who came to America, therefore, it would be useful to know more than birthplaces and ports of departure; one would like to know something of the sociogeographic experience of every shipload. (Meinig 1986:218)

Some social classes were more likely to migrate than others. Richard Hofstadter (1973:32) argues that the "aggrieved middle classes and the impoverished" made up a disproportionate share of the early migrants. Moreover, as many as two-thirds of them came to America as indentured laborers (Wolf 1982:363).

Most immigrants in the eighteenth century "landed in Philadelphia, went westward to the first unoccupied lands in the interior uplands and valleys, and, as those lands were taken up, migrated southwestward along the valleys" (McDonald and McDonald 1980:182–183). Many Scots and other migrants from northern Britain settled in western parts of Maryland and Virginia, having been encouraged by the Pennsylvania Quakers to populate the inland colonies. In 1731 one Quaker leader wrote that the new immigrants should be placed strategically in the west "as a *frontier* in case of any disturbance" with the Indians (Fischer 1989:633).

Those who continued south tended to follow a distinctive pattern of residential mobility: "Virginians kept on moving; their rates of internal migration remained high throughout the seventeenth and eighteenth centuries" (Fischer and Kelly 2000:74). This trend contrasted sharply with the traditional pattern in New England, where colonists had usually moved just once or twice while still young adults and had then settled down permanently. By comparison, in some counties of Virginia 20 percent of the population would relocate within a year and 50 percent within a decade (Fischer and Kelly 2000:317). The poor in particular moved frequently, from the time they were small children until their deaths.

Much of the migration beyond Virginia proceeded south along the Great Wagon Road into the Shenandoah Valley (Fischer and Kelly 2000; Williams 2002:45–48). From here thousands poured into the Appalachian "backcountry," a vast region extending from southwestern Pennsylvania to northern Georgia. Though significant numbers of Germans populated this landscape, a large majority of the settlers had come from the British Isles, especially the Celtic regions of northern Britain. In fact, by 1790 "90 percent of the backsettlers were either English, Irish or Scottish; and an actual majority came from Ulster, the Scottish lowlands, and the north of England" (Fischer 1989:635; see also McDonald and McDonald 1980:199). The Irish Protestants in particular exhibited an impressive degree of group solidarity, as extended families, church congregations, and neighborhoods tended to migrate together (Williams 2002:46). By the early nineteenth century these Protestants would come to identify themselves as "Scotch-Irish" to avoid being grouped with America's growing population of Irish Catholics.

From the Scotch-Irish population, one major stream of migrants would continue flowing south and west through Kentucky, Tennessee, or northern Alabama. Tennessee in particular served as a "funnel state" for those moving out of the Carolina backcountry and into the highlands of Arkansas (Walz 1958:265). But why Arkansas? It was certainly not the only option —Missouri, Illinois, and Texas were all competing for new settlers in the early nineteenth century. Some have argued that the Ozarks offered a terrain that was familiar to migrants from the Appalachian region (e.g., Owsley 1949:52; Blevins 2002:20). At nearly the same latitude and elevation as eastern and middle Tennessee, the Arkansas highlands were similar in physical geography, soil, rainfall, temperature, and appearance. Established patterns of subsistence were thus easily transplanted to the new setting. Another important factor was the widespread belief among antebellum Americans that their basic "constitution" was tailored to their latitude of origin. Medical treatises and guidebooks warned migrants "to be cautious in their destinations" (Valenčius 2002:28). Short migrations were preferred, based on the belief that slow biological acclimation to a new environment was crucial to an individual's health (Valenčius 2002:23). As a result, most of the settlers of the Ozarks had traveled across the highland South, making their way in a series of short moves over two or more generations (Bolton 1998:18). By the early nineteenth century, furthermore, most were following family members or acquaintances who had already established themselves in the Ozarks. Even unmarried men tended to move as satellites of larger groups that included relatives and friends.

This pattern is well illustrated by the case of Lorenzo D. Dunlap and his younger brother, Jesse Dunlap Jr., whose extended family would constitute a large proportion of the wagon train members in 1857. As young men, the Dunlap brothers had followed their sister, Nancy, from central Tennessee to the highlands north of the Boston Mountains.[1] Nancy had married William C. Mitchell in Tennessee, and in 1833 the couple with their infant son moved to Carroll County, Arkansas. Lorenzo and Jesse Dunlap did not immediately join their sister but settled first in neighboring Madison County. It was here that the Dunlap brothers married the Wharton sisters, Mary and Nancy. The sisters themselves were originally from Tennessee but as children had moved to Arkansas (Goodspeed Publishing Co. 1889:423). The Wharton family was the first to settle on what would become Wharton Creek, near the small town of Kingston (Figure 1.2). In 1838 Mary Wharton married Jesse Dunlap Jr. A year later Nancy Wharton, the younger of the two sisters, married Lorenzo Dunlap. The Dunlap brothers with their sister-wives settled on adjoining farmsteads near Wharton Creek (U.S. Bureau of the Census 1840). Some fifteen years later Jesse would form a partnership with his sister's husband, William C. Mitchell. By 1854 the two men were running a mill, a blacksmith's shop, and a general store in what is now Marion County.

The complexity of this case must not obscure the essential point: migrants to the Ozarks often maintained and cultivated a vast web of connections to kith and kin. In fact, such connections reflected a typical pattern of "chain migration" all the way back to the British Isles. Some have even suggested that Scotch-Irish and other "Celtic" settlers brought with them to America the "clannish" ideals and values of the British borderlands (McWhiney 1988; Fischer 1989; Nisbett and Cohen 1996; Webb 2004). We must be cautious, however, in assuming continuities across such expanses of space and time. Most of the settlers of northwestern Arkansas were already descended from

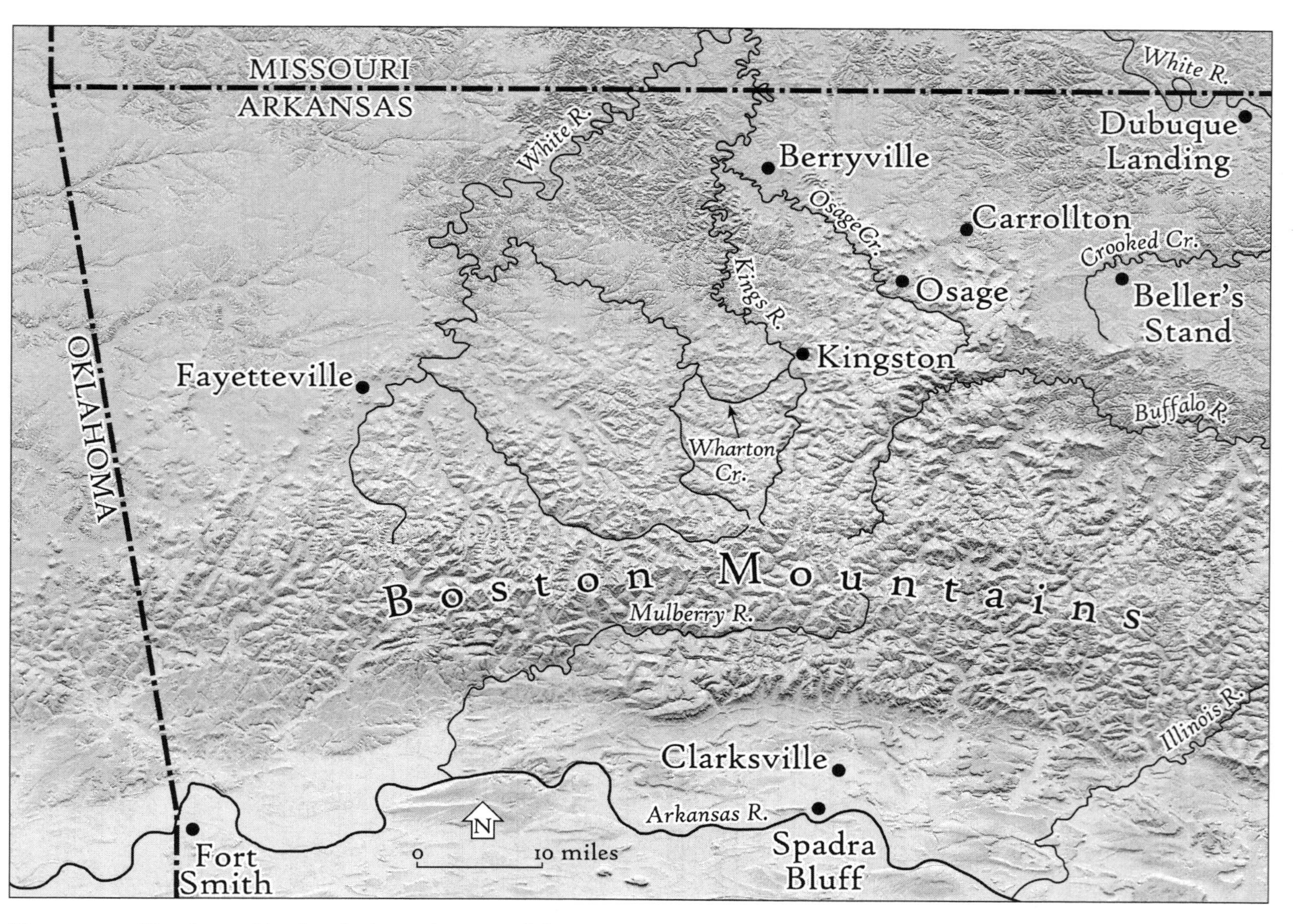

Figure 1.2. • Key sites and landmarks in northwestern Arkansas, c. 1850.

several generations of Americans on the move, and the very act of migration can be transforming. Although these pioneers were strikingly similar in their ethnic ancestry, "their culture and lifestyle reflected the southern backcountry, not Scotland, Ulster, or Wales" (Blevins 2002:19).

Obituary of Nations

Since the early eighteenth century the backcountry had been a zone of interaction between European Americans and Native Americans. The interaction in many cases had been violent, spilling into open warfare along the Pennsylvania and Virginia frontier in 1755, 1763, and 1774. As a result, "many of the settlers who moved south into the Carolinas' surging backcountry carried with them bitter memories that suppressed the differences between friendly and hostile Indians and merged them all into a racial enemy whose eventual removal became a popular goal" (Williams 2002:57). Though they had very different histories and cultures, the Cherokee, Seminole, Chickasaw, and Creek were all standing in the path of white expansion, especially for purposes of cotton production.

The Industrial Revolution in Scotland and England had been based on the manufacture of cotton textiles (Wolf 1982:278–285). To keep up with the growing British demand, American farmers had begun to exhaust the soils on the Atlantic seaboard, particularly in Georgia and the Carolinas. War with the Creek in 1813–1814 allowed settlers to seize tribal lands in Alabama and open these areas to cotton production. In the decades leading up to the Civil War the cotton crop accounted for more than half the value of all domestic exports from the United States (North 1961:68). Native Americans from Georgia to Arkansas felt the relentless pressure of agricultural expansion, setting off a chain reaction of tribal migration and intertribal conflict.

By the early nineteenth century the Ozarks and other regions west of the Mississippi were becoming refuges for fragments of eastern tribes that had lost their territories. In 1817 the U.S. government had promised the Cherokee a large tract in northwestern Arkansas, land that was still claimed by the Osage as their traditional hunting grounds. Chronic feuding between the two tribes forced the Osage to relinquish their claim in 1822, leaving the majority of the southwestern plateau in Cherokee possession. At the same time, white settlers continued to arrive and occupy the land, which had yet to be officially surveyed. With each delay in the completion of the survey, the Cherokee became more tightly circumscribed by white settlements. Eventually, tribal leaders were convinced that the only solution was for them to move farther west. In 1828 a western Cherokee delegation signed a treaty that relinquished their claims in Arkansas in return for a seven-million-acre tract in the Indian Territory (now Oklahoma). Although the treaty was designed to appease the western Cherokee, U.S. officials also inserted a clause stipulating that "their brothers yet remaining in the states may be induced to join them" (Mooney 2005:136).

The "brothers" were the eastern Cherokee, many of whom remained on their traditional lands in Georgia. In 1829 gold was discovered on these lands, and almost immediately calls went out for Indian removal. Georgia Congressman Richard H. Wilde argued, "What is history but the obituary of nations?" Should America, he asked, "check the course of human happiness—obstruct the march of science—stay the works of art, and stop the arm of industry, because they will efface in their progress the wigwam of the red hunter, and put out forever the council fire of his tribe?" (U.S. Congress 1830:1083). Such sentiments were shared by the Jackson administration, which encouraged white squatters to attack and seize Cherokee farms. In 1835, after a series of court battles, the last vestiges of the Cherokee in the East were forced to sign the Treaty of New Echota, ceding all their traditional lands. What followed was a succession of expulsions and forced migrations that have become known as the Trail of Tears. To avoid relocation, many eastern Cherokee fled to the Smoky Mountains, while others moved to Texas or Mexico. Some continued west and settled across a large expanse of California (Meinig 1993:97). Left in the wake were many "mixed-bloods," some of whom attempted to blend in with white settlers.

Such blending required creative maneuvering, however, to navigate shifting scientific, political, and popular views on race. Throughout the colonial period and the early nineteenth century many scientists believed that races were formed when biblical tribes migrated across the earth and "degenerated" into various states of savagery (Stocking 1968, 1987). A state of degeneration was not permanent, however, because exposure to different physical and cultural environments could alter one's race. Arguments for the mutability of race were used by some in the early republic to encourage acculturation and assimilation of native populations. But if Indians could be made white, was it possible for the reverse to occur? As frontier settlers moved deeper into the backcountry, many feared that they would degenerate as they were exposed to the same environments that had "created the Indians."

By the 1830s anxiety about "becoming Indian" was eclipsed by the new fear of miscegenation: "Indianness was a key element in white Americans' fears of mixed identity. Unlike the colonial French, Americans of the Mississippi Valley had no use for people of partial Native American heritage. Many saw in the racial intermixture of white and Native American groups a sign of inevitable and inalterable passing" (Valenčius 2002:249). Similar views came to be associated with the mixing of European and African "blood." In the Cotton South, even while skin tone and other "racial" markers were being blurred by miscegenation, blackness was defined in ever sharper opposition to whiteness (Stanton 1960; Horsman 1981; Jacobson 1998). The crystallization of fixed racial categories entered into public debate as many Americans sought to justify the enslavement of blacks or the confiscation of Indian lands.

Slow Amalgamation

In this context the state of Arkansas is an especially complex case because it represents a transition zone between the "Deep South" and the southern highlands. By 1840 slaves were held in nearly every Arkansas county, but the vast majority were in the river deltas of the southern and eastern portions of the state. The cotton culture was well established in areas such as Chico County, "which more closely resembled Washington County, Mississippi, directly across the river, than it did Washington County, Arkansas, in the state's northwestern corner" (DeBlack 2002:142). In the Arkansas Ozarks, for both climatic and logistical reasons, cotton was a minor crop before 1860. Most of the white settlers here were subsistence farmers, hunter-trappers, or herders rather than commercial planters. Yet the Ozarks' fertile bottomlands had been claimed by a small class of slaveholders who became the regional elite (Battershell 1999). Even though slaves constituted just 6 percent of the population in the mountainous counties (Bolton 1998:128), slavery was of great social and political significance.

Most of the slaves in the Ozarks, furthermore, were women and children. Adult males seem to have been sold for profit, perhaps because there was little need for field laborers on the region's relatively modest farms. "Whatever the reason for the paucity of adult male slaves, one noticeable result was the prominence of mulattoes among the Ozark slave population" (Blevins 2002: 278 n. 31). In Marion County, for example, more than half the Coker family's forty-two "servants" were listed in 1850 as "mulatto" (U.S. Bureau of the Census 1850, Schedule 2).

At the same time, many of the Cherokee who had been relocated from the East had one or more white ancestors. Throughout the eighteenth century many French, Spanish, British, and American colonists had taken Cherokee wives. "Moreover, children of mixed ancestry tended to marry their own kind, to raise their children as whites did, and to perpetuate a social group separate from rest of the [Cherokee] nation" (McLoughlin 1986:31). As a result, even the "white" populations of the Ozarks often contained persons of "mixed blood." [2]

To manage the blurring of racial categories, polite conversationalists made generous use of euphemisms such as "ginger-colored" and "Black Dutch" (Valenčius 2002:252). Children of "white" families may have heard rumors of relatives who were "Indian," but open discussion of such topics was still considered taboo, well into the twentieth century. In recent decades, however, many descendants of Ozark pioneers have come to emphasize their Indian heritage along with their Scotch-Irish or other European origins (e.g., Lair 1991; cf. Blevins 2002:277 n. 19).

On the 1857 wagon train Native American ancestry is clearly evident in one particular family line. John Twitty Baker, one of the leaders of the company, was born in Kentucky in about 1805, the third child of William Baker and Hannah Edwards.[3] Both William and Hannah were originally from North Carolina, and Hannah was half Cherokee (Baker 1982:160). When John Twitty (known as Jack) was about four years old, his family moved to a small farm in northeastern Alabama, near the town of New Market. Eventually, his father would purchase several hundred acres of public land from the government, develop a large farming enterprise, and acquire a number of slaves. Jack Baker in his turn would become a successful farmer, with at least one hundred acres near his father's estate.

In 1834, however, Baker killed three men in an hour-long brawl. On returning to his home, he found his barn burned and many of his cattle missing. The reasons for the fight remain unclear, but Baker was known to be a tough, competitive man with a fondness for drink (Baker 1982:161). At the same time, his Cherokee ancestry may have contributed to his troubles (Garrick Bailey, personal communication, 2003). White and Indian tensions in the southeastern states had escalated in the 1830s as the Jackson administration sanctioned harassment of Cherokee in Georgia, Tennessee, North Carolina, and Alabama in order to "encourage" westward relocation and the cession of Indian lands (Finger 2001:304–305). Even outside tribal territory, spillover violence was common in the region, especially where mixed-bloods had been successful in adapting to white society: "Indians who developed farms, built homes of European-derived architecture, owned slaves, and operated stores were prime targets for American criminals" (Myers 1997:153).

Jack Baker is unlikely to have flaunted his Cherokee heritage, but his mother's ancestry was probably well known to the local community in New Market. Also resident in the area was her brother, Silas Edwards, who was himself half Cherokee. In the aftermath of the murders Baker turned to Edwards as his principal ally in defending his family and property against retaliation. For more than a decade, he remained in Alabama, even after several of his neighbors and family members had moved to northwestern Arkansas.

Yet continuing tensions with the local community may have contributed to Baker's decision, at age forty-five, to leave the area. In 1849 he sold his farm and traveled with his wife and eight children by boat or raft down the Tennessee and Mississippi rivers to southern Missouri, where they began the overland journey to Arkansas (Baker 1982:161).[4] The Baker family—which had grown to eleven with the birth of another child in Missouri—soon arrived in Carroll County and settled near friends and family along Crooked Creek.

Baker's subsequent pattern of wealth acquisition presents an interesting contrast to that of Jesse Dunlap Jr., who by 1854 was living just to the east in Marion County. With seven slaves to work his property, Baker quickly emerged as one of the wealthiest farmers in the area. His pattern echoed the style of other slaveholding elites in the region. Dunlap, by contrast, was following a small entrepreneurial pattern, having established a mill and general store at Dubuque Landing on the White River. From the 1840s, steamboat service had begun to transform the agriculture of Marion County, where "cotton production ballooned from about 8 bales in 1839 to 1,100 in 1849" (Blevins 2002:25). Dunlap was representative of an incipient bourgeois class, seeking to turn a profit in a commercial economy that depended on swifter and more efficient modes of transporting both goods and people to market.

Perfect Terra Incognita

Because of its swampy lowlands, lack of roads in the interior, and often hazardous water routes, the Arkansas Territory was especially difficult terrain for early travelers. Before the 1830s most migrants were diverted to the south or to the north of Arkansas, into Louisiana or Missouri (Walz 1958:295). One early visitor, Reverend Cephas Washburn, was a missionary to the Cherokee Nation (Washburn 1869). Heading up the Mississippi in 1820, he tried to learn more about his destination from the local people on the river. He was startled to find that "Arkansas was a perfect *terra incognita*. The way to get there was unknown; and what it was, or was like, if you did get there was still more an unrevealed mystery" (Moffat 1954:187).

Remote and mysterious, Arkansas also had a reputation for "rude, boisterous, and violent" inhabitants, including Indians who had refused to give up their lands (Williams 1980:101). By 1834, however, the Cherokee had been forcibly removed to Oklahoma. Enticed by land grants from the federal government, new settlers surged into Arkansas, resulting in admission to statehood in 1836 (Walz 1958:309–315). Many of these early immigrants were attracted to the Ozark region, which was free of malaria and other health risks associated with the swampy lowlands. Most of those who would join the 1857 wagon train had first arrived in Arkansas during the immigration boom more than twenty years earlier.

Government subsidies encouraged much of the westward expansion. During the War of 1812 the United States recruited soldiers by promising 160 acres of land to each veteran. To fulfill this obligation, the government set aside six million acres as public domain, two million of them in northern Arkansas. Before the 1830s, however, the Ozarks saw only minor growth, in part because veterans often sold their claims to speculators or used their allotments to obtain land elsewhere (Bolton 1998:15; Rafferty 2001:50).

Open lands in Arkansas became more attractive when Congress passed the federal land law of 1832—known on the frontier as the "poor man's friend"—allowing settlers to purchase as little as forty acres at $1.25 per acre (Walz 1958:5). Public land sales peaked in Arkansas in 1836, with nearly a million acres sold (Bolton 1998:15). A second purchasing surge occurred between 1847 and 1856, following congressional appropriation of 160-acre bonuses to veterans of all wars and their heirs. By the end of the antebellum period nearly 1.5-million acres of public land in Arkansas were acquired through military warrants (Walz 1958:5).

To direct westward expansion in an organized manner, the federal government required that public lands be systematically surveyed, mapped, and recorded prior to being sold and settled. Few pioneers recognized these guidelines, however, and squatting became the rule rather than the exception (Meinig 1993:243). This was certainly the case for many antebellum families in Arkansas. In fact, the liberal land and tax laws may have been what attracted some settlers to the territory. As early as 1835, the Arkansas territorial legislature provided a tax exemption for houses built on public land, resulting in much of the state's inhabited property remaining public domain (Walz 1958:8). Although Congress made some early attempts to punish squatters with fines, forced removal, and imprisonment, settlement before survey became routine. The Preemption Act of 1841 "transformed the derisive term *squatter* into an honorable one" by legitimizing the frontier pioneers' claims to purchase lands they occupied *after* such properties had been surveyed and placed on the market (Meinig 1993:244).

Regardless of whether families occupied land prior or subsequent to survey, the grid system had little impact on the shape of frontier settlements. Hamlets would develop as "a loose string or cluster of such family homesteads along a creek or line of springs, connected with one another by paths and with the whole district by pack trails and droving roads with some commercial outpost" (Meinig 1993:245). Rather than the cadastral system, then, it was the "cultural traditions of kinship and resource use in association with natural patterns of woodland and prairie" that created the character of the frontier landscape (Faragher 1986:61).

Before 1850 more than 40 percent of the settlers of the Arkansas highlands were from Tennessee (Walz 1958:69). With no public land set aside, Tennessee real estate was becoming too expensive for most yeoman farmers (Finger 2001:186). Setting out from Nashville, most followed the Cumberland River to the Ohio Valley. From here some went up the Mississippi and overland through Missouri: "Such pioneers found the rough unglaciated hill country of the Ohio Valley and Missouri entirely familiar in kind and they readily worked their way back into the coves and recesses of the Ozarks" (Meinig 1993:229). An alternative route went down the Mississippi and up the Arkansas River, where some of the new arrivals settled in the nearby foothills. Others moved up the many tributaries of the Arkansas into the Boston Mountains (Sauer 1920:138).

Circuitous Routes

Although river travel was preferred by these early settlers, it was often necessary to cobble together a series of water and land crossings, frequently by quite circuitous routes. The favored seasons for overland migration were late fall and early winter, when the roads were dry and the insects at a minimum. Waterways saw the heaviest travel from February to May, when migrants could take advantage of the rising rivers but still reach their new homes in time to plant their crops. Migration in summer or early fall was to be avoided, not only for logistical reasons but because these seasons were believed to be inauspicious for the health of the traveler (Valenčius 2002:27).

Before 1850 most water transport was by dugout, flatboat, or keelboat. The third type was preferred by immigrants because it could hold more cargo (Walz 1958:11). What appeared to be a vast highway, however, proved to be less than reliable. Most streams "were far from the main routes of commerce, sometimes dangerous and only seasonably navigable" (Sauer 1920:130). Overland travel was even more precarious (Moffatt 1954:187). If travelers were lucky enough to find a trail, it was probably constructed with little care and located along high ground to prevent flooding (Sauer 1920:133). Road construction was often "do it yourself" and required the felling of enough trees to allow passage of a wagon. In general, "it was found cheaper to make a new road than to repair an old one" (Schoolcraft 1996:238). Bridges were rare and migrants would have to camp along the riverbanks, waiting their turn to cross on a primitive ferry (Bolton 1998:21). In 1818, for example, the Benedict family forded the White at Batesville, Arkansas, on "two canoes, lashed together with a few split clapboards laid across" (Benedict 1951:123). The family continued overland, but before long the road became impassable. They abandoned their wagon and proceeded on foot.

In March 1820, the Arkansas Post was visited for the first time by a steamboat—the *Comet*—which had traveled for eight days from New Orleans (*Arkansas Gazette*, April 1, 1820). Over the next decade, steamboats gradually increased in number and journeyed farther up the Arkansas, primarily to supply the army garrison at Fort Smith. They also brought manufactured goods to merchants along the river and carried cotton, hides, pelts, and pecans to market downstream (Moffatt 1954:195). Most steamboat passengers during the antebellum period were pioneers heading west. In 1831, for example, the *Industry* carried some 150 immigrants from Tennessee who settled the foothills of the Boston Mountains (*Arkansas Gazette*, July 4, 1837). Spadra Bluff, about one hundred miles from Little Rock, was one of the most popular landing points on the upper Arkansas. Immigrants here were usually welcomed by "some relative or friend who knew of the possible arrival of the new-comers" (Langford 1921:24).

Having landed at Spadra, many were persuaded to settle nearby in Johnson County, on the southern slopes of the Boston Mountains. The Tackitts—one of four Johnson County families on the 1857 wagon train—seem to have been typical of the settlers in this area. Both Martin and Cynthia Tackitt had been born in Tennessee, but they had met and married in Arkansas. By 1850 they were established in Spadra Township. Here they worked oxen and mules and grew wheat, corn, and potatoes. In one year their three milk cows produced 100 pounds of butter, which helped to feed seven children aged five to eighteen years (U.S. Bureau of the Census 1850, Schedule 4).

All seven of these children had been born in Arkansas. The oldest daughter, Eloah, married a young neighbor from Alabama, J. Milum Jones. The oldest son, Pleasant Tackitt, also married a neighbor, Armilda Miller. Because Armilda had been born in Tennessee, her general background and perhaps her network of friends and kin would have been familiar to those of her in-laws. Like their parents, the young couple relied mostly on subsistence farming, but Pleasant also became a preacher (Bagley 2002:65).

In 1856 or early 1857, while the Jones and Tackitt households prepared to leave for California, Martin Tackitt died. His widow, Cynthia Tackitt, was left to head the extended family. To make the overland journey, Cynthia relied on her teenaged daughters and sons as well as the kinship links afforded by the marriages of her older offspring. The Tackitt family would eventually rendezvous with the wagon train of John Twitty (Jack) Baker, who lived in Carroll County, on the far side of the Boston Mountains.

The Tackitts and the Bakers make for an interesting comparison in several ways. Both "clans" consisted of three generations, including in each case two young married couples with children. Whereas the Tackitts were headed by Cynthia, a forty-nine-year-old widow, the Bakers were headed by Jack, a fifty-two-year-old patriarch whose wife had refused to accompany him to California. Most important, Jack Baker was a wealthy landowner with seven slaves whereas Cynthia Tackitt had a few oxen and milk cows. According to the 1850 agricultural census, Baker's property, excluding his slaves, was worth at least four times what Martin Tackitt owned (U.S. Bureau of the Census 1850, Schedule 4). In 1855 Baker's slaves were assessed at $4,200. When this figure is added to the value of his farm and other property, the Baker estate was worth more than ten times the value of the Tackitt estate. In setting out for California, Cynthia Tackitt was probably obliged to liquidate all her assets whereas Jack Baker outfitted his company with a fraction of his total wealth.

Cosmopolitans in the Ozarks

In 1850 Arkansas had some 210,000 residents. The state's population had more than doubled, largely because of immigration to the Ozarks (Walz 1958:303). With only four persons per square mile, Arkansas was still underpopulated by national standards (Bolton 1998:19). Yet the Ozark Plateau was already too crowded for cattle herders, who required vast tracts of open range. The expansion of agriculture in particular had forced many herders "to settle as farmers or to withdraw into the mountains, hills, and pine barrens, or to seek other frontiers" (Owsley 1949:27). By 1850 one such frontier was drawing these cattlemen and thousands of others to a distant shore.

"HO! FOR CALIFORNIA," read a Fort Smith Company circular, which offered a checklist of supplies for overland travel (Bolton 1998:156–157): "Every man was to have a gun, ammunition, and a bowie knife. Livestock, including horses, mules, and oxen, were available in western Arkansas, but easterners were advised to bring their own wagons. Food per person included 100 pounds of bacon, 150 pounds of flour, 20 pounds of coffee, 30 pounds of sugar, and large quantities of salt, pepper, crackers, meal, rice, molasses, dried peaches, beans, tea, spices, saleratus, and vinegar." With the discovery of gold in the Sierra Nevada, Arkansas was promoted as a natural point of departure for California (McArthur 1986). From the Fort Smith area the forty-niners had a number of overland routes available: the popular southern route through New Mexico; the Cherokee Trail, which traveled through Indian Territory to the south of the Oregon-California Trail; and the Frontier Military Trail, which intersected the Oregon Trail via military forts in

Indian Country (Bagley 2002:58). In Fort Smith, by the end of 1849, "the cluster of people from different parts of the country gave rise to concerns about disease" (Bolton 1998:157). Yet the forty-niners kept coming, and they had a variety of ideas about how to get rich in California.

As the mining towns grew in the Sierras, so too did the demand for fresh beef. To meet this need, cattlemen drove herds from places such as northwestern Arkansas (Blevins 2002:27), including an 1850 expedition that was joined by Alexander Fancher. After moving from Tennessee to Illinois to Missouri, Alexander had arrived about seven years earlier in Carroll County, Arkansas. Here on the Osage Creek, a tributary of the Kings River, Alexander settled near his paternal uncle, James. Like Jack Baker, who lived on Crooked Creek some thirty miles to the east, James Fancher was a wealthy farmer and slaveholder. His estate helped attract to Carroll County a number of extended family members, including Alexander and his older brother, John. Already living nearby was James's younger brother (also named Alexander), who had a farm of his own. This gathering on the Osage was typical of many Ozark "hollers," where "friends and relatives living in the same or neighboring communities formed one or more parties and moved out together, and when they had reached the promised land they constituted a new community, which was called a 'settle-ment'" (Owsley 1949:62).

Such a community could be short-lived, however, for the promised land seemed always to be moving west. In 1850 Alexander and his brother John were following a classic trans-Appalachian pattern: "Before migrating, one or more representatives of a group spied out the land, whereupon the group—which was frequently a congregation or neighborhood—moved out together and became neighbors in the new country" (Owlsey 1949:75; see also Billingsley 2004). Such reconnaissance was usually made by related men, often brothers, who would send word back to other family members. In the case of the Fancher brothers, their 1850 cattle drive took a circuitous northern route that met up with the Oregon Trail, then turned southwest toward the Utah Territory (Bagley 2002:58–60). From here they traveled south, passing through a few Mormon hamlets, the most southern of which was Provo. Beyond this settlement the emigrants traversed a stretch of "wilderness," inhabited only by Native Americans, before reaching the Spanish Trail.

Meanwhile, Alexander's wife, Eliza, and John's wife, Ann, along with a combined brood of eleven children, also traveled to California. It is certainly possible that they went overland with their husbands and fathers. Thus Bagley (2002:58) claims that the "brothers John and Alexander Fancher, with their large families and a drove of cattle, set out on their first trip over the arduous road to California." Supporting this scenario is an account of the

Fancher brothers passing through Utah in October 1850 in a company of 92 men, 9 women, and 28 children (Peck 1850 in Bagley 2002:60).

According to Fancher family lore, however, Eliza, Ann, and their children followed a different route to the goldfields. Parting company with their husbands, the women took a riverboat to New Orleans, boarded a steamer to Panama, crossed the isthmus by mule, and steamed on to San Diego (Fancher 1999:244). Customhouse figures indicate that travelers by sea were beginning to prefer the Panamanian route to the arduous voyage around Cape Horn (Levy 1990:32). By the early 1850s the travel time via the isthmus had been reduced from six weeks to fewer than four, and the cost of passage had fallen from a high of five hundred dollars to approximately one hundred dollars (Unruh 1979:340). Numerous women made the water journey, and though many complained bitterly about cramped quarters, swarms of insects, and treacherous mule rides, they were often captivated by the exotic surroundings. As one woman described it in a letter, "The birds singing monkeys screeching the Americans laughing and joking the natives grunting as they pushed us along through the rapids was enough to drive one mad with delight" (Levy 1990:38).

In any case, by March 1851 the Fancher families had joined the 650 residents of San Diego, California. As small as it was, the settlement was marked by extraordinary ethnic and occupational diversity. Accustomed to farm life, the Fanchers now found themselves mixing with merchants, traders, wage laborers, and professionals. Their immediate neighbors included a blacksmith, carpenter, customhouse officer, physician, pilot, tanner, and "tobaccouist" (U.S. Bureau of the Census 1850, Schedule 1). Most of these neighbors were men. In the fourteen households adjacent to the Fancher residence, there were forty-eight males and only fifteen females.[5] Many households were composed entirely of men, and the Fancher brothers were among the few living with their wives and children.

Only a small fraction of their neighbors had come from the southern states. About a third were from New England or the mid-Atlantic region. At least a quarter had been born overseas, in Ireland, Germany, or the East Indies, and the physician hailed from Nova Scotia. Of the fifteen females, six had been born in California or Mexico, two in Pennsylvania, one in Texas, and one "on the frontier." The other five were Europeans. Such a neighborhood would have provided the Fanchers with a bonanza of new contacts and cosmopolitan information. These experiences might well have set Alexander and Eliza Fancher apart from their families and friends in the Ozarks.

In 1852 John and his family settled near Visalia, California, while Alexander, Eliza, and their seven children returned to the Ozarks. In 1854 Alexander drove a second herd of cattle to California (Fancher 1999:245–247) and returned with enough profit to buy two hundred acres in Benton County, Arkansas. Here, on the grassy Springfield Plain, Alexander accumulated more livestock and prepared to organize a final expedition to the West.

Even by frontier standards, Alexander Fancher was extremely mobile. Three interstate moves and two round trips to California probably gave him a rather worldly image among his Arkansas neighbors. Described by one of his descendants as "the first travel agent" in the Ozarks (Fancher 1999:245), Alexander was indeed a cosmopolitan figure whose local influence and prestige seem to have derived from his knowledge of an expanding, interconnected world.

Such a figure has typically resided in various local communities, maintaining long-distance contacts with several social networks (Hannerz 1990). Such contacts provide a "transmission-belt" for the movement of information—the cosmopolitan's key resource—from the wider world to the local setting (Merton 1968:461). In the case of Alexander, he had firsthand knowledge of overland routes and logistics, a realistic basis for assessing the land and cattle markets on the West Coast, and access to news and information from California residents, including his brother John.

Yet the Fancher brothers were not the only family members to have accumulated cosmopolitan knowledge and experience. Alexander's wife, Eliza, had also traveled to California. If we assume that she made the journey by sea—from New Orleans to Panama to San Diego—she would have passed through a series of "contact zones," busy intersections of peoples, goods, and information feeding in from Europe, Latin America, and the Pacific (Pratt 1992; Clifford 1997). On her return to Arkansas, Eliza would have been changed. Along with her husband, she is likely to have become something of a cosmopolitan in the Ozarks. When the Fanchers again set out for the goldfields in 1857, Eliza was apparently the only woman on the wagon train who had already seen California. She may well have been looked to by others—especially other women—as a source of knowledge and advice about the road ahead.

Conclusion

The white settlers of the Ozarks, according to Milton Rafferty (2001:46), fall into three broad categories:

> The first immigrants were southerners, mainly of Scotch-Irish descent and of the yeoman farmer type, mainly poor, nonslaveholders. Most were from Tennessee, North Carolina, Virginia, Pennsylvania,

> and Kentucky.... A wealthier group, slave owners from the South, occupied the better river bottoms, where slaves cleared timber and planted fields for hemp, tobacco, and corn. A third type was the townsperson, who usually had some capital to invest in commerce or in manufacture of commodities needed on the frontier.

Each of these categories is well represented by several families on the wagon train. The Dunlaps and Tackitts, for example, came to Arkansas as relatively poor "yeoman farmers" from Tennessee and North Carolina. The Bakers were wealthier slave owners from Alabama. Jack Baker in particular, overcoming the stigma of his Cherokee ancestry, would emerge as one of the wealthiest men in northwestern Arkansas. Meanwhile, Jesse Dunlap Jr. went into business on the river, eventually becoming a "townsperson" engaged in commercial manufacture and trade.

Yet there is a fourth category that must be considered. As Frank Lawrence Owsley (1949:24) emphasized many years ago, the first wave of immigrants to the Old South "consisted of herdsmen, who subsisted primarily in a grazing and hunting economy." These herdsmen were not only at the forefront of migration but remained more mobile than the farmers and townspersons who flooded in behind them. The Fancher family is an exemplary case of this herding pattern. Relocating every few years in search of open public land for grazing, the Fanchers were also quick to capitalize on new and distant markets. In the process, they tended to become "long-distance specialists" (Helms 1988), eminently qualified to organize friends and family for the next exodus.

CONFLUENCE

It was really a beautiful sight to see this company while on the march. The white topped wagons—the long line of cattle—the horsemen upon each flank, with their long rifles—the drivers with their big whips—all moving so regularly forward, that when viewed from a distance it seemed as if they were united and propelled by the same power.

—J. HENRY CARLETON, *THE PRAIRIE LOGBOOKS*, 1845

We have been left with a view of these trains shaped more by what emigrants wanted them to be than what they actually were.

—JOHN MACK FARAGHER, *WOMEN AND MEN ON THE OVERLAND TRAIL*, 2001

Most of the literature about the Mountain Meadows massacre tends to assume that the wagon train was a fairly coherent unit from the time it left Arkansas (e.g., Brooks 1962:44; Wise 1976:12; Bigler 1998:159; Denton 2003:100). In reality, however, there is little evidence for a unified group. All that is known for certain is that several parties, including two large networks from north and south of the Boston Mountains, eventually converged and camped together at Mountain Meadows (Figure 2.1). We must be careful not to project a unity that is based on knowledge of who was later massacred. Thus a serious question arises about those who camped at Mountain Meadows: were they an organized convoy or an incidental grouping—a kind of traffic jam on the Spanish Trail?

In the spring of 1857 families both north and south of the Boston Mountains were making final arrangements for the overland trek to California. Most of the travelers intended to relocate permanently and had spent months selling off their lands, purchasing supplies for the journey, and saying their goodbyes. Some of the men had purchased cattle with the intention

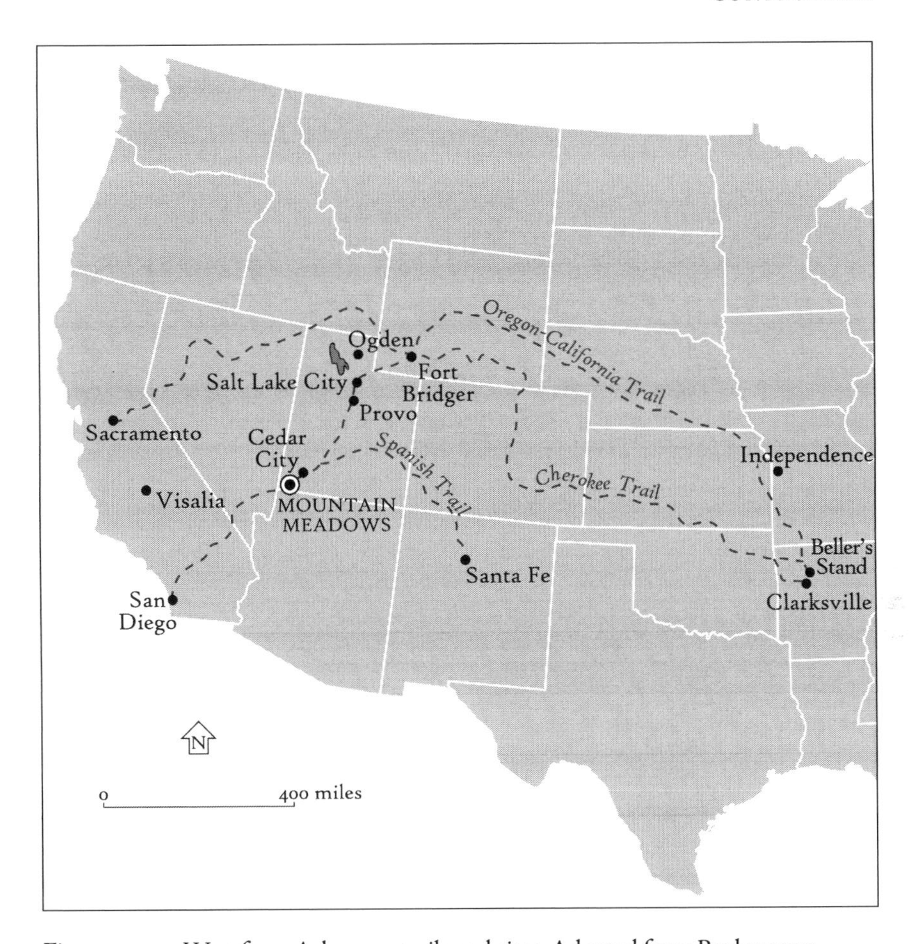

Figure 2.1. • West from Arkansas: trails and sites. Adapted from Bagley 2002.

of selling the animals in California and then returning to Arkansas with the profits. And a number of young men, like the Fancher brothers before them, were planning to scout out the land so as to relay word back to family who might follow.

Two large social networks fed into the wagon train. Each of these was a "party" in John Mack Faragher's (2001:32) sense: "a group of individuals and families bound together by agreement, prior acquaintance, or kinship." The two parties were extended kin groups from opposite sides of the Boston Mountains—one from Carroll County to the north, the other from Johnson County to the south. A smaller contingent, centered on the household of Alexander Fancher, provided a bridge between these two large parties. Not only did the Fanchers have contacts in both the large networks, but their friends and family in California could have provided vital information about the road ahead. At the same time, all the parties attracted a number of

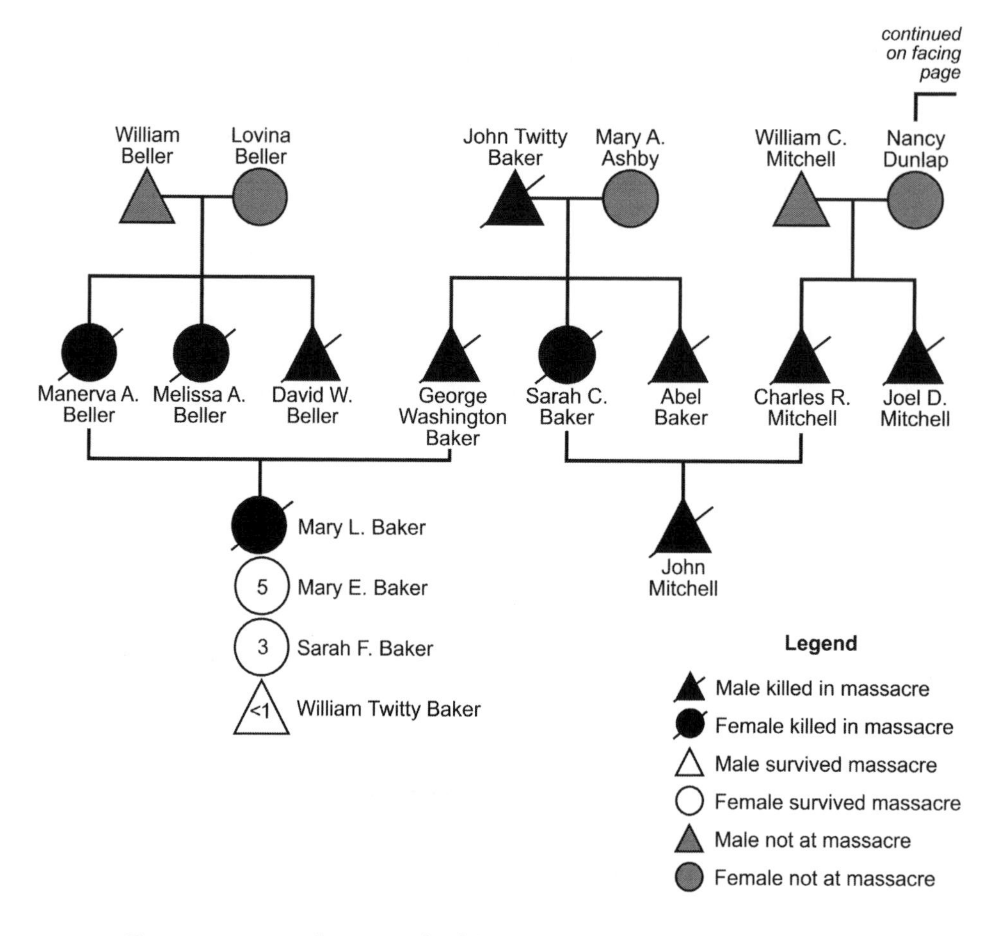

Figure 2.2. • Kinship network of the northern contingent, 1857.

satellite families and solitary men, most of whom were friends, neighbors, or distant relatives.

Not all the emigrants who left Arkansas together would ultimately camp at Mountain Meadows. A number of persons lagged behind or left the caravan, taking alternate routes to California. As a result, the contingent that camped at Mountain Meadows differed from the wagon train that left Arkansas.

Beller's Stand

In Carroll County the core of the party was formed by five extended families. Long before they set out for California, the Beller, Baker, Mitchell, Dunlap, and Wharton clans had been interwoven through marriages, friendships, and commercial partnerships (Figure 2.2).[1] For example, Manerva Beller

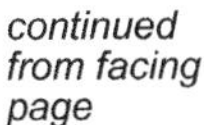

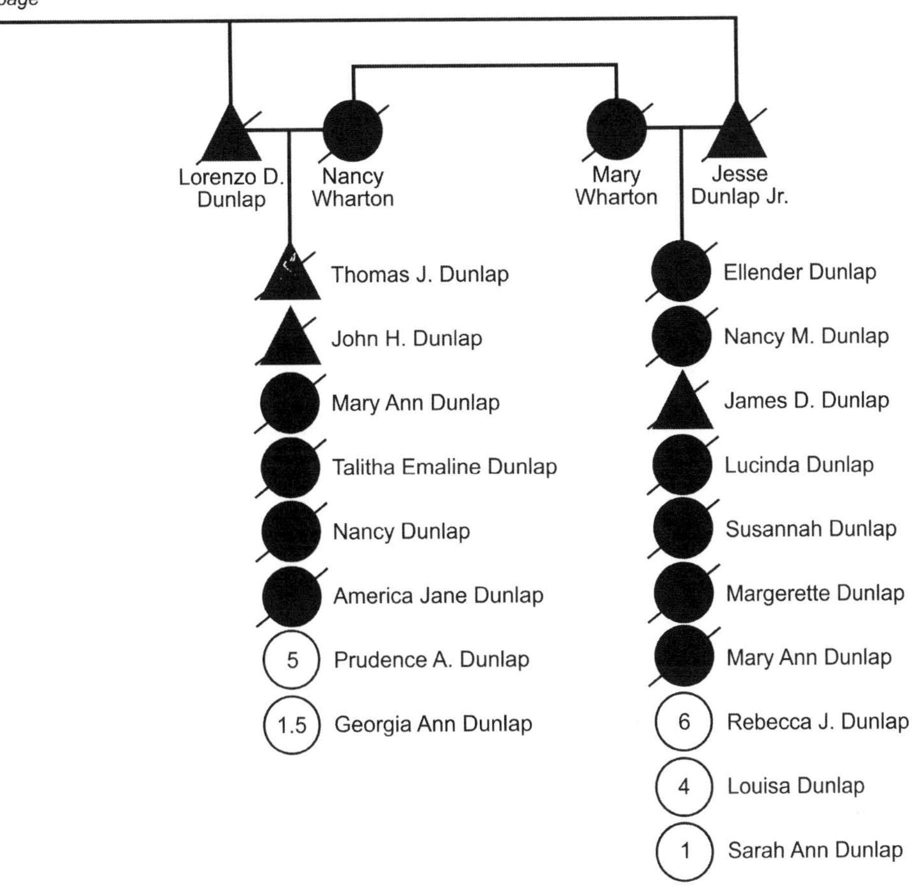

had married George Washington Baker, whose sister Sarah had married Charles Mitchell. Meanwhile, Charles's father had gone into business with Jesse Dunlap Jr., who had married into the Wharton family. Some of these links had been formed years before while the Bellers and Bakers lived in Alabama and the Mitchells, Dunlaps, and Whartons in Tennessee.

In April 1857 at least 36 members of these families gathered at a spot known as Beller's Stand, on the rolling meadow near Crooked Creek.[2] The eldest among them was 52-year-old Jack Baker. In fact, according to some accounts, Baker was the "captain" of the wagon train (e.g., Mitchell 1860 in Brooks 1962:45; Baker 1982). Logan (1992:227) provides one perspective on the historical evidence: "John T. Baker was the organizer and leader character in the contingent of the Mountain Meadows caravan that originated at Crooked Creek. Most of the depositions mention the other victims having

Table 2.1. • Northern Core Contingent: State of Birth.

	AR	MS	TN	AL	LA	KY	NC	TOTAL
Adults	1	1	4	4		1	1	12
Subadults	23				1			24
Total	24 (66%)	1 (3%)	4 (11%)	4 (11%)	1 (3%)	1 (3%)	1 (3%)	36

Source: U.S. Bureau of the Census 1850, Schedule 1.

Table 2.2. • Northern Core Contingent: Adult Kinship Relations.

Relationship	No.	%
Husband-Wife	8	67
Parent-Child	11	92
Sibling-Sibling	11	69
B-B	7	64
B-Z	4	36
Z-Z	4	36

Note: N = 17; 18+ years in age.

gone west in company with Baker. It is interesting to note that none of the 60 pages of depositions mentions Alexander Fancher, the person traditionally thought to have been the leader of the caravan." This point is echoed by Bagley (2002:65): "Ironically, although it is now usually remembered as the Fancher party, most of the emigrants recalled traveling with the Baker party." Denton (2003:97) has tried to split the difference between these two scenarios, suggesting that Fancher was "in charge of the people and wagons" and Baker was the "herd boss." Each of these men, according to Denton, "would be designated a 'captain.'" Whether Alexander Fancher might have been the leader of the wagon train is taken up below. In any case, Jack Baker was an obvious focal point for the contingent that gathered at Beller's Stand.

Baker's immediate circle included two sons, a daughter, and five grandchildren. One of his sons, George Washington Baker, is said to have already visited "El Dorado" in the early 1850s (*Daily Alta California* 1857b). This reconnaissance appears to have alerted the Baker family to commercial opportunities in the goldfields. According to Jack's wife, Mary Baker, "the object my husband...had in going to California was to sell a large lot of cattle with which he started" (Logan 1992:226). Mary would not accompany Jack but stayed home in Carroll County with eight of their offspring. Purportedly, "the old man intended...to return by water and bring out the remainder of his family" (*Daily Alta California* 1857b).

Table 2.3. • Northern Core Contingent: Surname Distribution.

	BELLER	BAKER	MITCHELL	DUNLAP	WHARTON	TOTAL	%
Female	2	4	0	15	2	23	64
Male	1	4	3	5	0	13	36
Total	3 (8%)	8 (22%)	3 (8%)	20 (56%)	2 (6%)	36	100

Source: U.S. Bureau of the Census 1850, Schedule 1.

Table 2.4. • Northern Core Contingent: Age Distribution.

AGE	BELLER	BAKER	MITCHELL	DUNLAP	WHARTON	NO.	%
0–4		m, f	m	f, f, f		6	17
5–9		f, f		f, f, f, f, f		7	19
10–14	m, f			f, f, f, f, f, f, m		9	25
15–19		m		m, m, f		4	11
20–24		f	m			2	6
25–29	f	m	m			3	8
30–34							
35–39				m	f	2	6
40–44				f	f	2	6
45–49							
50+		m				1	3

Who else was in the party at Beller's Stand? For the moment, let us consider only the party's core, consisting of the 36 persons known to belong to the five extended families (the satellite members are taken up later). All the adults, with the exception of 18-year-old Ellender Dunlap, had been born outside Arkansas (Table 2.1). Four had been born in Tennessee, the primary source of white migration to the Ozarks before 1850. Four others had come from Alabama, at the southernmost tip of the Appalachians, and the remaining three had made their way from North Carolina, Kentucky, or Missouri. Almost all the adults—11 of the 12—had at least one sibling on the wagon train, and the most frequent tie was between brothers (Table 2.2). Most of the adults, furthermore, were married and accompanied by a spouse.

Beller's Stand was flooded with adolescents and children—24 in all. The two Dunlap households accounted for 18. As a result, more than half the emigrants in the northern core had been born with the surname Dunlap (Table 2.3). Because 15 of the Dunlap children were female, the core of the northern party had an abundance of young women and girls (Table 2.4). In fact, the average female age in this group was only 13.[3] The males were considerably

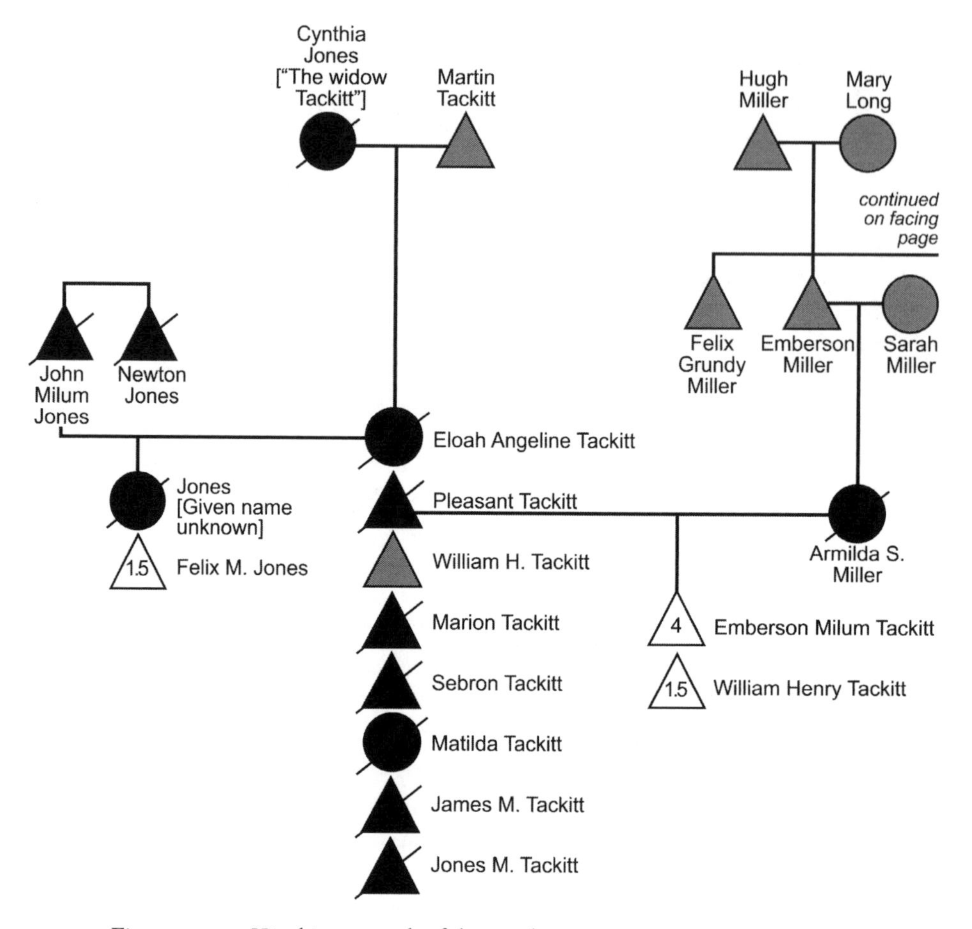

Figure 2.3. • Kinship network of the southern contingent, 1857.

older, with an average age of 22. Overall, however, the typical individual in this core group was an adolescent female.

Below the age of 16, everyone in this group had been born in Arkansas. Although a few of the children had experienced short residential moves to neighboring counties, none would have had memories of anything like the overland trek they were about to make. Nonetheless, these children would be following a pattern of migration that was well known to their parents: an initial move to the frontier as a child, followed by a move farther west as a young adult, with family in tow.

Spadra Suburbs

As the northern families gathered in April 1857, portions of the southern contingent from Johnson County were already on the trail.[4] Originating on the outskirts of two commercial centers, Spadra and Clarksville, the core of the

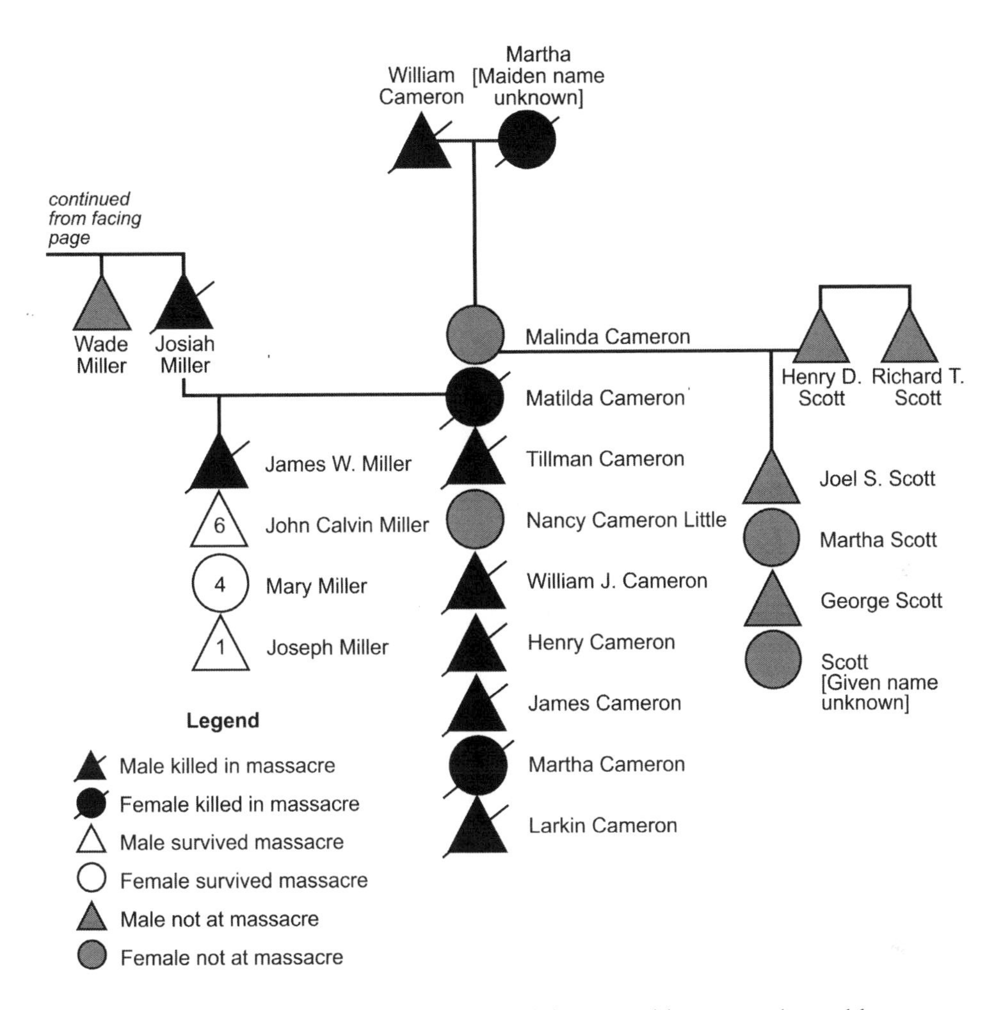

southern party was drawn from a few small farms and homesteads. Unlike the northern party, this contingent had no central gathering place. Instead, the group would pick up riders as the wagon train left Johnson County, continuing up the Arkansas River valley and into the Cherokee Nation (Bagley 2002:65–66).

Despite this pattern of recruitment, the southern contingent was held together by kinship and marriage (Figure 2.3). In fact, as defined here, the core of the southern group was strikingly similar to that of the northern group: a network of 36 persons from five extended families. In the southern case, the core families were surnamed Tackitt, Cameron, Miller, Scott, and Jones. Nearly 60 percent of the group contained either Tackitts or Camerons (Table 2.5). At the head of the Tackitt family was the recently widowed Cynthia Tackitt, 49 years old, who was joined by three adult offspring, four teenagers, and four grandchildren. The Cameron clan was headed by a

Table 2.5. • Southern Core Contingent: Surname Distribution.

	JONES	TACKITT	MILLER	CAMERON	SCOTT	TOTAL	%
Female	1	3	2	5	1	12	33
Male	3	7	4	6	4	24	67
Total	4 (11%)	10 (28%)	6 (17%)	11 (31%)	5 (13%)	36	100

Source: U.S. Bureau of the Census 1850, Schedule 1.

Table 2.6. • Southern Core Contingent: State of Birth.

	AR	MS	TN	AL	LA	KY	NC	TOTAL
Adults	5		4	7		1		17
Subadults	16			3				19
Total	21 (58%)		4 (11%)	10 (28%)		1 (3%)		36

Source: U.S. Bureau of the Census 1850, Schedule 1.

Table 2.7. • Southernern Core Contingent: Adult Kinship Relations.

Relationship	No.	%
Husband-Wife	10	59
Parent-Child	13	76
Sibling-Sibling	11	65
B-B	8	73
B-Z	7	64
Z-Z	2	18

Note: N = 17; 18+ years in age.

married couple, Martha and William Cameron, both 51. They were traveling with eight of their nine offspring, including two married daughters. The journey would be especially trying for the eldest daughter, Malinda, who had three young children and was pregnant with another, who would be born on the trail. Fortunately, she was accompanied by her husband, Henry D. Scott, and his brother, Richard T. Scott.[5]

Of the 17 adults in the southern core, only 5 had been born in Arkansas. The other 12 were originally from Alabama, Tennessee, or Kentucky (Table 2.6). Most of the adults—11 of the 17—had siblings on the wagon train, and the most frequent tie, as in the northern party, was between brothers (Table 2.7). The two parties were in some ways quite different, however. Most obviously, there is a striking reversal in sex distribution. Whereas the majority of the northern core consisted of young females, the southern party was mostly composed of young men and boys (Table 2.8). At the same time, as elabo-

Table 2.8. • Southern Core Contingent: Age Distribution.

AGE	JONES	TACKITT	MILLER	CAMERON	SCOTT	NO.	%
0–4	m	m	f, m		(m)	5	14
5–9	f	m	m, m	m	(f), m	7	19
10–14		m, m		m, f, f		5	14
15–19		m, f		m, m		4	11
20–24		m	f	m		3	8
25–29	(m)	m, f		f, f	m, m	7	19
30–34	m		m			2	6
35–39							
40–44							
45–49		f				1	2
50+				f, m		2	6

Note: Parentheses indicate an estimated age category.

rated in the next chapter, the northern group was led by a large landowner, Jack Baker, whereas the southern group was more loosely clustered around a widow and an older couple with only modest landholdings.

Boston Bridges

How did the two large networks come to be associated at all? No ties of kinship or marriage are known to have united the networks in 1857 (some of their descendants have intermarried since). The two parties set out from geographical points separated by more than sixty miles of extremely rugged terrain. According to one account (Thurston 1877), the Johnson County contingent traveled along the Arkansas River and met with the Beller's Stand group in Indian country. If a rendezvous had been arranged, it is likely that some kind of personal relationship served to bridge the parties ahead of time. What social links might have been involved? It turns out that three kinds of connections may have been important.

First, there may have been links generated by previous residence, either within Arkansas or in other states. Former neighbors now living on opposite sides of the mountains might have reconnected for purposes of a journey west. One possible example is the case of Jack Baker and William Cameron. When Baker arrived in Arkansas in 1849, Cameron had been living in the state for about a decade. In 1850 both men had holdings on Crooked Creek, probably within a few miles of each other, in what was then Carroll County (U.S. Bureau of the Census 1850, Schedule 1). Several other factors may have brought them together: both were in their mid-forties, both had seven offspring, and both had lived for some time in Alabama. What contact there may have been between the two is unclear, but they probably would have known of each other. Cameron certainly would have known of Baker, who had quickly established himself as a prominent farmer in the area, with more than four hundred acres and seven slaves. Cameron himself was only a modest landowner in Carroll County and by 1855 had moved on to an eighty-acre farm in Johnson County.[6] From here he may have served as Baker's link to a network of families south of the mountains.

Another kind of connection would not have required residential proximity. Instead, beyond the immediate "neighborhood," people may have been united by business dealings, military service, religious rituals, or political activities. Contacts developed over a wide area may have been renewed as people were recruited to the wagon train. An itinerant merchant, for example, may have spread the word about the train on both sides of the Boston Mountains. One emigrant who had been active in Carroll, Johnson, and Marion counties was Jesse Dunlap Jr. As described in the previous chapter, Dunlap had lived for a time on Wharton Creek in Madison County. By 1850, however, he was living in northern Johnson County and was listed on the census as a "merchant." As soon as steamboat service had arrived on the upper White River, Dunlap had relocated to Dubuque Landing, where he established a business with his brother-in-law, William C. Mitchell (Logan 1998:12). Just three years later he would join up with the wagon train at Beller's Stand. Through the activities of figures such as Dunlap—not a prominent leader but a mobile entrepreneur—the wagon train may have been constituted as a loose aggregation rather than a tightly organized hierarchy.

A third kind of link might have grown up with the prospect of commercial enterprises in California. Parties already established there served as focal points for the organization of some family members back in Arkansas. Felix Grundy Miller, for example, along with his wife, his children, and his younger brother Wade, had arrived in California by 1853 (Shirley Pyron, personal communication, 2003). In the south Central Valley, Felix and Wade settled on farmland near Visalia and set aside a parcel for kin who had yet to make the journey from Arkansas. Between them the brothers had a rich network of contacts on both sides of the Boston Mountains. Felix had come to California from his home on the Osage in Carroll County, and Wade had departed from Spadra in Johnson County. They had siblings in both counties and hoped that their youngest brother in particular would be persuaded to join them in Visalia. This brother, Josiah, had married into the Cameron family in Carroll County but had taken his wife and children to Johnson County by 1855. Miller family members and their neighbors likely passed on word about opportunities in Visalia, and many would have considered the prospect of a new life in California. In a sense, this case is just an extension of the much older pattern of stream migration that had drawn families such as the Millers through the Appalachians to northwestern Arkansas.

Fancher and Company

All three kinds of social connection—past residence, present affiliation, and future prospect—are illustrated by the case of Alexander Fancher. In fact, in many historical accounts and memorials Fancher is referred to as "Captain Alexander," under the assumption that he was the leader of the wagon train as a whole (e.g., Lee 1857 in Brooks 1962:151; Fancher 1999:248). This assumption is questionable. In early April, according to Benton County tax records, when the northern party was gathering at Beller's Stand, Fancher was still selling off his property on the Springfield Plain. This land was located in Benton County, some eighty miles west of Beller's Stand.

Ever since the massacre, many accounts have given the impression that Fancher and his household, along with other Arkansas families, set out from the same location in Carroll County (e.g., *Arkansas State Gazette and Democrat*, 27 February 1858; Wise 1976:12; Fancher 1999:249). Yet this is unlikely, if only because it would have required several days of backtracking by the Fanchers, with a large herd of cattle in tow. Some have even suggested that Fancher and Baker cooperated in organizing the wagon train (Denton 2003: 97). Yet there is no direct evidence that these two men even knew each other before 1857. What seems more plausible, in this light, is that the Fancher party proceeded west from Benton County and intersected along the way with some or all of the emigrants from Carroll County.

In any case, when he met up with the other travelers, Fancher was already linked to them in several ways. The Millers were his former neighbors in both Tennessee and Arkansas. William Mitchell, his former captain in the Carroll County militia, had married Nancy Dunlap. Their son was Charles Mitchell, who joined his maternal uncles, Lorenzo and Jesse Dunlap, at Beller's Stand. Most important, perhaps, both Josiah Miller and Alexander Fancher had a brother waiting in the vicinity of Visalia. The possibility arises that Miller and Fancher had coordinated their movements to arrive at neighboring homesteads in California. All this suggests that Alexander Fancher played an important role in the organization of the wagon train. At the same time, there is no solid evidence that he was present at Beller's Stand or that he was the leader of the train from the time it left Arkansas.

Yet Fancher, at age 45, had valuable experience in overland travel that may have won him followers as the train proceeded west. He had two successful

Table 2.9. • Fancher Core Contingent: Age Distribution.

AGE	FANCHER	INGRUM	NO.	%
0–4	f		1	8
5–9	f, f, m		3	23
10–14	m, f		2	15
15–19	m, m, m, f		4	31
20–24				
25–29	m		1	8
30–34		f	1	8
35–39				
40–44				
45–49	m		1	8
50+				

expeditions behind him, and preparations for such a trip must have become almost routine. This time it was likely to have been different, as he was escorting his wife, Eliza Ingrum, and their nine offspring. In Eliza's case, the destination was certainly familiar. Regardless of whether her previous trek had been by land or sea, she faced another journey with children in tow and must have worried about the arduous effects on their health.

Eliza had married Alexander when was she was remarkably young and had borne her first child by age 14. In 1857 she was only 32, and her children ranged from 19 to less than 2 years of age (Table 2.9). (Given this pattern of birth spacing, she may well have been pregnant as the wagon train departed.) Eliza's oldest offspring, Hampton, would have enjoyed the company of his paternal cousins, James and Robert Fancher, who were 25 and 19 years old. With the addition of these cousins, the Fancher party that set out for California consisted of 13 persons (Figure 2.4), with an average age of 17. The sex ratio of the party was nearly even—seven males and six females.

Satellites

The three social networks discussed so far comprised 85 persons, representing more than half the company that is supposed to have departed from Arkansas. At least a third of this company, however, is still to be accounted for. Who were the other 50 or 60 travelers? Here they are referred to as *satellites*, not because they were less important but because they were usually friends, neighbors, or distant kin of those in the core families.

One satellite household is likely to have joined the Fanchers in their

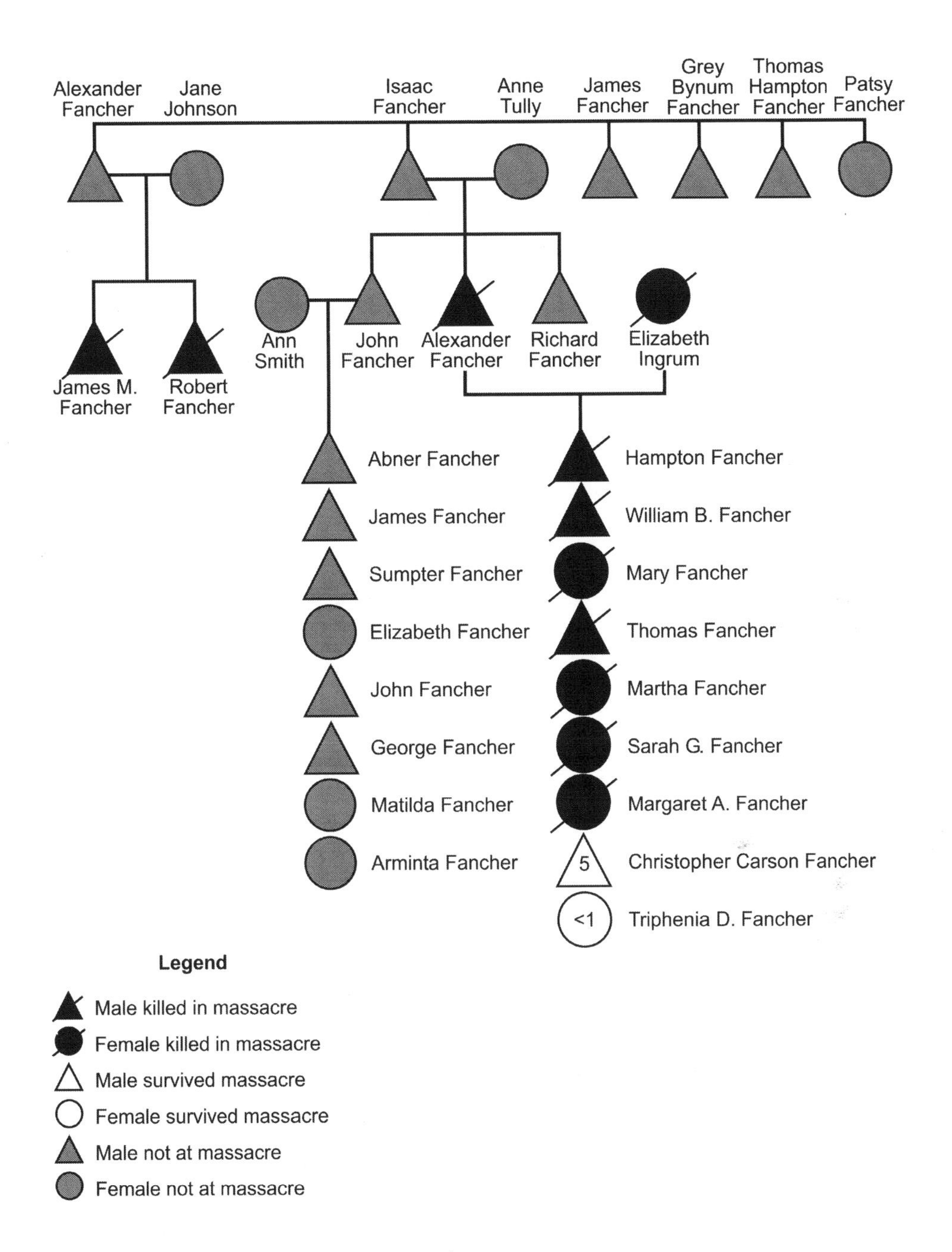

Figure 2.4. • Kinship network of the Fancher contingent, 1857.

departure from Benton County. Peter Huff and his wife, Saladia Ann Brown Huff, brought along four sons and a 4-year-old daughter, Nancy Saphrona. Little is known about the relationship between the Huffs and the Fanchers except that according to a land deed transfer, both families had moved to Benton County in about 1854. Peter Huff was about the same age as Alexander Fancher and had similar holdings on the Springfield Plain. Yet their fates on the wagon train would be quite different: by the time Fancher was murdered at Mountain Meadows, Huff had been dead for some forty days, possibly killed by a spider bite near Fort Bridger.

In the party that left from Beller's Stand, all the known satellites were men. Two of them, Milum Rush and Allen P. DeShazo, were Jack Baker's neighbors. Another was Silas Edwards, who was Jack Baker's maternal uncle, though there is no record of where he resided in 1857 or at what point he joined the train. From Marion County, adjacent to Carroll, came several other riders: two sets of brothers, the Woods and the Prewitts, and at least three others, Charles Stallcup, Richard Wilson, and Lawson A. McEntire. These Marion County men, who would have been neighbors to the Dunlaps and Mitchells, probably joined the train as drovers. Even among these satellites, ties of kinship were at work: Stallcup was a brother-in-law of the Woods, and Wilson was their cousin. Finally, three young men from the hills of Newton County—Peter Calmus Campbell,[7] Alf Smith, and Tom Farmer—joined the northern contingent in search of "adventure and to seek... fortune in the gold fields of California" (Niswonger 1992:38).

Although these men, as far as is known, did not travel with wives or children, they were not necessarily bachelors. Many had family members who remained in Arkansas and anxiously awaited their safe return. The majority of the Marion County riders, for example, left wives and children in the Ozarks. The wives, in particular, played a crucial role in maintaining the family farm. As Linda Peavy and Ursula Smith (1994:4) point out, "Although the women on the home frontier have remained a largely invisible sector,... their work directly supported a sizeable percentage of the men who explored and settled the American West." At the same time, such women had children "to be fed, clothed, housed, and educated; farms and businesses had to be managed; and creditors had to be paid or pacified—with or without a husband at hand" (Peavy and Smith 1994:4). One of these "women in waiting" was Manerva Jane Hudson Wood. When her husband, William Wood, joined the wagon train, Manerva was 18 years old, the mother of a 2-year-old son, and expecting a second child. Her waiting came to a devastating end when she learned of her husband's death at Mountain Meadows. On hearing the news, she suffered a miscarriage (Karin Heymer, personal communication, 2003).

In the southern contingent there were relatively few satellites, and little is known about them. For example, there was "a man named Basham, perhaps George D. Basham" (Bagley 2002:66), who seems to have associated with the Jones, Tackitt, and Poteet families (Logan 1992:231). The three Poteet brothers were reportedly cousins of the Tackitts (Charlotte Lucus, personal communication, 2003). "The oldest one of the Peteats [Poteets] was a married man, and had his wife and children along; They had a separate camp and wagon" (Rowan in Logan 1992:230). The separateness of this party was symptomatic of a more general pattern in the wagon train—a tendency for satellites to travel independently, with only a fluid connection to the core families.

In some cases there was no obvious connection of this kind. Nine named men, three of whom were with "families," have been associated with the wagon train but not with any of the core networks. In addition, several other "families," including the Laffoons, Sorrells, and Wassons, are sometimes linked to the caravan.

In considering such cases, we face a series of special problems. Satellite groups and individuals tend to be underrepresented in historical accounts. What might account for this historical obscurity? Is it because these people were truly marginal to the wagon train, perhaps camping only intermittently with the main parties? Or is it because they left behind no social network or powerful spokesperson to record and celebrate their participation? Those with few or no surviving descendants were especially unlikely to have their stories entered into the historical record. By comparison, descendants with large and densely connected kinship networks could regroup after the massacre and ensure that their kin were remembered (Novak and Rodseth 2006). In some cases, furthermore, the victims left behind a relative who was especially prominent or influential. Such a relative might work for many years to keep the story of the massacre in historical consciousness. The obscurity of some families and individuals may simply reflect their distance from those in a position to make and preserve history (Trouillot 1995).

Some 350,000 Others

At least 123 persons, and perhaps as many as 150, can be associated with the wagon train that left the Ozarks in 1857. This is just a tiny fraction, of course, of the estimated 350,000 overland travelers during the antebellum period (Jeffrey 1998:3). Compared with other companies, how typical was the structure and composition of the Arkansas wagon train? In particular, were the kinship patterns that characterized this train found in others during the same period?

In the early nineteenth century only a few overland trails crossed the American landscape. They ran either south along Spanish colonial routes or north along the paths taken by Lewis and Clark (Topping 1999:10). Only in 1841 did the first group of emigrants, the Bartleson-Bidwell party from Missouri, successfully complete the overland journey by wagon to California (Nunis 1959). During the 1840s, wagon trains tended to have a formal organization modeled on a military structure. The first trains were commercial caravans sponsored by fur traders William Ashley and William L. Sublette (Unruh 1979:29). Emigrant trains followed suit by electing officers, producing bylaws and codes of discipline, and subdividing their train into platoons. Under these guidelines some complained of autocratic train captains who monitored behavior to such a degree that "hardly a yoke of oxen could be permitted to drink without a command" (Carleton 1943 [1845]:182). Fear of unknown dangers on the trail, including Indian attacks, compelled most travelers to submit to such rigors. As a result, wagon trains were nominally under the control of experienced captains who could guide the emigrants safely to the West.

At the same time, as Faragher (2001:27) points out, "we have been left with a view of these trains shaped more by what emigrants wanted them to be than what they actually were." Despite their military organization, large trains were often rife with dissension. In many cases nuclear families had been recruited to join the train and had little connection to one another beyond the formal structure of command. There was scant loyalty to the wagon train as a whole, and smaller parties often split off (Faragher 2001:28–29).

In the 1850s, however, the organization of wagon trains began to change. Most companies had less formal organization but more extended kinship. Between 1856 and 1868 nearly half of all emigrant families traveled in extended family groups, many of which contained three generations of travelers (Faragher 2001:194). Perhaps the most important factor in this shift was the availability of reliable firsthand accounts of the trail ahead. Myths of unrelenting attacks by savage Indians and of the certain death faced by women and children in the Great American Desert were gradually dispelled (Unruh 1979:7–14). Furthermore, by the 1850s the need for trail guides diminished as more individuals made multiple trips and emigrants learned that most of the problems they might encounter could be dealt with by an extended family or other kin group.

Thus the kin-based organization of the Arkansas train was part of a wider trend in overland travel. Like the majority of emigrants in the mid-nineteenth century, the Arkansans traveled in small communities of neighbors and kin rather than regimented companies of nuclear families. The more fluid nature of the trains, offset by the extended kinship ties, ensured that "a quest for something new would take place in the context of the very familiar" (Faragher 2001:34).

For the adult emigrants, this kind of quest would have been familiar in another way. Most of them had memories of prior moves across significant distances: having been born in the East or the Appalachian region, they had moved at least once before their departure for California (Billington 1967:5). Of those men who made the overland journey during the mid-nineteenth century, most had moved west from their natal homes while in their early twenties; this was usually followed by a second move in their middle thirties (Faragher 2001:18). The decision to move, however, involved more than age. A man's stage in the family life cycle also came into play. He was especially likely to move in the first two years of marriage. After that, he tended to move while his children were still young and then again when some of them had reached adolescence (Faragher 2001:18).

Among the Arkansas emigrants, as far as is known, there were no newlyweds or other couples without children. All the married riders were embedded in what John Mack Faragher (2001:190) calls "young families" (with children under age 15) or "mid-stage families" (with some offspring 15 years or older). In this light, the Arkansas wagon train consisted mostly of established households or heads of such households who were traveling without their dependents. In general, the male emigrants had mobility patterns consistent with their stages of family life. Among them, only Alexander Fancher appears to have moved more frequently (at least four times) than would be expected on the basis of his life-cycle stage (a father of adolescent offspring).

In terms of sex ratios, how typical was the Arkansas train? During the gold rush single men or those traveling without their families were prevalent in the overland registers. Yet many men who traveled alone had wives and children who might follow them later or to whom they might return (Roberts 2000). As we saw, the previous overland journeys by Alexander Fancher were likely taken without his family, although his wife and children met him in California. Similarly, a number of the hired hands, such as William Wood, were family men who were traveling without their dependents.

Such men might have responded to an advertisement announcing the expedition. In most cases, however, they approached a known family member or local leader who was organizing a company of travelers. In the case of the 1857 train John T. Baker, his son George Baker, and Jesse Dunlap Jr. seem to have attracted neighboring men or distant kin who hoped to hire on as drovers or other laborers. Such hired hands were often considered part of the household. "Unattached men could and did group themselves into all-male companies, but many men preferred the well-understood and accepted divisions and unities of the family. These men...were attracted to a place where they could find 'bed and board' and have their 'washing and mending done' in exchange for masculine contributions to the family economy" (Faragher 2001:39). For men who were eager to reach California, the typical wagon train was an extremely slow mode of transport, and they often abandoned the company. Yet those who stayed with their host families tended to develop close attachments and were saddened to leave the household.

Except for the peak gold-rush years of 1849 and 1850, the majority of overlanders were women and children (Bagley in press; cf. Faragher 2001). Although husbands and wives continued to travel during this peak, they were overwhelmed by the flood of male migrants who were either unmarried or traveling without their families. On the 1857 train approximately 43 percent of the company was female, a fairly typical proportion in the mid-1850s (Bagley in press). It is worth remembering, however, that most of these females were girls or adolescents. Among the adults on the train, the ratio of males to females was nearly three to one.

Fragments

The wagon train that set out from Arkansas was reconfigured as it traveled west. At least one new rider joined the train, and there may have been other recruits who had become disenchanted with the Mormon theocracy and were attempting to leave the Utah Territory (Bagley 2002:104). More important, a number of riders left the train. In one case, this was the result of an accidental death. Most of the attrition, however, resulted from the strategic decisions of those who thought they might do better by following a different route or forming an independent party.

In July 1857 the various parties from northwestern Arkansas filtered through Fort Bridger, in what is now Wyoming. Since 1853 the fort had been under the control of the Mormons, so this point marked the train's entry into the domain of Brigham Young. Arriving as independent parties, some were delayed as they awaited a birth or suffered a death. Ellen Cecil, who was in the company of Basil Parker, was expecting a baby near the end of July, and this seems to have kept their party from accompanying the Fancher, Cameron, Dunlap, and Baker families (Bagley 2002:96). Meanwhile, somewhere near the fort, according to the *San Jose Pioneer* (21 April 1877), Peter Huff died after being bitten on the hand by a "venomous creature," probably a spider. Huff was buried on the trail. His widow, Saladia Ann, continued to Salt Lake City with her three sons and one young daughter.

Most of the Arkansans entered the Mormon capital in early August. Some apparently camped for weeks outside the city while waiting for cooler weather before taking the southern route (*Daily Alta California* 1857a). It was here that the Scott family separated from a larger contingent headed by William Cameron. Some twenty years later Malinda Cameron Scott provided the following account in a legal deposition (Thurston 1877):

> At the solicitation and under the advice of the Mormons and the representations that the stock could better be provided with feed, the train was divided, with the understanding that it was to be united outside of Salt Lake City and proceed by the northern route; and under said advice her husband, his brother-in-law, herself, and their three children and others started from Salt Lake and made one day's journey, on the third of August...and there encamped to await her father's part of said train; and that they remained in said camp until the seventh day of August in said year, when her husband was killed by one of the men of the train (but not by the Mormons).

Henry D. Scott was murdered somewhere between Salt Lake City and Ogden, Utah. The circumstances surrounding this event are obscure (Bagley 2002:99). Yet the decision to proceed along the northern route would eventually save the lives of Henry's wife and family. Three days after his death, Malinda gave birth to their fourth child. "After waiting for her father's part of the train a long and reasonable time the train proceeded on, and she eventually reached California" (Thurston 1877).

In addition to the Scott family, Basil Parker and the Poteet brothers (Parker 1902; McEuen 1996) separated from the main contingent and ultimately survived the overland journey. The three friends from Newton County—Campbell, Smith, and Farmer—became bored with the slow-moving train, and they too left at Salt Lake City, taking a shortcut to California. Such reductions in the original parties resulted in the loss to the company of at least 19 individuals: 9 men, 1 woman, and 8 children.

One of these vacant slots was filled by a young man from Tennessee. In mid-August, 19-year-old William A. Aden joined one of the Arkansas parties some fifty miles south of Provo, Utah. He too was en route to California, but rather than stay the winter in Provo (as he had written to his parents he would do), Aden decided to press on and join the Arkansas contingent (Bagley 2002:102). Along with Aden, a number of Mormon apostates were rumored to have joined the Arkansas contingent in an attempt to leave the Utah Territory. Whether such "back outs" were actually on the wagon train is a matter of debate (Bigler 1998:172; Bagley 2002:104).

In early September the Arkansans began to converge at Mountain Meadows, where they would water their cattle and rest before crossing the Mojave Desert. Spread out over the Meadows, the family units dispersed themselves informally in the same manner as they had traveled across the country. At the same time, what had been separate parties funneled into one high desert valley, perhaps forming a unified train for the first time. Husbands, wives, children, and grandchildren were joined by drovers and other laborers who were obliged to develop close friendships with their sponsoring families. A young man like William Aden would have found a ready cohort of other young men with whom to associate. Aden was described by his father as "quite uprightly, a good sign painter, writes poetry and some prose pretty well, makes a good speech—picks a Banjoe tolerably well—pretty good looking" (Bagley 2002:102). On September 6 Mountain Meadows hummed with the activity of some 140 people settling into their evening routine. Within five days, only 17 of them would remain alive.

NOURISHMENT

Eminent men represent a much better nourished class.

— Franz Boas, "Human Faculty as Determined by Race," 1894

Classes are not objects "out there," but there is something out there in the way of inequality, privilege, and social difference which the idea of "class" is meant to capture.

— Sherry B. Ortner, "The Hidden Life of Class," 1998

Most accounts of Mountain Meadows say a lot about the Utah Mormons and very little about the Arkansas emigrants. When they are described, these emigrants are generally depicted in one of two ways. That they were ill-tempered scoundrels was an image promulgated by the killers themselves and much of the Mormon history literature (e.g., Lee 2001 [1877]:225; Penrose 1884; Whitney 1892). The alternative image was suggested early on by Hubert Howe Bancroft (1889:545): "Most of them were farmers by occupation; they were orderly, sober, thrifty, and among them was not lack of skill and capital." This image of respectability has been adopted by several recent authors, including Will Bagley (2002:56): "Although long caricatured as a horde of faceless ruffians, the party's large number of women and children casts doubt on folklore that pictures its journey west as a drunken and murderous rampage. As these Arkansas travelers demonstrate, the typical overlander was not a shiftless vagabond, for crossing half a continent by wagon was an expensive proposition." Because the overland journey, in other words, required substantial financial investment, only a family with surplus wealth could fund an expedition of this kind.

Early guidebooks estimated that overland travel to California would cost a family of four more than $600. Throughout the 1850s the cost of travel increased as entrepreneurs imposed tolls and other charges along the route (Jeffrey 1998:39). Faragher (2001:21) suggests that transportation itself was the most expensive aspect of travel, requiring approximately $400 for a wagon, oxen, and gear. An adult's basic provisions, consisting of flour, bacon, and coffee, would have cost about $70 but would have to be supplemented by homegrown supplies. Another $65 for powder, lead, and shot, plus a bit of cash for the tolls, drained most families of their worldly assets (Faragher 2001:22).

Taken as a group, the Arkansans seem to have been better off than most. Their affluence was reflected especially in the enormous herd they were driving—at least 1,000 head by some estimates—but also in the gold, carriages, and racehorses they are supposed to have had in their possession (Denton 2003:98–99). Such wealth would seem to confirm that they were the prosperous bourgeois described by William Wise (1976), Bagley (2002), and others. Yet this kind of characterization raises a number of questions. What did it mean to be "middle class" in the antebellum context? What did it mean in Arkansas in particular, or in the Ozarks? In this chapter I explore such issues, drawing especially on census and tax records to assess the wealth of the core emigrant families.

Certain questionable images of American class structure have their beginnings in the early nineteenth century. Perhaps the most basic is the view of the United States as an egalitarian, even classless, society. When Henry Clay ran for president in 1824, he introduced the concept of the middle class as the basic identity of most Americans (Sellers 1991:238). Twenty years later the Reverend Calvin Colton (1844) summed up the ideology of America as a nation of "self-made men": "Ours is a country where men start from an humble origin, and from small beginnings rise gradually in the world, as the reward of merit and industry.... One has as good a chance as another, according to his talents, prudence, and personal exertions." According to this image, even the most common man could elevate himself to the class of a gentleman —or at least that of a free and equal frontiersman.

The reality, however, was that Americans were already deeply entangled in a global division of labor, based especially on cotton (Wolf 1982:278–285). As market forces penetrated the society, wealth was concentrated in fewer hands, giving rise to what Thorstein Veblen (1899) would call the "leisure class." "According to the best estimates, the share of national wealth held by the richest 10 percent jumped, mainly after 1820, from the 49.6 percent of 1774 to reach 73 percent by 1860.... Nor were the wealthy self-made. Overwhelmingly they were sons of rich and/or eminent families" (Sellers 1991: 238). It would be a mistake to generalize from national statistics such as these to every region of the country, however. In particular, we must avoid imposing the model of one region, such as New England or "the frontier," on specific settings such as northwestern Arkansas. It is important to remember how extremely fluid the social dynamics were in this region, as most of the adults on the train were not born in Arkansas and were probably not intending to stay there.

Social differences may show up in human bodies as well. The privileged of society, as Franz Boas reminds us, tend to be well nourished—though not without their own special disorders, such as gout or dental disease. Who the emigrants were biologically, in their bones, is a question that has not been considered in earlier accounts. What we have to draw on is not a perfect sample but only 28 of the estimated 120 bodies that were left at Mountain Meadows. Still, the skeletal remains that were analyzed in 1999 provide an unprecedented opportunity to assess skeletal indicators of dietary deficiency and excess. Triangulating from these data to the class identities of the victims, though not easy, is imperative to draw out as much variation within this sample of people as possible, so as not to return them to the state of anonymity from which they are just beginning to emerge.

Arkansas Divided

Attempts have been made to delineate class in the antebellum South, but it has proved to be a precarious task (Campbell 1987; Carey 2001). What is clear is that wealth was extremely unevenly distributed as early as 1840. In Arkansas, "despite its newly settled quality," economic stratification "was more similar to that of the late antebellum South than to colonial America" (Bolton 1984:628). Such inequality would continue through the antebellum period, with 10 percent of the white population holding 70 percent of the state's wealth (Bolton 1998:98). In this respect, at least, Arkansas resembled the national profile as described by Charles Sellers (1991:238).

By 1850 a familiar social hierarchy was emerging in the state, in part because the new settlers were intent on re-creating appropriate social norms (Moneyhon 1994:36): "Arkansas was no longer a frontier community.... Social institutions patterned upon those of the older states emerged, modified by local conditions." As in American society at large, the single most important determinant of social status was wealth. The rich, whatever their social backgrounds, were able to rise: "'Those claiming elite status possessed only a thin veneer of the cultural and other attainments that would distinguish them in an older society" (Moneyhon 1994:36). To the outsider, in fact, there was little in the speech or the demeanor of elites that would distinguish them from most other Arkansans. Only when one's possessions were on display or were already known to the observer would true social standing come to light.

The "best society" included professionals and businessmen, whose income would have allowed them to purchase considerable property, including livestock and slaves (Moneyhon 1994:37). Yet most of the elites were large planters. The great plantations were located in two areas of the state—along the Mississippi River in the east, and in the southwestern corner bordering Texas and Louisiana (McNeilly 2000:134). As in much of the Cotton South, the ownership of land and labor translated into social capital. The political sphere was dominated by a few elite families. These families kept parlors and displayed luxury goods, including dishes, silverware, sofas, ottomans, and French bedsteads with patent springs (*Arkansas Gazette*, 20 November 1844; *Arkansas State Gazette and Democrat*, 1 August 1857). They also traveled more widely, gave their children a better education, and in general flaunted their wealth more conspicuously than did the vast majority of the population.

According to Carl Moneyhon's analysis, nearly 90 percent of the white population of antebellum Arkansas belonged to the "middle class." This was the "backbone of society"—people who were "propertied, hard-working, and God-fearing, but without the wealth of the elite" (Moneyhon 1994:42). The majority were either Methodists or Baptists, with a significant minority of Presbyterians (Moneyhon 1994:48). In many ways this class embodied the bourgeois values that were now, according to Sellers (1991:237), becoming hegemonic in American society at large: "The so-called middle class was constituted not by mode and relations of production but by ideology.... A numerous and dispersed bourgeoisie of small-scale enterprisers pushed both themselves and their workers to staggering effort by mythologizing class as a moral category. Scorning both the handful of the rich and the multitude of dissolute poor, they apotheosized a virtuous middle class of the effortful."

In general, the members of this class were less ostentatious than the elites and tended to avoid conspicuous consumption. An inventory of households from Pulaski County in central Arkansas in the 1850s suggests that material possessions in most homes were quite humble (Bennett 1980). According to probate records, more than half the households in this sample had less than $100 worth of furnishings. The remaining homes, with one exception, had less than $500 worth. Rather than amass consumer goods, a farm family accumulated most of its wealth in the form of land, livestock, equipment, and slaves (Bennett 1980:3).

Within the middle class, different levels of wealth might be imperceptible to outside observers, but the prosperous farmer usually had more outbuildings around his home as well as more material goods inside. In light of such differences, we may differentiate between an "upper" and a "lower" middle class. The upper middle class included small planters and successful farmers as well as some professionals, merchants, and craftsmen. The leadership of local communities and churches tended to be drawn from this segment of society. Moneyhon (1994:42) distinguishes the upper from the rest of the middle class in terms of the assets needed to mobilize labor: "In 1860 the minimum worth for this group was about $1000. That amount was significant because the farmer or merchant who achieved it had made the first step toward controlling the labor of others and had the potential to go further."

The lower middle class, by contrast, was mainly composed of subsistence farmers who owned or rented small plots. At the same time, many in this stratum moved in and out of skilled occupations, such as blacksmith, wagon maker, miller, ginwright, and carpenter. Rather few were merchants. Lower-middle-class Arkansans tended to move frequently and held land of their own only intermittently.

For people of such modest means, falling out of the middle class altogether was a real possibility. Some who did so lived hand-to-mouth, taking on odd jobs or moving to the margins to follow a hardscrabble existence (Moneyhon 1994:49): "At the bottom of white society were those who possessed no property at all. Contemporaries often identified them in terms of their life-style and occupations; the 'peddler class' and 'backwoodsmen & Mechanics' were typical descriptions." In 1860 about 10 percent of Arkansans had no taxable property (Bolton 1998:99). Not all of them, however, were truly destitute. Some held wealth that was not taxable or were waiting to inherit property. Furthermore, squatters who appeared on tax lists to be propertyless were often self-sufficient and would eventually register to own the land.

Although a statewide class structure of this kind may be discerned, it is often too crude to capture the most important social differences. Historically, Arkansas has been a region divided between the highlands of the northwest and the low plains that extend to the Mississippi delta. This geographical division is reflected in wealth differences, with highland farmers holding only one-third of the taxable assets: land, slaves, horses, and cattle.[1] By the mid-nineteenth century, as documented by S. Charles Bolton (1998:53–54), "two somewhat different societies were emerging. The highlands area was becoming a society of small farmers, while the lowlands region was gradually developing a small class of market-oriented planters." Lowland taxpayers had a bimodal distribution—either rich or poor—and many had no taxable "humid subtropical," although numerous microhabitats pock the region as a result of topographic variation. Temperature, in particular, can fluctuate dramatically with the time of day, the slope of a mountain face, and the distance to water.

The families that joined the wagon train had made their homes in the valleys and foothills either north or south of the Boston Mountains. To the north is the vast plateau carved by the White River and its tributaries. To the south, gentle slopes converge on the Arkansas River and its rich alluvial valley. These two waterways dominate the landscape in their respective regions, each forming a distinct topography, ecology, and settlement pattern. Such geographical differences between north and south would give rise, in turn, to different patterns of mobility, kinship, and economy in the two primary social networks on the wagon train.

Long before these networks had assembled, however, there were people who had visited both sides of the Boston Mountains. Native Americans and European explorers had passed through this region, though few had settled here for more than a few months or years at a time. The Osage and other indigenous peoples had hunted here in small mobile bands. Later arrivals, such as the Cherokee, would establish more permanent settlements. The French explorers Marquette and Jolliet would make contact with local tribes and begin the process of colonial interaction. Before turning to the history of the wagon train, we must consider the flow of both Native Americans and Europeans into the Ozarks and how this contact zone changed in relation to population growth and government policies in the East.

Downstream People

In 1673, while traveling from Quebec along the Mississippi River, Father Jacques Marquette and Louis Jolliet questioned a group of natives about access to the sea. They were told that "at the next great village, called Arkansea, eight or ten leagues farther down the river, we could learn all about the sea" (Reynolds 1906). Continuing south, the explorers did indeed come upon an Indian community at the mouth of the Arkansas River. The Quapaw, a Siouan-speaking people (Morse 1991:53), had settled on the banks, constructing palisaded villages of large, multifamily dwellings. Marquette's account of his journey gave the region its name: Arkansas, or "land of the down-stream people" (Baird 1980).

By 1686 French traders had established the Arkansas Post at the confluence of the White and Arkansas rivers. The post became a busy intersection for missionaries, trappers, and merchants who exchanged the precious commodities of the day: salted buffalo meat, buffalo tallow, and bear oil. When property (Bolton 1984:631). In the Ozarks, by comparison, wealth was more evenly distributed, giving rise to a substantial majority of yeoman farmers.

Ozark Society

Such farmers were not necessarily concentrated in the highlands as opposed to the lowlands; instead, their social role was more prominent in the hill country because here they escaped the shadow of a dominant planter class. In the southeast corner of the state as much as 70 percent of all taxable land was owned by slaveholding planters (Bolton 1998:62–63). In the northwest, by contrast, most of the land was not suitable for cotton, and the few large plantations were concentrated along narrow bottomlands surrounded by rugged topography. Where cotton could be grown, it was generally too expensive to transport unless there was ready access to a river landing.

Thus even within the Ozarks there was a major economic divide between areas along navigable waterways and those that were cut off from such waterways by mountains and hollows. In particular, on the Arkansas River the southern Ozark counties of Crawford, Franklin, Johnson, and Pope developed a significant cotton industry whereas the counties directly to the north—Washington, Madison, Carroll, and Newton—produced almost no cotton at all (Blevins 2002:38). The southern counties also developed a more commercial culture, oriented toward market centers far downstream, from Little Rock to New Orleans. In the backcountry, by contrast, most people "were involved in subsistence agriculture, feeding themselves by applying the labor of large families to abundant land and by exchanging services and homemade goods with their neighbors" (Bolton 1998:49). Such bartering was the dominant form of exchange, though most farm families would have sold some products to a country store for cash. In turn, they purchased commercial goods such as tea, coffee, or sugar and paid their annual taxes (Sellers 1991:14–15). In general, however, these "hill folk" were less likely than their southern neighbors to rely on markets for their livelihood.

This intraregional contrast is encapsulated in the difference between Carroll and Johnson counties, the two areas that provided most of the emigrants on the 1857 wagon train. Carroll County, north of the Boston Mountains, was remote from the established arteries of commercial trade. Its social economy tended to be inward-looking, with an emphasis on subsistence agriculture and herding, though there were some regional markets in goods and services. Johnson, to the south of the mountains, was a watershed that invited goods and people to flow into the network of the Arkansas River and on to the Mississippi.

A closer look at these two counties reveals a sharp contrast in occupations. By the mid-nineteenth century 94 percent of the men in Carroll County identified themselves as farmers (U.S. Bureau of the Census 1850, Schedule 1). Only 5 percent called themselves merchants or artisans, and 1 percent professionals. Although the countryside saw little occupational diversity, even small settlements tended to have a blacksmith, post office, and gristmill. One such hamlet was in Prairie Township, near present-day Berryville, where 7 percent of the men were artisans and merchants in 1850. There were three "professionals": a physician and two schoolteachers. The busiest market center, however, was the town of Carrollton. Founded in 1833, the county seat had a bustling public square surrounded by businesses and a courthouse. Here resided a brickmason, carpenter, chair maker, four blacksmiths, three merchants, a wagon maker, a wheelwright, and a saddler. A few luxury items could be purchased from the town's wool carder, shoemaker, and two tailors. Interestingly, only one man in Carrollton identified himself as a professional—a 55-year-old schoolteacher from Tennessee.

In Johnson County, by contrast, less than 80 percent of the men said they were farmers. Merchants and artisans made up 13 percent of the adult male population, twice as many as in Carroll County. A full 5 percent were professionals. The remaining fraction described themselves as "laborers" or said they had no occupation. The county seat of Clarksville had become especially market-oriented. Here the vast majority of men were artisans, merchants, or professionals whereas only 3 percent identified themselves as farmers. The professionals included numerous clerks and lawyers, one justice of the peace, a registrar, a receiver, and a judge, as well as a full-time preacher, three physicians, and two teachers.

These figures represent what we know as of 1850, based on the U.S. census. In 1850, most of those who would depart for California seven years later were living in Carroll County. During these years at least three families—the Camerons, Millers, and Scotts—would relocate to Johnson County and would help form what I have called the southern contingent. Why these families moved, only to head west in 1857, is uncertain. What is clear is that the gold rush, in this same period, had begun to transform the corridor of the Arkansas River that ran through Johnson County. Whereas the traditional routes of travel and trade had connected the Ozarks to the Mississippi, the magnet of the goldfields began to pull from the west. People began to follow the Arkansas River to Fort Smith and then traveled on by various routes to El Dorado. This westward flow was itself a source of income for entrepreneurs who outfitted the forty-niners, supplied them with room and board, and charged them fees and tolls as they passed through. The Camerons, Millers, and Scotts, who had never owned much land, may well have been enticed by the emerging market opportunities, first in Johnson County and later in California itself.

Another set of market opportunities was created by steamship travel, especially along northern tributaries that had been inaccessible before the 1840s. The greatest of these tributaries, the White River, was especially tempting to Jesse Dunlap Jr., who described himself in the 1850 census as a "merchant." At the time, however, he lived with his wife and ten children on a pig farm in Johnson County. Four years later he moved his family to Dubuque, some eighty-five miles to the northeast, in what was then Marion County. Here he went into business with his sister's husband, William C. Mitchell. The collaboration between Dunlap and Mitchell was an enterprise typical of the antebellum South: "The source of capital for most Southern businesses was family based. Banks were available, of course, in larger communities, but naturally, family resources were preferred" (Wyatt-Brown 1982:213). Mitchell brought to this business both economic and social capital. Though not a slaveholder, he seems to have been affluent, with property in the town of Carrollton, and had held various positions in local and state government. For more than a decade, he served as an Arkansas state senator (Lair 1983:340) before moving in 1854 to Marion County. "Family tradition says that Mitchell and Jesse Dunlap, Jr. had a store and mill at Dubuque landing which was at the mouth of West Sugarloaf Creek on White River" (Logan 1998:307). Together the politician and the self-described merchant would put their entrepreneurial skills to the test on the new steamboat circuit. This partnership did not last long, however, as Dunlap was soon drawn to a new market opportunity far from the Ozarks.

Emigrant Society

Based on Moneyhon's (1994) criteria, all the core families on the wagon train would fall into the middle class. In 1855 the taxable wealth of these families ranged from $50 to over $7,000 (Table 3.1). None were entirely without property, and none were "elites" in Moneyhon's sense. Nevertheless, there were significant economic distinctions among the riders on the train.

The wealthiest emigrant was John Twitty Baker, who in 1855 had taxable assets of approximately $7,100. His property included almost five hundred acres of farmland near Crooked Creek. A large farm such as this was especially characteristic of upper-middle-class status. Baker also had human property. His seven slaves alone were worth some $4,200, more than half his total wealth. By the standards of the southern planter class, these holdings were small, but Baker was one of only 61 slave owners in all of Carroll County. Of these owners, the majority had fewer than three slaves. In this

Table 3.1. • Taxable Assets of the Core Families, 1855–1856.

HEAD OF HOUSEHOLD	YEAR	COUNTY	ACRES	SLAVES	CATTLE	HORSES	MULES	$ VALUE
Baker, John Twitty	1855	Carroll	472	7	22	7	2	7,106
Baker, George W.	1855	Carroll	100		19	4		1,198
Cameron, William	1855	Johnson	120		5	2		535
Cameron, Tilman	1855	Johnson				1		100
Dunlap, Jesse Jr.	1855	Marion			10	3		370
Fancher, Alexander	1856	Benton	210		4	3	1	895
Huff, Peter	1855	Benton	160		22	3	1	925
Jones, John Milum	1856	Johnson			1	1		50
Miller, Josiah	1855	Johnson			3	1	1	335
Mitchell, Charles R.	1855	Marion	200		2	2		1,220
Scott, Henry D.	1855	Johnson			3	1		115
Tackitt, Pleasant	1855	Johnson			2	1	1	140

Source: County tax records.

light, Baker was not only the most prosperous rider on the train but perhaps a social notch above the average farmer in the area.

On highland farms slaves would often labor alongside their owners to clear land, build structures, and tend livestock (Bolton 1998:128). Slaves could be cheaper to maintain than hired laborers and might be rented out to other farmers (Taylor 1958:82–91; Battershell 1999:45). In many ways, slaves served as "a long-term speculative investment for backcountry farmers" (Otto 1980:47). While large planters preferred to maximize their labor force, farmers in the Ozarks were more inclined to keep a "breeding population" of younger slaves who might produce offspring (Phifer 1962). These offspring could be profitable. A slave worth less than $400 in the 1820s was worth more than $700 by the 1850s.

Just such a pattern of investment seems to be characteristic of Baker's slaveholdings. In 1850 he owned one 18-year-old mulatto male, three black males (16, 8, and 4 years old), and three black females (16, 12, and 6 years old). Such capital accumulation appears to indicate that Baker was investing for future generations of his family. On the eve of his journey to California, Baker willed to his youngest son, Pleasant Madison Baker, "a certain negro boy named Charles." Neither Charles nor any of the Bakers' slaves would ride on the wagon train.[2]

Meanwhile, Baker's oldest son, George Washington Baker, and his son-in-law, Charles R. Mitchell, were the next wealthiest men on the train (Table 3.1). In 1855, at age 25, George Baker did not own slaves, but he had

Table 3.2. • Household Size and Property Holdings of the Core Families, 1850.

HEAD OF HOUSEHOLD	AGE	ADULTS	CHILDREN	COUNTY/ TOWNSHIP	ACRES IMPROVED/ ACRES UNIMPROVED	$ VALUE OF FARM IMPLEMENTS	$ VALUE OF FARM MACHINERY	NO. OF SLAVES
Baker, John Twitty	45	2	7	Carroll/ Crooked Creek	55/385	2000	150	7
Baker, George W.	25	2		Carroll/ Crooked Creek	18/40	150		
Beller, William[a]	dec.	1	8	Carroll/ Crooked Creek	65/300	2000	125	8
Cameron, William	44	2	7	Carroll/ Crooked Creek	20	150	10	
Dunlap, Jesse Jr.	32	3	7	Johnson/ Mulberry	13/40	500	125	
Dunlap, Lorenzo	35	2	6	Johnson/ Mulberry	18	300	15	
Fancher, Alexander[b]	38	2	7	[San Diego, CA]				
Fancher, Jane[a]	40	4	6	Carroll/ Carrollton	30	150	5	
Emberson, Miller[a]	38	2	3	Johnson/ Spadra	40/40	600	60	
Miller, Josiah[b]	31	2	1	Crawford/ Mountain				
Mitchell, William C.[a]	43	4	7	Carroll/ Crooked Creek	110/40	1000	40	
Scott, Henry D.	19	2	1	Carroll/ Crooked Creek	10/250	150	10	
Tackitt, Martin	40	3	6	Johnson/ Spadra	40	300	175	

Note: Data consolidated from U.S. Bureau of the Census 1850 (Schedules 1, 2, and 4).
[a]Descendants of this household joined the 1857 train.
[b]No agriculture census found for this household.

considerable holdings in land, cattle, and horses, amounting to $1,220 in taxable wealth. He had married into an equally prosperous family, the Bellers, who had at least eight slaves in 1850 (Table 3.2). Two years younger than George Baker was his sister's husband, Charles R. Mitchell. The oldest son of William C. Mitchell, the prominent politician mentioned above, Charles had spent much of his childhood in the county seat of Carrollton. His was a background of official and professional duties in addition to the chores and routines of rural life. His father had been, in turn, a postmaster, an officer in the militia, a county clerk, and a state senator. By marrying Sarah Baker in 1856, Charles Mitchell effectively combined his own family's prestige and influence with the considerable property and social power of the Baker clan. This union was in keeping with the general tendency of affluent southerners "to increase the bonds of family reliance and to enhance both career and marital success by concentrating wealth" (Wyatt-Brown 1982:217).

If the Bakers, Bellers, and Mitchells formed the affluent core of the wagon train from Carroll County, there were at least two fairly prosperous families that departed from Benton County farther west. In the mid-1850s Peter Huff and Alexander Fancher each held approximately $900 in taxable assets (Table 3.1). In Moneyhon's terms (1994), this figure would indicate a status just below the threshold between upper middle and lower middle class. Yet the farmland held by Huff and Fancher suggests that they were both comfortably situated on the Springfield Plain. On Huff's 140 acres, he grazed three horses, a mule, and twenty-two cattle. Fancher kept three horses, a mule, and four cattle on 210 acres. These farms were about the same size as those owned by George Washington Baker and Charles R. Mitchell, though considerably smaller than John Twitty Baker's.

The wagon train also included a number of less affluent families that would clearly fall into the lower middle class. Most of these families, interestingly, belonged to the southern contingent from Johnson County. Their taxable assets ranged from the $50 held by John Milum Jones to the $535 held by William C. Cameron (cf. Denton 2003:98–99). In fact, Cameron was the only one in this contingent who is known to have owned land (Table 3.1). On average, a core family departing from Johnson County had just $235 of taxable wealth. By contrast, a comparable family departing from Carroll or Benton County had $2,270 in assets—a ten-fold difference. Though all the riders on the train may have been, in a general sense, middle class, there was a marked distinction between the relatively affluent northern contingent and the relatively humble southern contingent.

The only exception to this pattern would seem to be Jesse Dunlap Jr. Though he departed with the northern contingent, he appears on paper to have had little to his name. Dunlap, as we have seen, had a history of shifting residence and occupation. Born in Tennessee, he had been a pig farmer in the backwoods of Johnson County and a storekeeper on the banks of the White River. His case also provides a good example of how fluid taxable assets could be from year to year. In 1850 Dunlap had a farm and livestock worth about $1,000 (Tables 3.2 and 3.4), enough to place him in the upper middle class. In 1855, however, he was assessed for just three horses and ten cattle and did not pay taxes on land at all (Table 3.1). As a merchant, Dunlap may well have liquidated most of his assets in anticipation of an upcoming enterprise.

In this context, it is worth remembering that Dunlap's brother-in-law and business partner was William C. Mitchell. Though he did not travel on the wagon train, Mitchell seems to have been as important to its socioeconomic core as John Twitty Baker and Alexander Fancher. Through both kinship and marriage, Mitchell had dense ties to various households on the train. He had married into the Dunlap family, and his oldest son had married into the Baker family. While Mitchell and his wife remained in Arkansas, the Dunlaps and Bakers were decimated at Mountain Meadows. As a result, William and Nancy Mitchell lost at least twenty-four members of their extended family, twelve of whom were children.

Many Mouths

The large kin groups that constituted the wagon train were to some extent the ideal arrangement in the American South: "Large, healthy families enhanced paternal prestige by displaying power, will, and wealth in the rearing of so many dependents" (Wyatt-Brown 1982:205). These dependents, in turn, represented the principal workforce of the household (Sahlins 1972; Merrill 1977). As Sellers (1991:10) notes, "Experience taught American farmers that the optimum divisions of labor and scale of production could be achieved—with considerable variation for time and place—on as little as twenty improved acres, employing a labor force of father, mother, and six to eight surviving children out of eight or ten pregnancies." In the Ozarks large families allowed farmers to rely on children as seasonal laborers and avoid the cost of hiring outside help (Blevins 2002:50). By 1840 Arkansas had a distinct demographic profile (Yasuba 1962:61–63). "The refined birth rate, calculated as the number of children under ten for every one thousand women aged sixteen through forty-four, was higher in Arkansas than any other state or territory and a startling 43 percent higher than in the United States as a whole" (Bolton 1993:81).

Over her reproductive life, a woman on the Arkansas frontier could expect to have on average nearly nine children. Because women married young and started families almost immediately, households grew quickly. By the time she was in her twenties, a mother was caring for an average of three children under ten years. When she had reached her thirties, her household was likely to include "five or six youngsters, three or four of them under ten" (Bolton 1993:82). She was responsible for feeding not only her offspring but her husband and sometimes other adult males as well.

In 1840 there were three adult males for every two females in Arkansas. Many of these men were bachelors, but they did not necessarily form independent households. In fact, most "were normally attached to someone's family" (Bolton 1993:82). Such attachments were generally based on some degree of kinship, by either blood or marriage. The extended Dunlap family again provides a striking example. Jesse and Lorenzo Dunlap, it may be recalled, married the Wharton sisters and lived on neighboring farms. As their households grew, they took in two unmarried brothers of Mary and Nancy. As a result, each of the wives was directly responsible for her children, a husband, and a brother. Both Wharton brothers would have subsidized their board with farm work, but they also required of the women more domestic labor, especially the processing and preparation of food.

What did these Arkansas women prepare for their families? Corn and pork would have been considered the staple foods. At nearly every meal, corn was eaten in one form or another: on the cob (even while still green), creamed, roasted in the shuck, but most commonly dried and ground into meal. Mush, porridge, and griddle cakes were cornmeal variations that supplemented the ever-present corn bread (Hilliard 1972:48–49). While Americans in the Northeast reduced their intake of corn in the first half of the nineteenth century, "southerners retained the eating habits of seventeenth- and eighteenth-century America by clinging to corn for food throughout the nineteenth century and, indeed, well into the twentieth" (Hilliard 1972:151).

Corn was grown throughout Arkansas, but in the Ozarks it was the primary crop. On many farms in the highlands, all or most of the cultivated acreage was devoted to corn. Because it was so abundant, corn had little monetary value, generally going for less than 18 cents a bushel (Blevins 2002:26). Surplus corn could be sold or exchanged as food, but a considerable portion was turned into corn whiskey or beer. These products were easy to transport, provided supplemental calories, and were often safer than milk or water. Before 1830 most men and women consumed alcohol in "drams," small amounts that might be taken throughout the day. By 1850, however, this practice had been greatly discouraged by the early temperance movement (Thornton 1995:156).

Table 3.3. • Core Households' Production of Grain, Produce, and Animal By-Products, 1850.

HEAD OF HOUSEHOLD	COUNTY	WHEAT (BU)	RYE (BU)	INDIAN CORN (BU)	OATS (BU)	WOOL (LB)	PEAS & BEANS (BU)	IRISH POTATOES (BU)	SWEET POTATOES (BU)	BUTTER (LB)	$ VALUE OF HOMEMADE MANUFACTURE
Baker, John Twitty	Carroll			1,650	40	15	3	15	50		75
Baker, George W.	Carroll										10
Beller, William[a]	Carroll			2,000		30					60
Cameron, William	Carroll			500	100			5	30	8	45
Dunlap, Jesse Jr.	Johnson			200	120	6	5			50	20
Dunlap, Lorenzo	Johnson			200	6	4			50	50	20
Fancher, Alexander[b]	[San Diego, CA]										
Fancher, Jane[a]	Carroll			350	25			3			20
Emberson, Miller[a]	Johnson				90	15			6	25	5
Miller, Josiah[b]	Crawford										
Mitchell, William C.[a]	Carroll		50	2,000	1,000			30	100		21
Scott, Henry D.	Carroll			150							45
Tackitt, Martin	Johnson	60		800				10	15	100	40

Source: U.S. Bureau of the Census 1850, Schedule 4.
[a]Descendants of this household joined the 1857 train.
[b]No agriculture census identified for this household.

The corn-centered diet was usually supplemented with garden produce, especially Irish and sweet potatoes, as well as greens, peas, turnip roots, and melons. Surplus fruits were often dried or turned into preserves, jams, and jellies for winter use. Garden surplus that could not be preserved might be fed to animals.

But like farm families themselves, most livestock were fed primarily corn. Each year, an average southerner consumed an estimated 13 bushels of corn; a pig ate 5 bushels, a horse or mule another 5, a cow 1 bushel, and a sheep ¼ bushel (DeBow 1848:149; Hilliard 1972:158). In 1850 Arkansans produced nearly 9 million bushels of corn, with Carroll and Johnson counties contributing over 250,000 bushels each. Even after all humans and animals had been fed, there was a surplus of more than 90,000 bushels in Carroll County and 50,000 in Johnson County.

The demand for fodder was significantly reduced in the highlands because livestock were often allowed to range freely. Cattle and hogs could forage in the hardwood forests for grasses, acorns, hickory nuts, walnuts, and beechnuts. In fact, farmers in the Ozarks were more likely to fence in their crops than to fence in their animals. Though some families grew no crops at all and relied exclusively on livestock, most subsisted on a mixed economy of farming and herding. The uses of animals on the farm were multiple and varied: "Horses, mules, and oxen pulled stumps, plows, and wagons. Cattle provided milk and beef, though hogs and wild game provided the majority of smokehouse meat" (Blevins 2002:28).

Between 1830 and 1880, annual consumption of meat in the United States was approximately 175 pounds per capita (Cummings 1941:15). The demand for beef as opposed to pork was relatively modest (Hilliard 1972:130; cf. Horowitz 2006:20). In fact, it was not until after the Civil War that beef consumption increased substantially (Wolf 1982:321). Milk, butter, and cheese were dietary by-products from cattle, but "considering the quality and treatment of the woods-grown cows, it is unlikely that dairy production was more than enough to supply minimum needs. A few quarts of milk per day was a likely yield from each cow" (Hilliard 1972:199). In all of Carroll County in 1850, only 166 pounds of butter and 42 pounds of cheese were produced. Yet there was an enormous range of variation from one part of the Ozarks to another. In the same year, Johnson County produced nearly 30,000 pounds of butter and 300 pounds of cheese. The Tackitt family alone produced 100 pounds of butter in 1850.

In general, however, the wagon train's core families were producing nearly identical kinds of goods on their farms. Nearly all grew corn, oats, and potatoes and kept some cattle (Tables 3.3 and 3.4). According to the 1850 census,

Table 3.4. • Livestock Holdings of the Core Households, 1850.

HEAD OF HOUSEHOLD	COUNTY	HORSES	ASSES & MULES	MILK COWS	WORK OXEN	OTHER CATTLE	SHEEP	SWINE	$ VALUE OF LIVESTOCK	$ VALUE OF LIVESTOCK SLAUGHTERED
Baker, John Twitty	Carroll	4		5	6	5	5	100	715	70
Baker, George W.	Carroll	1								15
Beller, William[a]	Carroll	14	11	6	8	5	15	25	825	30
Cameron, William	Carroll	2		3	2	3	5	15	119	40
Dunlap, Jesse Jr.	Johnson	4		2	6	3	3	60	465	50
Dunlap, Lorenzo	Johnson			3		1	3	15	46	20
Fancher, Alexander[b]	[San Diego, CA]									
Fancher, Jane[a]	Carroll	3	1	9		2	8	20	178	10
Emberson, Miller[a]	Johnson	3		3	7	7	19	11	233	16
Miller, Josiah[b]	Crawford									
Mitchell, William C.[a]	Carroll	7	1	10	8	20		150	675	120
Scott, Henry D.	Carroll			1	2	2	3	30	150	40
Tackitt, Martin	Johnson		1	3	4			1	123	50

Source: U.S. Bureau of the Census 1850, Schedule 4.
[a]Descendants of this household joined the 1857 train.
[b]No agriculture census identified for this household.

the majority of these households were producing a surplus of corn, and those farms with the greatest corn surplus were also growing other grains such as wheat, oats, and rye. In 1850, at least, most of the core families seem to have had more than enough to feed themselves.

In particular, a surplus of swine was produced by every household but one, the Tackitts of Johnson County. For the most part, the core families were corn and pig farmers. Of those who kept cattle, John Twitty Baker and Peter Huff had the largest herds, with a modest 22 head apiece, according to Carroll and Benton county tax records in 1855. This reality contrasts with the usual image of Baker, for example, as both a farmer and a "cattleman" who became the "herd boss" on the train (Denton 2003:97), or of Alexander Fancher, who is supposed to have had "ranching in his blood" (Bagley 2002:56). Of course, the Baker-Fancher train was driving cattle—as many as 1,000, according to David L. Bigler (1998:160)—but most were apparently purchased specifically to cash in on the California market. Back in the Ozarks the people who formed the wagon train were less likely to be grazing cattle than to be running pigs.

Disorders of Porkdom

Pork was the complement to corn in the southern diet. The average southerner is estimated to have consumed about 150 pounds of pork per year, nearly four times the amount of beef consumed (Hilliard 1972:105). In both Carroll and Johnson counties there were nearly four pigs for every human being. Surplus swine were profitable, going in the antebellum period for about $3.50 per animal. Pigs were also easily transportable, as they could walk themselves to market. The demand for pork was ubiquitous and gave rise to market centers "as far away as St. Louis and Kansas City or as close as Arkansas Post and Little Rock" (Blevins 2002:27).

Although hog meat was regarded as the ideal food for working people, some physicians were concerned about the amount of pork being ingested:

> The United States of America might properly be called the great Hog-eating Confederacy, or the Republic of Porkdom. At any rate should the South and West...be named dietetically, the above appellation would be peculiarly appropriate; for in many parts of this region, so far as meat is concerned, it is fat bacon and pork, fat bacon and pork only, and that continually morning, noon, and night, for all classes, sexes, ages, and conditions. (Wilson 1860:178)

Though pork supplied high amounts of energy-producing fat, its protein content was lower than that of other meats. This protein deficiency may have been ameliorated by limited amounts of beef, mutton, chicken, eggs, and wild game.

Nevertheless, the typical southern diet was deficient not only in protein but in several vitamins and minerals. A lack of vitamins A and C, in particular, resulted from seasonal and regional shortages of fruits and vegetables. Iron deficiency was an especially prevalent condition in the South (Hilliard 1972:66). Iron from muscle is easily absorbed by the intestines. In the pork-based diet of the time, however, more fat than muscle was consumed. Iron from plants, furthermore, is difficult to absorb. A diet high in corn, in particular, actually inhibits iron absorption through the effect of compounds called phytates (Roberts and Manchester 2005:226). A common medical result of iron deficiency is anemia.

In the nineteenth century iron-related anemia was described by physicians as "chlorosis." Folk treatments ranged from dandelion leaf tea and blackstrap molasses to one's own blood diluted with water (Hatfield 2004:13). Symptoms of anemia include fatigue, pallor, shortness of breath, palpitations, and gastrointestinal disorder. Chronic or severe cases can lead to skeletal abnormalities. Such abnormalities are of special interest here because they may be present in the human remains from Mountain Meadows.

Let us look more closely at the skeletal manifestations of anemia. Bone lesions associated with iron deficiency appear primarily on the cranial vault, eye orbits, and the joints of long bones. In these locations marrow proliferates as the body struggles to produce more red blood cells (Aegerter and Kirkpatrick 1975; Goodman and Martin 2002:27). As the marrow expands, it begins to weaken the bone's outer structure, or cortical bone. Eventually, perforations appear in this smooth surface, exposing the spongy internal structure known as trabecular bone. This process produces tiny pits and eventually a worm-eaten appearance. When such lesions appear in the eye orbits, the condition is known as *cribra orbitalia*.

From the skeletal evidence, what can we tell about the incidence of anemia among the emigrants on the wagon train? Several of those in the mass grave had anemia-related lesions. Cribra orbitalia was found in one older woman and three young men. It also appeared in five fragments of orbits that were indeterminate for age and sex. Most of the porosity was mild, although one young man had lesions that were moderately severe. None of the orbits showed signs of healing, indicating that the condition was active at the time of death (Figure 3.1). Only a single individual, an older male, had lesions in the postcranial skeleton, that is, in the bones beneath the skull. The proximal joints of this individual's lower legs (fibulae) were spongy and expanded in

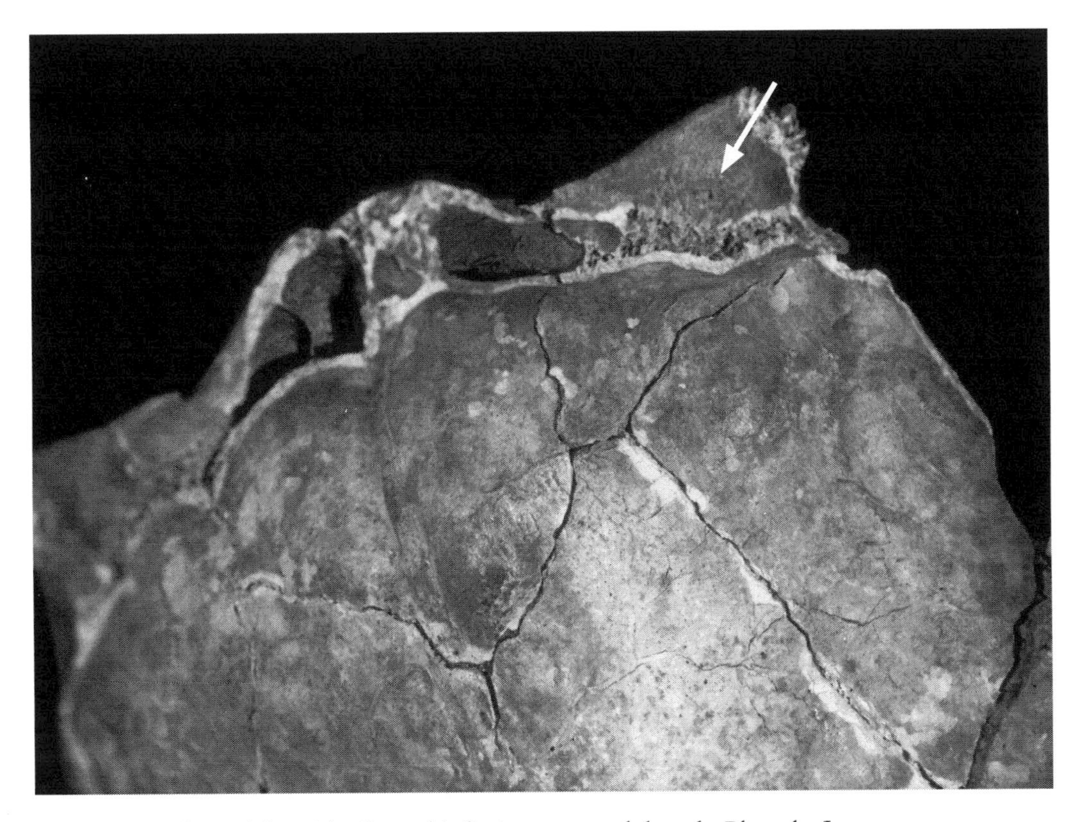

Figure 3.1. ◆ Active bilaterial cribra orbitalia in a young adult male. Photo by Laurel Casjens.

appearance (Figure 3.2). His condition was moderately severe and was active at the time of death.

To what extent can such lesions be attributed to the diet of the Arkansans before they departed on the wagon train? Diet alone cannot account for anemia, since serious blood loss can be caused by many factors. Accidents, menstruation and childbirth, vitamin C deficiency, gastrointestinal ulcers, and intestinal parasites have all been shown to induce anemia in contemporary populations (Wapler et al. 2004:337). From the skeletal evidence, furthermore, it is difficult to distinguish between a metabolic condition and an infection, or to trace any possible interconnection between the two. Infectious disease, as we shall see in the next chapter, may well have contributed to the skeletal lesions found in this sample.

The present analysis is further complicated by the fact that the emigrants had been on the trail for some five months just before their deaths. In this period some foods were probably in short supply, exacerbating any existing

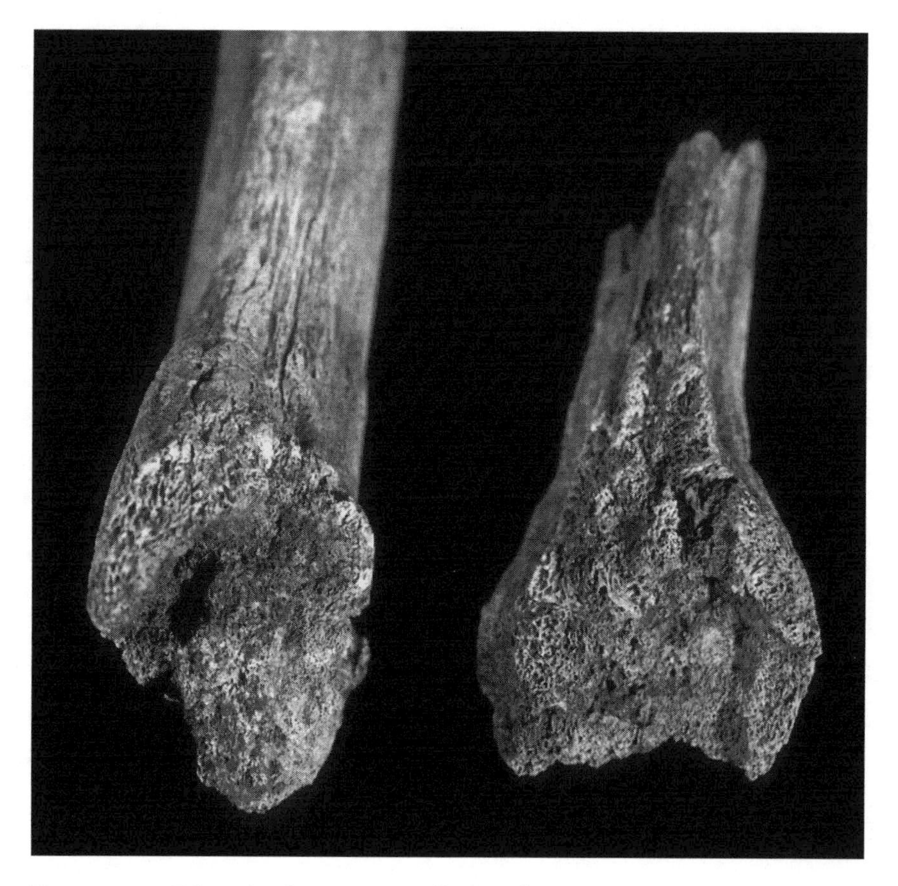

Figure 3.2. • Bilateral inflammation in fibulae of an old adult male. Photo by Laurel Casjens.

deficiencies of iron or other nutrients. Interestingly, the skeletal analysis uncovered no evidence of scurvy, perhaps the most common nutritional disorder in overland migrants. To prevent scurvy, the prudent traveler carried vinegar, pickles, dried fruit, or other foods rich in ascorbic acid. While many emigrants were "prepared to exist on the staples of bread, bacon, and coffee," they tried to diversify their diets by making cheese and butter, gathering berries and other plant foods, and even baking the occasional cake or pie (Faragher 2001:21, 78). Interestingly, wagon trains that included women tended to have fewer nutritional deficiencies (Grob 2002:137–138).

The Big Fix

Along with corn and pork, an array of stimulants—especially sugar, tobacco, coffee, and tea—rounded out the diet of the antebellum South. What Eric R. Wolf (1982:332) called the "Big Fix" was a global phenomenon that accom-

Table 3.5. • Tobacco Stains on Adult Dentition in the Mountain Meadows Sample.

	NO.	TOBACCO STAINED	%
Maxilla			
Incisor	59	13	22
Canine	15		
Premolar	42	7	17
Molar	82	22	27
Subtotal	198	42	21
Mandible			
Incisor	50	2	4
Canine	16		
Premolar	44	9	20
Molar	58	6	10
Subtotal	168	17	10
Total	366	59	16

panied the spread of capitalism. The premier stimulant of British laborers, both urban and rural, was sugar (Mintz 1985). Its popularity spread rapidly in North America, "which had battened upon molasses and its yield, rum, even before the thirteen colonies revolted. By 1880–84, the United States was consuming thirty-eight pounds of sucrose per person per year—already well ahead of all other major world consumers except the United Kingdom" (Mintz 1985:188). Sugar and other "drug-foods" could be found throughout the Arkansas Ozarks. Tobacco, honey, maple sugar, and sorghum were all accessible from local farms. Refined sugar and caffeine products were occasionally imported.

In 1850 none of the core families reported producing stimulant foods on their own farms, but such foods were probably accessible. Tobacco was grown in both Carroll and Johnson counties and was commonly consumed as a remedy for pain as well as for its stimulant effects. It grew well on newly cleared land, but soil infertility after two or three seasons often discouraged farmers from growing the crop. Nonetheless, in 1850 Carroll County produced more than 7,800 pounds of tobacco while Johnson County produced a bit less than 7,000 pounds. In the sample of skeletons from Mountain Meadows, some 16 percent of the adult teeth were banded by tobacco resin (Table 3.5, Figure 3.3). Most of the stains were localized on the molars. In the remains of one young man, the incisors were carious, abscessed, and stained brown, suggesting the use of tobacco as a palliative.

Figure 3.3. • Tobacco stains on a maxillary second molar of an old adult male. Photo by Laurel Casjens.

In 1850 both honey and maple sugar were produced in Carroll County, but in Johnson County only honey was reported. In fact, honey was collected in Johnson County at a volume nearly six times that of Carroll County's. By the mid-nineteenth century homemade sweeteners such as honey, maple sugar, and molasses were often supplemented by refined sugars. In the forty years following 1830 the yearly per capita consumption of processed sugar doubled (Sledzik and Moore-Jansen 1991). When these sweeteners were consumed in tea, coffee, or alcohol, the teeth would be bathed in sugar. Combined with corn and other complex carbohydrates, secondary sugars from these foods produced a "highly cariogenic diet typical of most preindustrial populations of the period" (Sutter 1995:190).

Compounding the problem was the general lack of oral hygiene in the nineteenth century. To ward off toothaches, people often carried amulets, such as the tooth or bone of an animal, nutmeg, a pewter ring, a bead, or a bullet (Hatfield 2004:347). A variety of home remedies were used to treat tooth pain. Onion strips might be worn around the wrist, for example, or tobacco smoke inhaled. If the condition persisted, the diseased tooth might be extracted and the abscess lanced. This procedure was advised as a last resort, however, because "it is a painful operation, and oftentimes a dangerous one, when attempted by an unskillful and clumsy hand" (Gunn 1986 [1830]:227).

Carious lesions develop when the tooth's surface is decalcified by bacteria, especially *Lactobacillus acidophilus* and *Streptococcus mutans* (Pindborg 1970). The funnel-shaped lesions pierce the enamel, then the dentin, and eventually the pulp chamber. Once the pulp chamber is exposed, the bacterial infection moves through the root and begins to damage the bony tissue (alveolar bone) that holds the tooth itself. As the infection and inflammation increases, bone is resorbed and a pocket, or abscess, forms around the root. Eventually, the tooth may be lost. Secondary infections of the sinuses and a systemic spread of bacteria can also develop from a dental abscess. As a result, an individual's overall health can be further compromised and may lead to seemingly unrelated infections, such as heart disease. Tooth development is also affected by nutritional shortages. Like iron deficiency, then, dental disease results from a complex etiology of environmental factors (e.g., trace elements in food and water) and the shape and structure of an individual's teeth, as well as diet and oral hygiene (Ortner and Putschar 1981; Powell 1985).

Nearly all the emigrants had surplus corn on their Arkansas farms, and the distribution of carious lesions suggests that other sugary foods were obtained for consumption by all members of the family. Furthermore, given the extent of dental pathology, secondary infections would have certainly been a possibility for a number of the emigrants. A total of 366 erupted permanent teeth and 11 deciduous teeth were recovered from the mass grave. Many of the adult teeth were fractured by bullets. Such trauma precluded analysis of some tooth crowns, but the bony sockets could be evaluated for disease. Of the permanent teeth, 19 percent had dental caries, most of which were located in the molars (Table 3.6). The emigrants' caries were usually in the small spaces between the teeth (the interproximal surfaces) and in the natural fissures on occlusal (biting or chewing) surfaces. Here food particles can accumulate in small recesses, become trapped in dental plaque—created

Table 3.6. • Pathology of Permanent Dentition in the Mountain Meadows Sample.

	NO. OF TEETH[a]	CARIOUS	NO. OF SOCKETS[b]	ALVEOLAR ABSCESS	ANTEMORTEM LOSS
Maxilla					
Incisor	59	10 (17%)	37	3 (8%)	1 (3%)
Canine	15		17		
Premolar	42	5 (12%)	37		4 (11%)
Molar	82	32 (39%)	48	2 (4%)	1 (2%)
Subtotal	198	47 (24%)	139	5 (4%)	6 (4%)
Mandible					
Incisor	50	2 (4%)	33		
Canine	16		13		1 (8%)
Premolar	44		31		
Molar	58	19 (33%)	39	3 (8%)	7 (18%)
Subtotal	168	21 (13%)	116	3 (3%)	8 (7%)
Total	366	68 (19%)	255	8 (3%)	14 (6%)

[a]Number of erupted permanent teeth.
[b]Number of sockets with erupted teeth.

Table 3.7. • Pathology of Deciduous Dentition in the Mountain Meadows Sample.

	NO. OF TEETH[a]	CARIOUS	NO. OF SOCKETS[b]	ALVEOLAR ABSCESS	ANTEMORTEM LOSS
Maxilla					
Incisor					
Canine	2	1 (50%)	2	1 (50%)	
Molar	1	1 (100%)	2		
Subtotal	3	2 (67%)	4	1 (25%)	
Mandible					
Incisor					
Canine			1		
Molar	8	2 (25%)	2		
Subtotal	8	2 (25%)	3		
Total	11	4 (36%)	7	1 (14%)	

[a]Number of erupted deciduous teeth.
[b]Number of sockets with erupted deciduous teeth.

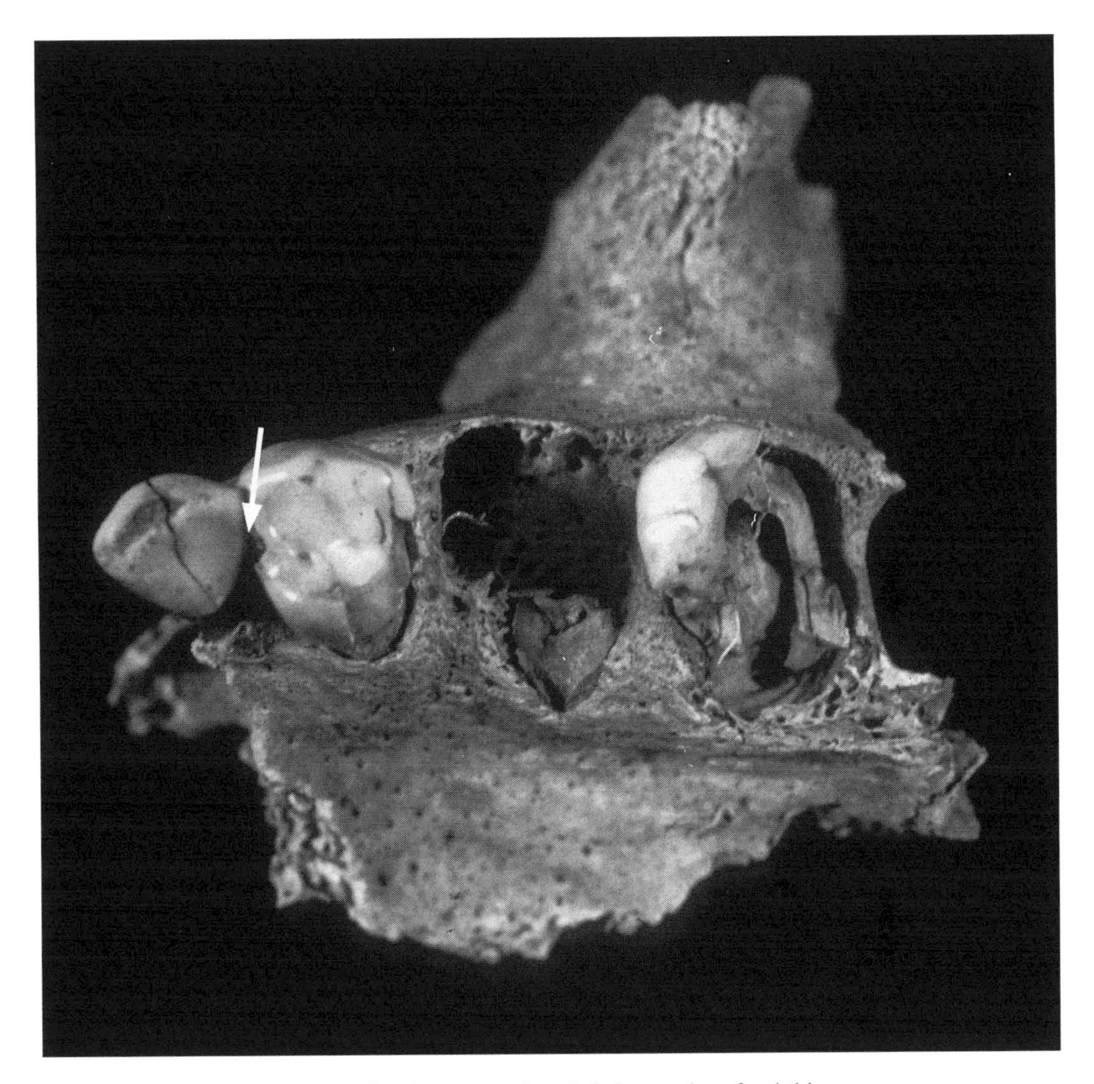

Figure 3.4. • Carious lesion in deciduous maxillary left first molar of a child, 5.5 to 6.5 years old. Photo by Laurel Casjens.

from microorganisms and proteins in the saliva—and ultimately become mineralized as calculus (Hillson 1996).

In the emigrants these deposits seem to have started at an early age. Calculus buildup was apparent even on the deciduous ("baby") teeth. In the sample, only 11 deciduous teeth could be identified, but 4 of them had caries (Table 3.7, Figure 3.4). This finding suggests that children, by 20 months of age, had been weaned on sugary foods similar to those eaten by adults.[3]

Not surprisingly, dental pathology was more severe in the older adults. Even with the young demographic profile of the train, 9 percent of the tooth

Table 3.8. • Antemortem Alveolar Pathology in the Mountain Meadows Sample, by Age.

	Age <15			Age 15–34			Age 35+			Total		
	No. Sockets	Alveolar Abscess	Antemortem Loss	No. Sockets	Alveolar Abscess	Antemortem Loss	No. Sockets	Alveolar Abscess	Antemortem Loss	No. Sockets	Alveolar Abscess	Antemortem Loss
Maxilla												
Decid incisor												
Decid canine	1			1	1 (100%)					2	1 (50%)	
Decid molar	2									2		
Incisor	2			30	1 (3%)		5	2 (40%)	1 (20%)	37	3 (8%)	1 (3%)
Canine	1			13			3			17		
Premolar	3			25			9		4 (44%)	37		4 (11%)
Molar	5			32			11	2 (18%)	1 (9%)	48	2 (4%)	1 (2%)
Subtotal	14			101	2 (2%)		28	4 (14%)	6 (21%)	143	6 (4%)	6 (4%)
Mandible												
Decid incisor												
Decid canine	1									1		
Decid molar	2									2		
Incisor	4			18			11			33		
Canine				9			4			13		
Premolar				21			10		1 (10%)	31		1 (3%)
Molar	1			24			14	3 (21%)	7 (50%)	39	3 (8%)	7 (18%)
Subtotal	8			72			39	3 (8%)	8 (21%)	119	3 (3%)	8 (7%)
Total	22			173	2 (1%)		67	7 (10%)	14 (21%)	262	9 (3%)	14 (5%)

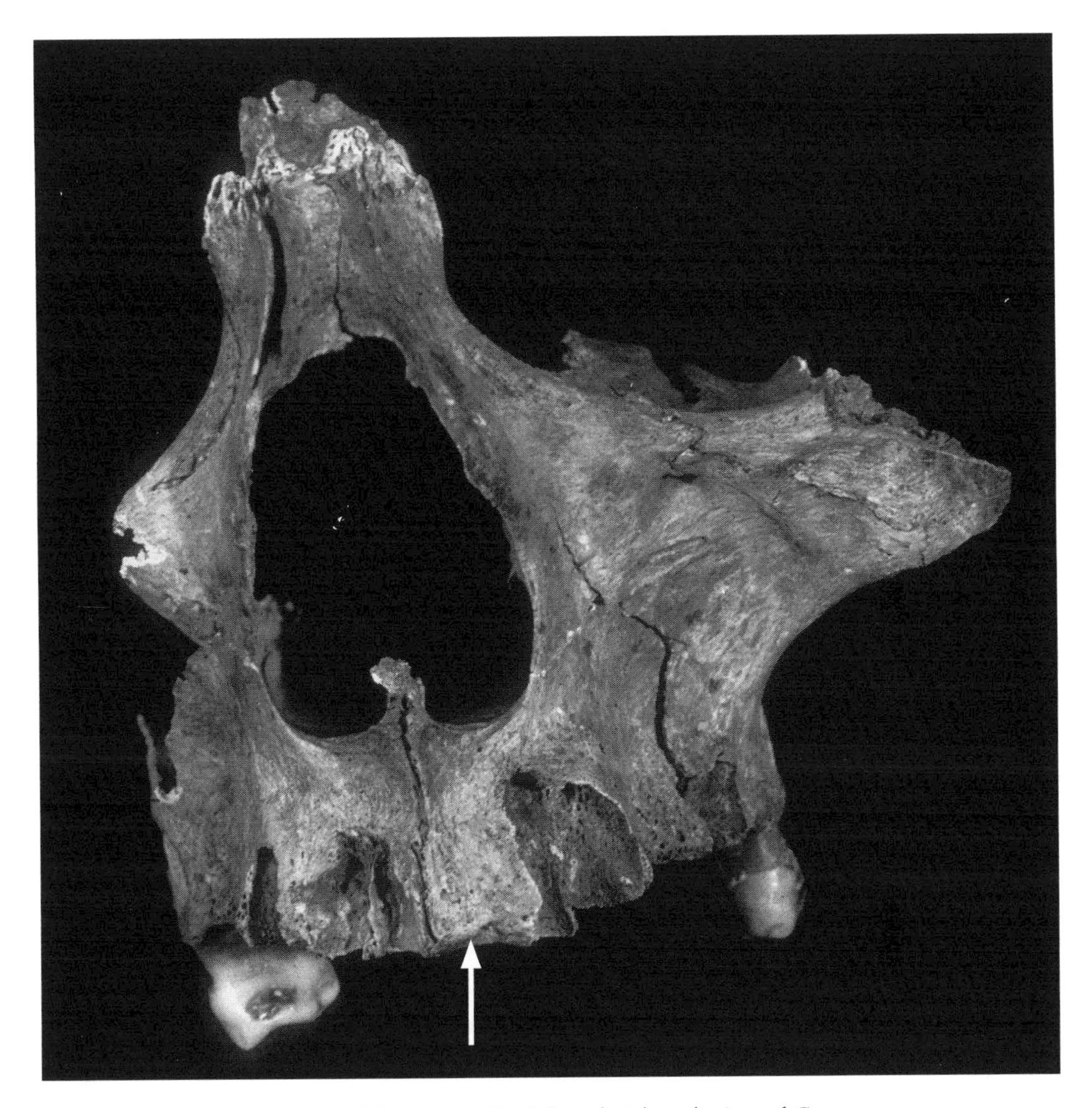

Figure 3.5. ✦ Antemortem tooth loss in an old adult male. Photo by Laurel Casjens.

sockets had either active abscesses or teeth that had been lost before death (Table 3.8, Figure 3.5). The mandibular molars were particularly at risk, but so too were the incisors. These anterior teeth are especially prone to developmental defects that create linear horizontal furrows (enamel hypoplasia) in the enamel crown. In one young adult male, for example, the hypoplastic bands he developed in childhood predisposed him to serious dental disease. At the time of his death, both maxillary incisors had large carious lesions that traversed the enamel defect. The caries perforated the pulp chambers, and abscesses were forming at the root tips (Figure 3.6). Adding to the

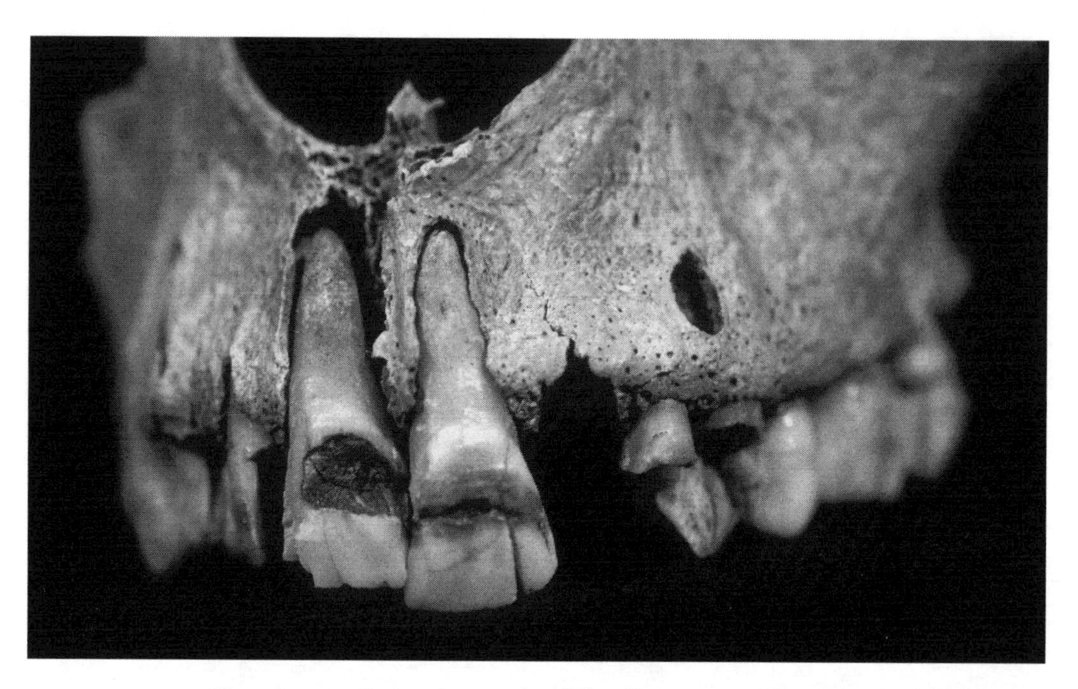

Figure 3.6. • Carious lesions that follow linear enamel hypoplasia in a young adult male. Note the bands of tobacco stains across the crowns. Photo by Laurel Casjens.

high bacteria load from these two diseased teeth was a severely abscessed deciduous canine. This tooth was retained from childhood, which resulted in destruction of the crown by a large carious lesion and the formation of an abscess in the bone.

From our perspective, the dental health of the emigrants was poor. From what we can tell about their antebellum contemporaries, they were just about average. One comparable skeletal sample was excavated at the Cross family homestead cemetery, near Springfield, Illinois. The 29 excavated graves were dated between 1820 and 1846 (Larsen et al. 1995). The Cross family skeletons had a frequency of carious teeth (19.6 percent) nearly identical to that of the Mountain Meadows remains (19.1 percent). This comparison is especially interesting because the two samples represent white Americans living in the rural interior before the Civil War. In many other settings around the same time, dental disease was much worse. For example, families living in the Monroe County Almshouse in Rochester, New York, between 1826 and 1863 had caries in almost 33 percent of their teeth (Higgins et al. 2002). Some of the worst dental pathology has been found in the remains of Mormon pioneers who lived in the Salt Lake Valley between 1847 and 1856. Here nearly 43 percent of the teeth were carious (Tigner-Wise 1989).

Movers and Stayers

Between 1830 and 1860, amid rapid economic growth in the United States, mortality rates rose and adult stature decreased. The paradox of increasing affluence alongside what appears to be deteriorating public health has been described as the "Antebellum Puzzle" (e.g., Steckel 1995; Komlos 1996, 1998). Yet this deterioration was not uniform across the country or in all occupations. According to Michael Haines et al. (2003:409), "the 'Antebellum Puzzle' seems to have resulted from a complex set of factors, including urbanization, increased population mobility, worsening mortality conditions, greater contact via improved transport infrastructure, and deteriorating nutrition."

The literature on the Antebellum Puzzle is relevant to a number of issues in the present context. After all, the people killed at Mountain Meadows had participated in the economic growth of the antebellum period. In principle, this skeletal sample ought to be an ideal one for testing the various hypotheses that have been proposed in the literature. Unfortunately, the determination of stature in this sample is complicated by the lack of complete long bones (those of the arms and legs). All these bones had been severely damaged and were commingled in the grave. With only fragments to work with, estimates of stature become notoriously unreliable.

The Antebellum Puzzle will not be solved by the Mountain Meadows sample. On the other hand, the literature on the puzzle sheds an interesting light on the lives of the Arkansas emigrants. What this literature suggests is that large samples of people, even within the same country and historical period, must be broken down as much as possible according to region, occupation, and mobility patterns. Only a fine-grained analysis that is sensitive to many local conditions is likely to enhance our understanding. In this regard, three key insights have emerged from the debate about the Antebellum Puzzle.

First, the change in stature varied according to region of the United States. Men born in New England and the mid-Atlantic states were less likely to reach the adult stature of their forefathers (Haines 1998:170). In contrast, southern men, especially those who grew up in Tennessee, were least likely to decline in stature during the antebellum period (Komlos 1987:905 n. 21). Given that adult stature is, in part, a reflection of childhood environment, we must know something about where people grew up before we can predict any outcome. In the case of the emigrants the first point to make is that most of them were not Arkansans by birth. In fact, with eight exceptions, all the adults on the wagon train had been born in other states, notably North Carolina, Alabama, Kentucky, and Tennessee. What is especially suggestive about the findings of John Komlos (1987) is that there were interesting differences even among southerners, with Tennesseans exhibiting the least diminishment of stature.

Second, change in stature varied by pattern of residence and occupation. Rural residents tended to be taller than urban dwellers, and farmers tended to be taller than nonfarmers. Mortality also varied according to certain aspects of geographic position (Haines et al. 2003:396): "Both transportation access and urbanization directly and significantly affected death rates. Access to regional transportation networks via a water route increased the death rate by four per thousand. And a ten percentage point increase in the share of a county's population living in an urban area resulted in an increase of 1.3 to 1.4 deaths per thousand." These distinctions are especially interesting in the case of the Arkansans because of the contrasts between Carroll and Johnson counties. Though a number of the riders on the wagon train had lived in both counties, there were important social and economic differences between the northern contingent and the southern contingent. As I have suggested, some of these differences may be related to the geographic landscape. Carroll County was relatively remote from navigable waterways before the 1850s; Johnson County, by contrast, was increasingly tied into the mercantile economy of the Arkansas River corridor. As pointed out by Haines et al. (2003:409), access to water transport increased one's exposure to both market forces and contagious diseases.

Finally, change in stature varied with one's pattern of geographic mobility. In particular, Haines et al. (2003:401) examined "the difference between 'movers' and 'stayers'—that is, between those who probably spent their entire formative years in one location and those who did not." The disparity in stature was slight but enough to suggest that "the economic advantages of moving might have yielded nutritional advantages for the children of movers." Be that as it may, in the case of Mountain Meadows all or nearly all the adult emigrants had made long-distance moves at least once before the departure of the wagon train. In this sense the Arkansans were "movers" rather than "stayers."

For generations, Americans had filled the frontier with settlements and offspring. As the population grew and land became more expensive, sons and daughters were challenged to acquire farms near their parents. With such an agrarian crisis, young people who remained in their birthplaces could be squeezed out of the middle class. Only the most affluent households, under these conditions, could sustain an agricultural "firm" that provided for the entire extended family. Often the heirs were expected to fend for themselves —by waiting patiently for their inheritance, marrying well, or taking their chances on cheap frontier land, where it might take years to reestablish a family estate.

> Many a far-sighted father preferred an alternative strategy that also fed the western migration, but without fragmenting the stem family and undermining patriarchal authority. Selling the family farm well in advance of the children's maturity, he used the proceeds to acquire a much larger tract of cheaper land farther west, on which the maturing children's labor could provide support for aging parents and farms for adult sons. Often many households of kin migrated as a clan, or related households followed a lead household in chain migration. (Sellers 1991:16)

Among the emigrants at Mountain Meadows were a number of these far-sighted fathers—and mothers. The problem was not just "many mouths" but many conflicting interests, shaped by various social, political, and economic contexts. Whether this problem would have been solved by the likes of Alexander Fancher and Jesse Dunlap will never be known.

CONSTITUTION

Had I entered upon my career—with a weakly constitution and unsound stomach *caused by the Ignorance and bad management of a Mother, I should long ago have been in my Grave.*

—Everard B. Dickinson to Mr. and Mrs. Philo Dickinson, June 21, 1850

Thus we find that certain moral values are upheld and certain social rules defined by beliefs in dangerous contagion, as when the glance or touch of an adulterer is held to bring illness to his neighbours or his children.

— Mary Douglas, *Purity and Danger: An Analysis of Concepts of Pollution and Taboo*, 1966

Many traditional accounts of Mountain Meadows have claimed that the Arkansas emigrants were, in some sense, diseased. Some two weeks after he participated in the massacre, John D. Lee described the victims as syphilitic: "Many of the men & women was ro[tten?] with the pox before they were hurt by the Indians" (transcribed in Kenney 1983:5:103). Soon it was reported in the *Los Angeles Star* (1857a) that William H. Dame, colonel of the Iron County militia, had examined the bodies of the Arkansans and determined that all the women were prostitutes. As Bagley (2002:165) points out, such stories seem to have been transmitted to reporters by William Mathews, a leading Mormon official in California, as part of a "systematic defamation of the murdered emigrants."

This conclusion is no doubt correct. To understand such defamation, however, we must consider what it meant to be "diseased." This is a complex topic, especially in light of the burgeoning literature on public health and conceptions of disease in Victorian America (e.g., Rosenberg 1992; Porter 1996; Leavitt and Numbers 1997; Humphreys 2001; Grob 2002).

In the nineteenth century a person's physical, mental, and moral states were thought to be amalgamated. Each individual had, in effect, an essence, an innate "constitution" that manifested itself daily in both behavior and health (Valenčius 2002:99). Such constitutional tendencies were both heritable and malleable. In this respect, mothers bore a special burden. Women in the nineteenth century were seen as "innately suited to be the nurturers of young children" (Allured 1988:250). Maternal care was credited for the production of successful and healthy adults. One Arkansas immigrant, Everard B. Dickinson (1850), complimented his New England mother for raising him in a "wholesome—cleanly manner" that produced in him a "healthy—sound Constitution & capacity."

Not all Arkansans, however, were as lucky as Dickinson. Given the high rates of morbidity and mortality, someone, or something, usually got the blame. Before the bacteriological revolution late in the nineteenth century (Duffy 1971), a debate raged over how disease was spread. Some believed that disease was contagious, others thought that environmental factors were responsible. Regardless of the mechanism, "social reformers and social scientists of the early nineteenth century did not draw a qualitative distinction between physical and moral causes of disease" (Dorn 2000:269). Chronic illness, in particular, became entangled with an individual's identity.

When evaluating morbidity and mortality in the nineteenth century, then, we are challenged not only by the lack of discrete diagnoses but by the moral overtones associated with illness. Such factors must be considered when we attempt to reconcile our present understanding of disease with antebellum representations. Even the most systematic source, the mortality schedule from the 1850 U.S. census, requires careful interpretation. Although statistics on age, sex, place of birth, and cause of death are used in this chapter to establish disease patterns in the Ozarks, we must keep in mind a number of caveats. We know that various illnesses were collapsed into broad categories, and the census accounted only for a single year of deaths (Savitt 1978:135–139). Moreover, it has been estimated that the censuses conducted between 1850 and 1900 undernumerated deaths by about 40 percent (Condran and Crimmins 1979; Haines 1979). Conditions that were chronic or endemic, and were likely to have caused long-term suffering and disability, do not show up in these records. Furthermore, because of the moral overtones and beliefs of disease heritability, informants may have been reluctant to reveal certain illnesses (e.g., "pox"), especially those that reflected on the character of surviving family members.

Nonetheless, the mortality census gives us some insight into the demographic and geographic distribution of certain diseases, ultimately allowing us to assess health risks for people living in the Ozarks and for those emigrants traveling on the overland trail. Such patterns can be evaluated in relation to the disease patterns identified in the Arkansans' skeletal remains. At the same time, the skeletal findings may supplement what is known about nineteenth-century disease, shedding light especially on chronic conditions that were likely to affect the bone.

Morbid Miasmas

In 1850 fewer than half of those Americans who had managed to survive to age five lived to see their sixtieth birthday (Haines 1998). White males in a rural setting had the best chance of survival (Grob 2002:123). At much greater risk were women or children born into large families (Steckel 1988; Bean et al. 1992). The primary cause of morbidity and mortality was infectious disease. Yet "germs" were not recognized as a cause of illness until the 1890s: "As twentieth-century Americans would come to fear 'germs,' so antebellum Americans feared 'miasmas': they were the useful catch-all for disease worries" (Valenčius 2002:114).

Miasmas, in themselves mysterious and protean, were harbored by the physical environment. "Exhalations from the bowels of the earth, extreme degrees of heat or cold, sudden temperature fluctuations, and rapid changes in the weather" all signaled potentially noxious conditions (Jones 1967:255). Because characteristics of the soil, water, air, and temperature varied regionally as well as seasonally, so too did the expected patterns of illness. In the heat of late summer and early fall, for example, decaying vegetation near lowlands and swamps was believed to produce miasmic gases that caused fevers. Although higher elevations were considered more salubrious, the night air was deemed unhealthy, even in the Ozarks (Jones 1967:266 n. 65). Such natural insults to one's constitution were further exacerbated when the settlers themselves disturbed the land. Felled trees, tilled soil, and their putrefied byproducts created an environment teeming with miasmas.

When these infectious agents entered the body, the natural equilibrium of fluids, or "humors," was altered. The theory of humors went back to the fifth century BCE (Hays 1998:10). According to this doctrine, four humors —blood, phlegm, yellow bile, and black bile—flowed through the body, creating a fine balance that established one's health. As diseases moved through the body's channels, some were believed to be specific, settling in a particular organ, while others could be altered as they made their journey (Warner 1997:89).

The balance of humors was specific to an individual, so treating disease required close assessment of the patient's peculiarities. These were based on biological factors such as age, sex, and diet, combined with environmental variables of season, temperature, and altitude (Warner 1997:87). The analysis of these environmental variables was the domain of medical geography. This field sought to establish correlations between natural regions and climate-sensitive diseases so that patients could be advised about the best latitude or altitude to treat their condition (Rupke 1996:304). Detailed observations of temperature, atmospheric pressure, winds, moisture, and the distribution of plants and animals filled medical treatises and handbooks for doctors and laypeople alike.

Based on these guides, patients were counseled to remove themselves to areas where the atmosphere was pure, especially near the sea, in the pines, and on the prairies (Thompson 1976:146). This kind of "travel therapy" favored regions such as the Great Plains and California and emphasized distance from urban centers. American cities, as Noah Webster (1799:253) put it, "are great prisons, built with immense labor to breed infection and hurry mankind prematurely to the grave."

Escaping from such prisons was perhaps the best therapy, but many patients were obliged to submit to more "heroic" treatments. As described by John Harley Warner (1997:88), these treatments included "extracting blood by opening a vein with the lancet (venesection) or drawing blood by suction from scarified skin (wet cupping); producing drastic catharsis by mercury-containing drugs (such as calomel) or other cathartics; causing debilitating vomiting by drugs such as tartar emetic; and prescribing a low diet." Such therapies were based on the principle that illness in general resulted from "overstimulation," and "lowering therapy" was required to restore equilibrium to the body.

The therapy was tailored, furthermore, to the "natural state" of the patient, which depended on place of residence. In particular, southern and northern climates were seen as requiring different treatments. Northerners were supposed to be more tolerant of bloodletting because their cold climates were invigorating and made them more robust. Southerners, on the other hand, were exposed to malaria and heat, which "continually stimulated the liver, ... exhausting that organ and leaving it debilitated" (Warner 1989: 181–182). To stimulate "torpid southern livers," doctors administered calomel, a derivative of mercury. Whereas northerners were more likely to be bled, southerners were more likely to be poisoned.

Such regional differences were reflected in both the professional and lay medical literature. Literate laypeople who wanted guidance in the domestic treatment of disease could choose from scores of popular manuals. Between 1807 and 1860 at least eleven such texts were published for a southern audience alone (Keeney 1989:277 n. 2). Perhaps the most popular was John C. Gunn's *Domestic Medicine, or Poor Man's Friend,* which promoted the layperson's ability to treat disease as well as a doctor. First published in 1830, the book went through one hundred editions by 1870 (Rosenberg 1986:vii).

Such bootstrap medicine was characteristic of many alternative sects that developed during this period, most of which were reacting to the medical profession and their heroic practices (Haller 1994). In the South the most popular of these movements were the Thomsonians. Founder Samuel Thomson called "every man his own physician" and emphasized the use of hydropathic and homeopathic therapeutics. These principles, popularized in *The Southern Botanic Physician* (Abbott 1844), were hailed as a doctrine for the "laboring class" because they eliminated fees for doctors and patent medicines.

In rural locations alternatives offered by Gunn and the Thomsonians were particularly enticing. Not only was it difficult to locate a doctor in these areas, but their services were extremely expensive. A dollar or two might be charged for simple services such as bleeding or cupping. The fee increased when the physician was called to treat fractures, pregnancies, or hernias (Moffatt 1951:90–91). These conditions could cost between $20 and $300, plus the charge for the doctor's mileage and hourly attendance. As a result, most families called on a physician only as a last resort, attempting first to treat illness through their own methods, guided by self-help manuals.

Such manuals never entirely displaced the professional physician, however. The most common form of medical training in the early nineteenth century was practical experience with a preceptor (Shryock 1930:66; see also Stowe 2004). Before 1800 those who sought more formal credentials often traveled to Europe. By the 1830s medical schools and colleges were available in larger American cities such as Philadelphia, New York, Charleston, and New Orleans. At midcentury even Arkansas had a thriving medical profession. In 1853 a resident of Lewisburg wrote, "We have enough doctors here to kill all the world in twelve months" (McMillen 1990:71). In Carroll County there were three physicians practicing in 1850. Johnson County had even more medical practitioners—there were eight physicians just within Spadra and Clarksville townships.

Some middle-class households were beginning to call on professionals and to purchase patent medicines, but most families in the Ozarks would have continued to rely on domestic care (McMillen 1990:69). Those charged with administering such care were usually women. As Bolton (1991:276) argues, female health provisioning in the sparsely populated frontier created important social networks among women. These women were often unrelated and a great distance from their natal kin. The common discourse of health—biological, psychological, and behavioral—would have enlivened all their conversations and activities (Bolton 1991:282). In view of the fact that women in the Ozarks were giving birth about every two years and nursing their families through continuous cycles of illnesses, they would have had a lot to talk about.

In the rest of this chapter I consider symptoms of disease that would have been recognized and talked about by laypeople in the antebellum South. The same symptom, of course, may have different underlying causes, but let us begin by setting aside what we know from modern medicine. In the writings of the day, five major categories of illness crop up again and again: (1) "fevers," including what was sometimes diagnosed as "ague" or malaria, (2) "flux," "worms," and other gastrointestinal disorders, (3) "coughs," especially pneumonia and tuberculosis, (4) endemic childhood diseases, such as diphtheria and scarlet fever, and (5) venereal diseases, including "pox" (syphilis).

Movers and Shakers

In the mid-nineteenth century the highlands were generally considered to be healthier than the lowlands. To some extent, this folk belief is borne out by mortality statistics—at least for the white populace. In 1850 there were 2,160 deaths reported in Arkansas. With more than 40 percent of the state's population, the Ozarks accounted for only one-third of the deaths. To put this another way, while the Ozark region had one death for every 98 residents, the rest of the state averaged one for every 65. Within the Ozarks the highest death rates were reported in the southern counties along the Arkansas River and in the eastern counties near the Mississippi Valley (Figure 4.1; Table 4.1).

Throughout the region many deaths were attributed to nonspecific "fevers." The author of *Gunn's Domestic Medicine* (1986 [1830]:128, 136) believed it was "almost impossible to describe *fever* correctly; because it shows itself in so many various ways and forms." When chills and shaking came in cycles, the condition was described as ague, or "the ager." Because the symptoms were so common, many settlers considered the illness to be part of the "seasoning process" in their new environments. "He ain't sick, he's only got the ager" was a typical refrain on the frontier (Pickard and Buley 1945:13–14). The shaking often began in late summer and early autumn—the "sickly season"—and continued until the first frost provided relief (Valenčius 2002:78).

This seasonal pattern is suggestive of malaria, though it was difficult to distinguish this disease before the discovery of the malaria protozoan late in the nineteenth century (Grob 2002:129). *Plasmodium vivax* and *P. falciparum*

Figure 4.1. ◆ Death rates in Ozark counties, 1850. These county boundaries were in place from 1836 to 1860. Data from U.S. Bureau of the Census 1850, Schedule 3.

are the two most common species of malaria. The less virulent *P. vivax*, which generally causes outbreaks in the spring, seems to have been imported by English colonists. The more lethal *P. falciparum*, which sets in during the autumnal heat and kills 20 to 40 percent of its victims, arrived with the African slave trade (Dunn 1965; Kiple and King 1981; Merbs 1992; Humphreys 2001). Both species move from one human host to another through an insect vector, the *Anopheles* mosquito.

The success of *Anopheles* in transmitting the parasite depends on both the environment and the behavioral patterns of the human host. Most spe-

Table 4.1. • Mortality Ratios in the Arkansas Ozarks, by County, 1850.

COUNTY	POPULATION	DEATHS	RATIO
Benton	3,509	20	1:176
Carroll	4,401	24	1:183
Crawford	7,027	88	1:80
Franklin	3,500	54	1:65
Fulton	1,769	28	1:63
Independence	6,939	115	1:60
Izard	3,017	14	1:216
Johnson	4,496	31	1:144
Lawrence	4,886	69	1:71
Madison	4,659	31	1:150
Marion	2,182	9	1:242
Newton	1,711	15	1:114
Pope	4,231	54	1:78
Randolph	3,032	46	1:66
Searcy	1,950	16	1:122
Van Buren	2,761	37	1:75
Washington	8,771	52	1:169

Source: U.S. Bureau of the Census 1850, Schedule 3.

cies of this mosquito prefer standing or slow-running water and midsummer temperatures greater than 58 degrees F. Their breeding is encouraged by deforestation. Acting as a "delayed time fuse," endemic malaria would often strike some ten or twenty years after forests had been cleared and farms established (Watts 1999:219; see also Humphreys 2001). For example, by 1770 malaria had become endemic to the Upper Mississippi Valley in Illinois (Grob 2002:130). Missouri, by comparison, had later and slower rates of immigration and was not ravaged by malaria until after 1820.

In the Arkansas Ozarks only nine deaths in 1850 were attributed specifically to malaria (Table 4.2). At the same time, however, 86 deaths were the result of fatal "fevers." Since nearly 70 percent of these fevers appeared during the late summer or fall, malaria was the likely culprit. Even though the Arkansas highlands saw fewer cases of malaria because of the cooler summers and earlier onset of winter, nearly all the settlers in the region had traveled from or through malarial zones.

In fact, all the core families on the wagon train had at some point traveled through the Mississippi lowlands. Alexander and Eliza Fancher, for example, had lived in Illinois and Missouri, where malaria was already endemic.

Table 4.2. • Reported Causes of Death in the Arkansas Ozarks with Special Reference to the Core Families' Counties, 1850.

REPORTED CAUSE	NUMBER (N = 655)	AR OZARKS (% ALL DEATHS)	CARROLL COUNTY	JOHNSON COUNTY	MARION COUNTY	BENTON COUNTY	CRAWFORD COUNTY
Unknown	98	15.0	8 (8.3%)	7 (7.1%)			
Fevers, unclassifiable	86	13.1	2 (2.3%)	1 (1.2%)	2 (2.3%)	3 (3.5%)	11 (12.8%)
Respiratory disease	71	10.8		2 (2.8%)	2 (2.8%)		1 (1.4%)
Diphtheria	46	7.0	2 (4.3%)	3 (6.5%)			
Scarlet fever	45	6.9	1 (2.2%)	1 (2.2%)			
Digestive system	40	6.2		2 (5%)			5 (12.5%)
Diarrheal diseases	41	6.3			1 (2.4%)	3 (7.3%)	7 (17.1%)
Tuberculosis	35	5.3	3 (8.6%)			2 (5.7%)	4 (11.4%)
Nervous system	29	4.4		6 (20.7%)		1 (3.5%)	4 (13.8%)
Skin lesions	27	4.1	2 (7.4%)	2 (7.4%)		1 (3.7%)	3 (11.1%)
Cholera	22	3.4	1 (4.6%)			2 (9%)	4 (18.2%)
Accident	22	3.0			1 (4.6%)	2 (9.1%)	2 (9.1%)
Typhoid fever	15	2.3			1 (6.7%)	1 (6.7%)	3 (20%)
Maternity	16	2.0		1 (6.3%)		1 (6.3%)	1 (6.3%)
Worms	12	1.8					1 (8.3%)
Dropsy	12	1.8	1 (8.3%)	2 (16.7%)			2 (16.7%)
Malaria	9	1.4					
Measles	7	1.1		5 (71.4%)			
Smallpox	7	1.1	2 (29%)				
Old age	7	1.0	2 (28.6%)	1 (14.3%)	1 (14.3%)		
Homicide	4	0.6			3 (75%)		
Whooping cough	3	0.5					1 (33.3%)
Neoplasms	1	0.2					

Source: U.S. Bureau of the Census 1850, Schedule 3.

Based on these local patterns of exposure, as well as migration and mobility patterns, it is quite likely that a number of the 1857 wagon-train members had contracted malaria at some point in their lives. Some of these survivors would have been carriers of the disease, as were many others on the trail. By 1830 "fevers" were prevalent on all the overland routes (Olch 1985:201; Rieck 1991:13; Grob 2002:126).

Malarial fevers are often associated with anemia. Once a mosquito infects a human host, the malaria plasmodium occupies the liver, multiplies, and moves into the bloodstream. Attaching itself to red blood cells, the parasite consumes one-quarter to three-quarters of a cell's hemoglobin, undergoes division, and eventually ruptures the cell. This later stage produces the repetitive symptoms of malaria—fevers, chills, headache, and muscle pain. The process of cell destruction, combined with further blood cell loss from the body's immune response, creates severe anemia in the malaria victim. Over the long term, even as the parasite load decreases, an anemic state can persist (Aufderheide and Rodríguez-Martín 1998:230).

Anemia, as we saw in the previous chapter, triggers the production of more red blood cells in the vertebrae, flat bones, and long bones. This process can create skeletal lesions, especially in the eye orbits (cribra orbitalia) and cranial vault and near the joints of long bones (Aegerter and Kirkpatrick 1975). Unfortunately, because skeletal anemia can also result from dietary deficiencies and certain gastrointestinal parasites, among other conditions, it is not a reliable indicator of malaria.

Wee Beasties

A diverse range of parasites, from worms to bacteria, are responsible for both chronic and lethal infections of the gut. In the antebellum period, epidemics that killed suddenly and seemingly at random presented a challenge to the medical community. The physician's failure to diagnose and cure these epidemics helped undermine the authority of an already suspect profession. Increasingly, the American public turned to alternative medicines and therapies. Local governments attempted to stop epidemics at their source by promoting what came to be known as "public health."

Yet there was little agreement on what did in fact cause outbreaks of disease. Traditional theorists argued that disease was contagious, spreading directly from person to person by some ill-defined entity such as "animalcules" or "wee beasties" (Hays 1998:137). Such terms went back to the seventeenth century, but two hundred years later some medical authorities continued to argue that "corpuscles" or "fungous tribes" were the underlying cause of infectious disease (Rosenberg 1960:343–346). In 1832, for example,

Kentucky physician Daniel Drake attributed cholera to "poisonous, invisible, aerial insects, of the same or similar habits with the gnat." According to this school of thought, epidemics should be managed through the quarantine of patients and others suspected of carrying disease. In contrast, the "environmentalist" camp contended that airs flowing from open sewers, cemeteries, and other miasmas carried disease. According to this logic, which was endorsed by most authorities in the nineteenth century, these odiferous miasmas were the true root of the problem and should be cleansed or removed from public contact (Hays 1998:138; McNeill 1998:270–271).

In retrospect, of course, both schools of thought had a point. Quarantine and improved sanitation are both effective measures against infectious disease. At the same time, there are obvious costs to both strategies. Quarantine of ships, for example, was a hindrance to trade and was detested by merchants and consumers alike. Public health measures were hardly practical on a farm or ranch. As a result, both urban and rural conditions were conducive to digestive-tract infections (Savitt 1997:359): "Flies transported bacteria such as *Vibrio* (cholera), *Salmonella* (food poisoning and typhoid), and *Shigella* (bacillary dysentery), the virus which causes infectious hepatitis, and the protozoan *Entameba histolytica* (amebic dysentery) from feces to food.... Finally there were the large parasitic worms, a concomitant of primitive sanitation."

At a time when most illnesses were attributed to rather nebulous causes, worms were a discrete and observable enemy that could be put on display. Many physicians exhibited jars of tangled masses to promote their therapeutic success (Moffatt 1951:91–92). The roundworm (*Ascariasis*), threadworm (*Trichuris*), and tapeworm (*Taenia solium*) would have been recognizable to laypersons as well as professionals. All these nematodes share a long symbiotic relationship with humans and are generally asymptomatic in their hosts (Aufderheide and Rodríguez-Martín 1998:238, 241).

In contrast, a smaller but more dangerous nematode—hookworm (*Necator americanus*)—became endemic in the rural South but was not independently recognized until 1903 (Etting 1993). Like the malarial parasite, hookworm appears to have traveled on slave ships from West Africa (cf. Ferreira et al. 1983, 1987, for precolumbian origins in South America). First occupying the colonial Atlantic seaboard, hookworm was distributed across the Cotton South by the early nineteenth century (Grob 2002:196). The heaviest infestations occurred in Louisiana, Mississippi, Alabama, and Florida, but the disease reached as far as "the northern boundaries of Virginia, Kentucky, Arkansas, and the boothill of Missouri" (Brinkley 1997:119). Deciphering exposure to hookworm during the antebellum period is especially problematic because it may have been spread throughout the South by Civil War soldiers (Brinkley 1997:127 n. 57). Antebellum accounts are ambiguous because some hookworm symptoms, especially fevers, may have been misdiagnosed as malaria or typhoid (Stiles 1903).

Eggs of the hookworm are introduced into the soil through human stools. Preferring warm and moist tropical or subtropical zones, the eggs mature rapidly through a series of larval stages. Whereas most worms follow a pattern of fecal-oral transmission, hookworms burrow through skin. Barefoot travelers on damp ground provide a new host for the larvae, which move through the blood and lungs to the upper small intestine. Here the larvae attach to the mucosa and suck blood, grow, mate, and release new eggs through their host's fecal matter (Coehlo and McGuire 1998:186). On average, these worms live one to five years, but they can survive up to twenty years in the intestines.

The health impact of hookworm infestations can be substantial. Symptoms include "anorexia, abdominal pain, geophagy, nausea, headache, rash, weakness, fever, vomiting, diarrhea, dysentery, and intestinal bleeding" (Coehlo and McGuire 1998:186). Such conditions were unlikely to kill the patient but tended to cause chronic poor health, including anemia (Patterson 1989: 156). As we have seen, anemia may well show up in the skeleton, but the hard-tissue lesions indicative of hookworm are difficult to distinguish from the effects of dietary deficiency or malaria. Once again, cribra orbitalia and other symptoms of anemia found in the Mountain Meadows remains are suggestive but not definitive. What we do know is that several adults in the mass grave had mild to moderate anemia at the time of their deaths.

Another condition that probably affected the emigrants was diarrheal disease of various origins. Like "fever," the terms used to describe bouts of gastrointestinal distress were generalized and ambiguous. In particular, "flux"—sometimes "lux"—could refer to various strains of influenza, dysentery, and cholera. The virulence of the disease was often attributed to the patient's constitution and behavior. Dr. Gunn (1986 [1830]:192–193), for example, described a form of diarrhea that "prevails among persons of weakly constitutions; persons advanced in years; and those who have lived *intemperately*" (see also Rosenberg 1960:333).

In 1850 gastrointestinal afflictions were reported in 20 percent of the deaths in the Arkansas Ozarks (Table 4.2). Males and females died at approximately the same rate, but most of the victims were young—on average, just 13 years old. All the counties occupied by the wagon-train families in 1850 experienced some deaths as a result of gastrointestinal infections. Cholera was specifically indicated in twenty-two deaths across the Arkansas

Ozarks. Males were twice as likely as females to die from cholera, and most of the victims were men in their twenties. This distribution probably reflects the greater mobility of young men and their risk of exposure.

In the mid-nineteenth century cholera was a relatively recent import from Asia. In 1832, only a year after reaching England, the disease first appeared in Canada and North America. Once in the United States, cholera quickly spread, particularly along water routes, producing periodic outbreaks during the antebellum period (Grob 2002:105). Although the Ozarks avoided cholera epidemics, surrounding areas suffered major outbreaks. Illinois had been especially hard hit in the mid-1830s when "the sick frequently outnumbered the well and the dead accumulated so quickly that people had to bury them in blankets, two to a grave" (Faragher 1986:89). In 1849 St. Louis alone lost 10 percent of its population; half the victims were children (Valenčius 2002:6). The death rate in Arkansas never approached these extremes, although cholera appeared intermittently across the state.

The Arkansas emigrants of 1857 would have been well aware of epidemics in the region, as well as those that awaited them on the overland trail. Most fatalities on the Oregon-California route were attributed to diarrheal infections, and historians estimate that some 20,000 persons (about 6 percent) died in the crossing (Rieck 1991:14). Some stretches of the trail were sicklier than others: "The road from Independence to Fort Laramie is a graveyard" (Mattes 1969:84). If the travelers reached Wyoming in good health, they knew that the worst had passed; less than 9 percent of the cholera cases occurred west of Fort Laramie (Rieck 1991:13).

Departing from various disease-ravaged areas, emigrants carried the cholera bacterium (*Vibrio cholerae*) with them, infecting thousands of others through defecation on the trail. When the live organism entered the intestines, the onset of symptoms could be sudden and dramatic: "David Ayers, one of our company, puked and purged all night and upon examining his condition this morning found he had the cholera, as much so as any case I ever saw. All the symptoms were present even to the rice water discharges. I went to work on him faithfully, he lying in his wagon while we were moving on, and now he is very much better, circulation restored, discharges altered, etc." (Crane 1852 in Olch 1985). Such symptoms are caused by the rapid replication of the bacteria in the intestines and secretion of toxins that inhibit water and mineral absorption. In extreme cases, profuse vomiting and diarrhea leads to circulatory collapse. The victim's skin turns blue as the heart or kidneys fail, sometimes within hours of the onset of symptoms (Hays 1998:136). Less than 50 percent of the adults contracting cholera survive, and mortality is often higher for children and the elderly (Grob 2002:104).

The graves that lined the trail would have been observed firsthand by Alexander Fancher on his overland journey in 1850. On this same journey William Bedford Temple, from Carroll County, Arkansas, wrote home to say that he had seen four or five fresh graves every day (Temple 1850b; Bagley 2002:59). As the caravan waited to cross the Big Blue River in Nebraska Territory, Temple reported that a man "died of diareer as many others done."[1]

Graveyard Coughs

Between 1800 and 1859 yellow fever was responsible for some 55,000 deaths in the United States (Humphreys 1992; Patterson 1992). Between 1833 and 1866 cholera claimed about 250,000 Americans (Chambers 1938:285–286). These fatalities, however, represent only a small fraction of the disease-related deaths, though their impact was often exaggerated in the public imagination (Grob 2002:108). "In terms of mortality," as Duffy (1971:419) argues, "consumption (tuberculosis of the lungs), and pneumonia, should have caused the greatest outcry."

From Virginia to Louisiana, the American South was ravaged by respiratory diseases in the mid-nineteenth century (Patterson 1989:159). Such diseases were given various names, including pneumonia, congestion, and "winter fever." In the Arkansas Ozarks these diseases accounted for at least 10 percent of the deaths in 1850, striking four men for every three women. In general, the victims died in their prime, at age 29 on average, and quickly, within days or weeks of the onset of symptoms.

Meanwhile, tuberculosis was rampant in the Northeast. As a result, one out of five deaths in the United States was attributed to "consumption" in the first half of the nineteenth century (Rothman 1995:13). In its terminal stage, tuberculosis is easy to identify by a bloody hollow cough, wasting of the body, night sweats, and intermittent fevers. Yet tuberculosis is a biphasic disease that involves a primary infection followed by a reactivation or reinfection. The disease's tendency to attack, recede, and sometimes disappear for years was especially mysterious (Rothman 1995:13–15).

Tuberculosis is transmitted by two bacilli of the genus *Mycobacterium*. While *M. tuberculosis* is usually contracted by inhaling bacilli expelled into the air by another lung-infected human, the *M. bovis* host is an animal—especially the cow—and is contracted through the consumption of infected milk or meat. Once in the body, the *Mycobacterium* triggers an immune response that encapsulates the bacilli in tubercles—masses of "white blood cells," or lymphocytes. Such tubercles contain the infection, and this is where the bacilli stay—as long as the body's immune system remains sufficient. At this stage the disease is usually symptomless, but its victims continue to carry the infection. If such carriers are reinfected or if their immune systems are compromised, the bacilli disseminate from the tubercles and the wasting symptoms begin. Human-to-human transmission of *M. tuberculosis* is the most common form of infection, resulting in the classic symptoms of pulmonary distress (Aufderheide and Rodríguez-Martín 1998:119–121; Grob 2002: 18–20; Roberts and Buikstra 2003:4–7).

In the nineteenth century early symptoms of tuberculosis were easily confused with pneumonia, influenza, or just the common cold. Whether a cold would develop into a deadlier condition was believed to depend on the patient's heredity and manner of living (Gunn 1986 [1830]:204–205):

> Persons of delicate constitutions are most subject to colds; and from the carelessness of such persons, in neglecting to avoid exposure, and to remove the early symptoms of disease, more than two thirds of the whole number of CONSUMPTIVE CASES, in all countries, arise and become fatal.... Here I repeat, because it is all-important, that most of the CONSUMPTIONS of *this country*, originate in *neglected colds*, brought on by exposure to the night air, by damp feet; by changing warm clothing for thin; by becoming warm from exercise, perhaps in a crowded ball room, and suddenly exposing the body to a cold current of air; and by many other imprudent courses of conduct.

Ballrooms were rather rare in the Ozarks, but small cramped housing—especially during the winter months—would have facilitated transmission of pulmonary infections, including TB.

In certain circles, ironically enough, the symptoms of tuberculosis became almost fashionable. Although the disease was found throughout the country, it was especially associated with the urban areas of the Northeast (Rothman 1995:4). In particular, the dying young woman—gaunt, pale, with flushed cheeks—became a source of literary and operatic inspiration (Hays 1998:157–158). Consumptive men were sometimes associated with creative genius. Such imagery spilled over from the upper classes, which had the privilege of retiring from ordinary work schedules to nurse the long-incubating disease. In a sense, this type of figure became symptomatic of the leisure class, an especially appropriate example of what Veblen (1899) called "conspicuous consumption."

Beyond New England and the Northeast, the romance of tuberculosis touched even the western and southern states, which provided the principal readership of *Gunn's Domestic Medicine* (1986 [1830]:164): "I hardly know an object of more tender concern to the anxious parent, or the medical advi-

Table 4.3. • Reported Causes of Death among Infants and Young Children in the Arkansas Ozarks, 1850.

	DEATHS, AGES 0–5 (%)	ALL DEATHS (%)	AVERAGE AGE (YR)
Diphtheria	15.0	7.0	0.57
Scarlet fever	10.0	6.9	5.1
Fevers	10.0	13.1	17.1
Diarrhea	7.7	6.3	12.9
Skin lesions	7.4	4.2	3.0
Digestive	5.5	6.2	21.6
Respiratory	4.5	10.8	29.2

Source: U.S. Bureau of the Census 1850, Schedule 3.

sor, than a young and beautiful female in the pride and spring of youth, and strength of intellect, borne down by the invasion of a malady, which has so often selected for its sacrifices the most amiable and interesting beings of God's creation." Although the young female victim of consumption was the most familiar image, tuberculosis struck men as well as women, the old as well as the young. In the Arkansas Ozarks nearly equal numbers of males and females died of consumption in 1850, and the average victim was almost 35 years of age.

Tuberculosis leaves characteristic scars on the spine, ribs, or joints (see Aufderheide and Rodríguez-Martín 1998; Santos and Roberts 2001; Roberts and Buikstra 2003). Rib lesions have been associated with pulmonary tuberculosis in some 9 percent of patients with the disease (Kelly and Micozzi 1984; Roberts et al. 1994). Given the high rate of pulmonary infection during this period, we might expect to see some of these lesions in the emigrants' remains. No such lesions, however, were identified on any of the 260 rib fragments that were exhumed from the mass grave. In fact, only one individual, an older adult male, had skeletal lesions consistent with a chronic and widespread infection (see Figure 5.3). This infection, however, was unlikely to be tuberculosis.

What is striking, then, about the victims at Mountain Meadows is their apparently robust pulmonary health. These were people who had seen tuberculosis and other respiratory diseases run rampant in their country and on the trail. In fact, on a national basis, tuberculosis rates increased over the course of the 1850s, leveling off only in the following decade (Grob 2002:110). Yet the study sample of 28 people buried under Carleton's cairn had no obvious signs of "graveyard coughs." They were heading to California with the expectation of new lives and a change of air.

Suffering Children

Across the United States, infant mortality was high throughout the nineteenth century. Especially noxious were the urban areas, where 43 percent of newborns would not survive to their first birthday (Steckel 1988:342). By comparison, infants in rural households were at an advantage but still died at a rate of almost 19 percent. This was true whether the household was in the Northeast, in the South, or on the western frontier, which extended in 1850 from Minnesota to Texas (Steckel 1988:337). Children who survived to age one, however, had a different chance of dying, depending on their geographic region. Now the Northeast held the smallest risk, with young children dying at a rate of 13.3 percent, as opposed to 16.3 percent in the South and more than 23 percent on the frontier.

Yet these large regional characterizations turn out to be very poor predictors of child mortality in northwestern Arkansas. Here the infant mortality rate, according to the 1850 census, was just 7 percent. Among children ages one to five, the risk of death was less than 2 percent. Young juvenile death rates appear to have been significantly lower in the Ozarks than in the rest of the South. In fact, the Ozarks do not resemble any of the national regions that were evaluated by Richard Steckel (1988). The pattern here diverges most sharply from the pattern on the "frontier," where children died at a rate more than ten times that of the Arkansas Ozarks.

While the risk of death varied dramatically from region to region, the infections most likely to kill infants and children were similar across the country. One of the greatest child killers was laryngeal diphtheria (West 1989:233). Diphtheria results from a bacteria bacillus (*Corynebacterium diphtheriae*) that spreads easily by air or physical contact, causing headache, lethargy, high fever, cough, and a painfully swollen throat. In the Ozarks 15 percent of the young juvenile deaths were attributed to diphtheria in 1850 (Table 4.3). Whereas this disease claimed infants in particular, scarlet fever killed many toddlers and older children. Like diphtheria, scarlet fever is caused by a bacterium, in this case a hemolytic streptococcus (Grob 202:80–81). Both diseases are highly contagious, nasopharyngeal infections with similar symptoms that were often confused. In 1850 one or the other was blamed for the deaths of three children in Carroll County and four in Johnson. Nonetheless, 1850 was described in the Johnson County census as an "unusually healthy" year (U.S. Bureau of the Census 1850, Schedule 3).

Gunn (1986 [1830]:344) recognized that many childhood diseases could be prevented by changes in daily routines: "If you are desirous of preserving your children's health, and giving them good constitutions, give them exercise, and let them be frequently in the open air, so as to accustom their bodies to the various changes of the atmosphere." Given Gunn's counsel, overland travel should have been considered advantageous to the children's health. The trail, however, was "a congested human stream," according to Elliott West (1989:216): "Never before or again would most pioneers come into contact with so many people in so short a time." Though the majority of adults on the trail had survived and developed immunity to childhood diseases, the young were at risk of multiple exposures within days of their departure.

In the core wagon-train families, women were giving birth every 2.3 years on average and the birth spacing ranged from one to three years. There are no obvious age gaps in any of these households, indicating few, if any, child deaths. Such findings are especially interesting, considering that Steckel (1988) found that the greatest predictor of childhood death on the frontier was the number of siblings in the household. Young children, in particular, were less likely to survive if they had four or more siblings in the household.[2] These large frontier families provided a predictable pool of newly susceptible infants—one every two years on average (Steckel 1988:344). Among the core families on the 1857 wagon train, however, even those children born into households with four or more siblings seem to have survived.

Ironically, surviving a childhood illness increases the likelihood of dental and skeletal lesions (on this "osteological paradox," see Ortner 1991; Wood et al. 1992; Steckel and Rose 2002; Wright and Yoder 2003). Defects in the tooth enamel, or hypoplasias, are useful for assessing growth disruption during childhood because this is when the crowns of the teeth are forming. Hypoplastic bands are created when enamel apposition ceases due to a period of chronic stress, usually associated with infectious disease or nutritional imbalance (Cutress and Suckling 1982; Hillson 1996). Once the child recovers, normal growth of the crown begins again, but a permanent scar is left on the tooth.

In the Mountain Meadows sample 6 percent of the teeth had enamel defects. Most were located in the anterior dentition of adults (Table 4.4). Because permanent crowns of incisors, canines, and premolars have completed their development by about six years of age, any growth arrest in the enamel is indicative of infant and childhood illnesses.[3] Given that enamel disruptions in adult teeth reflect childhood conditions, most of the defects in the Mountain Meadows sample resulted from illnesses contracted in Alabama, Illinois, Kentucky, Tennessee, or North Carolina, states in which the "Arkansans" had lived as young children.

A few of the emigrants had in fact grown up in Arkansas. They were teenagers or children, and the evidence for their dental health is incomplete. Of the 63 teeth that were not fully developed, there were just 3 with enamel

Table 4.4 • Dental Hypoplasia in the Mountain Meadows Sample.

	NO. TEETH	NO. TEETH W/ HYPOPLASIA	%
Maxilla			
Decid incisor			
Decid canine	2		
Decid molar	1		
Incisor	59	10	17
Canine	15	2	13
Premolar	42	4	10
Molar	82		
Subtotal	201	16	8
Mandible			
Decid incisor			
Decid canine			
Decid molar	8		
Incisor	50	3	6
Canine	16	2	13
Premolar	44		
Molar	58		
Subtotal	176	5	3
Total	377	21	6

defects, suggesting that the "home-grown" Arkansans had been relatively free of prolonged illnesses. There was at least one exception, however: the youngest child in the grave, no more than five years old, had four distinct enamel defects in two canine teeth. Such a pattern of defects indicates a series of illnesses that disrupted growth. This child had survived at least four serious bouts of sickness, only to suffer a violent death far from home.

Poisonous Pox

"Social reformers and social scientists of the early nineteenth century did not draw a qualitative distinction between physical and moral causes of disease" (Dorn 2000:269). Chronic illness, in particular, became entangled with an individual's identity. As medical historian Charles Rosenberg (1997a:37) explains, "Each case constituted a unique aggregate of circumstance and responsibility, of morality and imprudence, of countless decisions (and thus behavior) repeated over time." Allowing one's cold to turn to consumption, for example, or a bruise to become cancer, was believed to be the result of moral and behavioral failings. Thus the language of disease and illness could be used as a social weapon (Craddock 1995; O'Brien 2003; Wray 2006).

Syphilis, in particular, had long been linked to sexual immorality. It was generally believed that "those who suffered from it got their just desserts" (Hays 1998:257). Even *Gunn's Domestic Medicine* (1986 [1830]:267), which was usually sympathetic to victims of disease, took a hard line when it came to treatments for "pox": "This caustic will sting you a little; but never mind this; you are now on the stool of repentance; and are only learning the salutary moral lesson, that 'the penalty always treads upon the heels of the transgression,' and that the sacred laws of nature and her God, can never be violated without punishment to reform the offender!" In the case of syphilis the afflicted were expected to suffer. "The POX," according to Gunn (1986 [1830]: 263), "is a most corrupting, dangerous, and destructive disease; and is suffered to progress in its ravages on the human body, never fails in desolating the human constitution, and destroying life at its very *core*."

Syphilis is caused by a bacterium, *Treponema pallidum*. The first clinical symptoms of venereal syphilis are inflammatory changes in the soft tissue. Localized pustules develop where the bacteria enter the body. As the bacteria spread, so do the lesions. In the later stages of syphilis, destruction may extend to the heart, arteries, brain, spinal chord, and bones (Roberts and Manchester 2005:209–210; Aufderheide and Rodríguez-Martín 1998:158). Bone lesions in the tertiary stages are most likely to develop two to ten years after infection. These lesions tend to appear bilaterally on a number of bones, especially the tibiae, cranial vault, and facial bones around the nose (Ortner 2003:280). Moreover, any mother who has been infected may pass the bacteria on to her unborn child, resulting in skeletal and dental abnormalities in the infant (Lewis 2007:151–159).

Syphilis is evident in several skeletal populations from the nineteenth century (for precolumbian context, see Powell and Cook 2005; Hutchinson and Richman 2006). The disease was detected, for example, in the bones of adult residents at the Monroe County Almshouse in Rochester, New York (1826–1863) (Higgins et al. 2002:176). Skeletal and dental lesions consistent with congenital syphilis were found at two African American cemeteries: Freedman's Town (1869–1902) in Dallas, Texas (Condon et al. 1994), and Cedar Grove Baptist Church (1881–1927) in rural southwestern Arkansas (Rose and Hartnady 1991). These cases were probably not unusual. "Indeed, before effective methods to treat or cure the disease developed in the early twentieth century, syphilis was likely endemic within any nineteenth-century population center" (Davidson et al. 2002:254).

The remains at Mountain Meadows, however, tell a different story. In the study sample of at least 28 massacre victims, there was no evidence of lesions that would be consistent with a diagnosis of venereal or congenital syphilis. Once again, we are struck by the apparent vigor of this population.

These findings are in sharp contrast to claims that were made in the immediate aftermath of the massacre. As we have seen, John D. Lee maintained that members of the Arkansas party were syphilitic. Furthermore, William H. Dame, colonel of the Iron County militia, had examined the bodies of the emigrants and claimed that all the women were prostitutes.[4] Though the skeletal evidence from the mass grave at Mountain Meadows cannot decisively refute the claims of Lee, Dame, and others, it casts doubt on the image of an emigrant party that was "rotten with pox," as Lee put it (Kenney 1983:5:103).

For the sake of argument, however, let us grant the possibility that the victims' bodies might have been examined for evidence of disease and other abnormalities. How would anyone have been able to tell that they were infected with syphilis? Unless the victims were in the advanced stages of the disease, only a close examination of their genitalia would have revealed any symptoms. Needless to say, none of the newspaper accounts or journal entries provides details about how such a procedure was conducted. It is known that the bodies were stripped of their clothing soon after the massacre. So the possibility remains that the perpetrators, under the guise of a medical examination, committed a final outrage on the killing field.

To question the health and physical condition of the massacre victims was to question simultaneously their moral constitution. By claiming that the emigrants were syphilitic, Lee and his confederates were commenting on more than the physiology of the Arkansans. Sexual impropriety was only the most obvious lapse in a wider discourse of moral causality. In many cultural contexts, according to Richard Shweder and colleagues (1997:122–123), such causality

> is notable for its references to transgressions of obligation: omissions of duty, trespass of mandatory boundaries, and more generally any type of ethical failure at decision making or self-control. It is associated with the idea that suffering is the result of one's own actions or intentions, that a loss of moral fiber is a prelude to misfortune, that outcomes—good or bad—are proportionate to actions.

Perpetrators of the massacre seem to have been justifying an especially "bad outcome" for the Arkansas emigrants. In their version of events the emigrants themselves bore responsibility for their deaths. Such reasoning allowed even children to be viewed as morally corrupt.

In this respect, mothers bore a special burden. From the moment of conception a pregnant woman was expected to monitor her behavior so as to ensure the proper growth and character development of her child. If an expectant mother, for example, allowed herself to be frightened by the sight of a man with a severed limb, her baby might be born with only one arm (McMillen 1990:73). Negative feelings in general were discouraged, "for all could be communicated to her child and create lasting moral damage" (Rosenberg 1997b:28). In the popular imagination, maternal care was both credited for the production of successful and healthy adults and blamed for any number of character flaws and physiological deficits.

Thus, in the case of Mountain Meadows, to insinuate that parents were afflicted with disease—especially one such as syphilis—was to comment on the character, or future character, of their offspring. It was especially offensive to claim, as Dame was purported to do, that "all the women were prostitutes." Because an infant was "dependent upon the state of the mother's blood from the moment of conception till weaned from the breast," emotional states such as anger, sexual desire, or envy "could potentially injure the nursling by contaminating its milk" (Rosenberg 1997b:193). Such logic allowed the perpetrators of the massacre to deny the innocence even of the surviving children. Thus, on September 29, 1857, Wilford Woodruff wrote in his journal (Kenney 1983:5:103): "Brother [John D.] Lee said that He did not think their was a drop of innocent Blood in their Camp for he had too of their Children in his house & he Could not get but one to kneel down in prayer time & the other would laugh at her for doing it & they would sware like pirat[e]s."

In Utah many have claimed that the Arkansans were, in some sense, *adulterated*—that they had inferior constitutions and carried moral as well as physical impurities. Such accusations redirect attention from the behavior of the murderers to the putative failings of the victims themselves. Even today, as Rosenberg (1997a:44) argues, "our bodies reflect cumulative behaviors and impart worth, with the specter of disease serving as sanction for accepted behavioral norms."

DOMAINS

Woman—In every age and clime she has smoothed the asperity and softened the ferocity of man.

— Fourth of July Toast, *Arkansas Gazette*, 1831

Woman, representing the highest type to which men aspired, had no reason to experience ritual.

— Mark C. Carnes, *Secret Ritual and Manhood in Victorian America*, 1989

The victims at Mountain Meadows, however anonymous they remain in most historical accounts, are always assigned to three categories: men, women, and children. Whatever else we are told about them, we are led to believe that the men acted "like men" while the women and children remained "offstage" in a protected, quasi-domestic domain. Thus only the men are portrayed as behaving badly (or heroically) on the trail, and only they were involved in the negotiations to resolve the standoff with their Mormon assailants (who were themselves, of course, all men). Throughout most of the story, in fact, women and children are conspicuous by their absence—right up to the hour of their deaths. By all accounts, the women and children were physically separated from the men before being lured to the killing fields. The style of execution was also strictly gendered. The emigrant men were purportedly shot by other men whereas the women and children were bludgeoned to death by "Indians."

What are we to make of this narrative as a portrait of men, women, and children in Victorian America? Does this starkly gendered story accurately reflect the reality of American life, or is it just one more idealized image of Victorian sex roles? This chapter takes up such questions in the antebellum context, especially in the Arkansas Ozarks. Often assumed to be a cultural backwater, the Ozark region was surprisingly open to wider social currents flowing from distant sources.

In particular, as many historians have noted, the first half of the nineteenth century witnessed the emergence of a so-called cult of domesticity, according to which civility, education, and morality came to be defined as especially female concerns (e.g., Cott 1977; Smith-Rosenberg 1985; Sellers 1991; Stanley 1996). In a world increasingly tainted by selfish materialism and greed, only women seemed capable of safeguarding the traditional ideals of domestic virtue and civic responsibility.

Yet men were deeply affected by the market revolution and its social repercussions, and sought ways to restore a sense of authentic camaraderie apart from their regimented lives in the industrial economy. According to Gilbert Herdt (2003:10), "a new idea of male 'human nature' was growing popular among the aspiring middle class—that it was 'normal and natural' to join segregated secret clubs and to be initiated through special or esoteric rites. A new cultural reality was created—albeit hidden from the public, and particularly those public or domestic spaces trafficked by women." The result was a proliferation of so-called fraternal orders, such as the Freemasons and the Odd Fellows, which offered a decidedly masculine critique of market values (Clawson 1989:212): "Fraternalism stood as an alternative to domesticity because it identified men as the principal moral actors and proposed to extend the moral economy of kinship beyond the nuclear family to a larger sphere of social relations. The bonds of mutual obligation, the image of a self-regulating, caring community, were central to the concept of nineteenth-century fraternalism."

The tension between fraternalism and domesticity was played out in various ways across the country and up and down the social hierarchy. In some contexts, fraternalism gained the upper hand, restoring to men some of their traditional status as patriarchs (Carnes 1989; Clawson 1989). By and large, however, domesticity tended to set the tone of gender relations in Victorian America, eventually spawning the anti-Masonic movement (Bullock 1996), the temperance movement (Bordin 1981), and the first wave of feminist activism (Berg 1978).

Perhaps the most creative *synthesis* of fraternalism and domesticity was the institutionalized form of Mormonism that emerged in the 1840s in Nauvoo, Illinois. As R. Laurence Moore (1986:36) points out, "Most of the distinctive features of Mormon theology, the plurality of Gods, the baptism for the dead, marriage for eternity, and plural marriage, all date from the Nauvoo period." The apparent novelty of these beliefs and practices belies the way in which they merged the fraternalism of Freemasonry with the cult of domesticity, giving rise to a moral framework that enshrined both masculine hierarchy and feminine duties. This moral framework survived the assassination of the Mormon prophet in 1844 and was successfully transplanted to the Intermountain West. Here the Mormons hunkered down, hoping to avoid further entanglements with the decadent culture of American capitalism (Rodseth and Olsen 2000).

When the Arkansas emigrants arrived in Utah in 1857, they confronted a theocratic state preparing for war to preserve its unique synthesis of fraternalism and domesticity. In the aftermath of Mountain Meadows, lurid stories of Mormon barbarity became standard fodder for the penny press and the booming market in sensational gothic imagery (Cohen 1993, 2003:54). At the same time, Mormons fought back with their own caricatures of the emigrants as ruffians, murderers, and thieves, whose women were prostitutes and whose children could "sware like pirates" (Kenney 1983:5:102).

A Semi-barbaric State

The frontier is often considered an untamed space where single men roamed the land, filling their days with hunting, drinking, gambling, and brawling. As industrialization produced a rigid landscape of daily routines in the East, tales blossomed of the western wilderness and its equally wild inhabitants (Slotkin 1985; Roberts 2000:201). Arkansas, in particular, had a reputation for attracting "the fringe elements of society" (DeBlack 2002:113, 115; see also Harkins 2004:25–29). This image was promulgated in part to feed the nation's growing appetite for romantic literature of frontier life. As D. Fred Williams (1980:102) points out, "Most Americans based their perceptions of Arkansas on travel accounts and feature stories in popular magazines." In 1849 a newspaper editor in Van Buren, Arkansas, wrote about the persistent negative image of its citizens: "People at a distance easily come to the conclusion that...a typical Arkansan is...a person in a semi-barbaric state, half alligator, half horse...armed to the teeth, bristling with knives and pistols, a rollicking daredevil type of personage, made up of coarseness, ignorance and bombast" (*Arkansas Intelligencer*, 3 November 1849). To some extent, this reputation was deserved. As Bolton (1993:2) remarks, "Arkansas Territory was a violent place where duels occurred frequently, brawls were commonplace, and murder was something about which the average citizen might reasonably worry."

Some have emphasized that this propensity toward violence may be related to the unique demographics within territorial Arkansas and other frontier states. David Courtwright (1991, 1996) has proposed that in many of these remote places the sex ratio was heavily biased toward single young men. He argues that because more men than women migrated west, the surplus men "could not all marry and establish families; and that, lacking wives and families, they were more likely to behave in unhealthful and destructive ways" (1991:457). In addition to being more prone to violence and antisocial behavior, bachelorhood often compromised men's health. They were "less likely to eat nutritious food or pay attention to personal hygiene," according to Gerald Grob (2002:137), and furthermore, they "frequently succumbed to disease and accidents, and perhaps fell prey to psychological despair."

Yet when the first mortality census was conducted in 1850, there was little evidence for deaths related to such vice in the Arkansas Ozarks. Here only a single bachelor purportedly died from scurvy, while three other *married* men died from intemperance or drunkenness (U.S. Bureau of the Census 1850, Schedule 3). This rather surprising pattern may be explained, in part, by demographic change. Though there were still three males for every two females in Arkansas in 1840 (Bolton 1998:118), by 1850 the sex ratio for whites was nearly equal.

There were, however, four murders recorded that year in the highlands. Three of the victims were close kin. William Y. King (50), William King Jr. (33), and Loomis G. King (26) were killed in a roadside ambush in August 1849. Their deaths were part of a string of homicides since 1844, resulting from a feud between the Tutt and Everett families of Marion County. The so-called Tutt-Everett War is of special interest here because it brought together a number of men who would eventually organize the 1857 wagon train. For the moment, however, this feud provides an opportunity to look more closely at patterns of male violence and male bonding in the context of nineteenth-century America, especially in the southern highlands.

The Everett family was "old stock" from Kentucky that had settled the area before 1836. With the creation of Marion County, the Everetts monopolized most of the political offices, including those of judge, sheriff, and militia colonel (Flippin 1958:155). The Tutt family also settled the area in the 1830s, and Hansford "Hamp" Tutt, from east Tennessee, would come to own the only public house in the village of Yellville. Hamp's growing popularity and political aspirations brought the Tutts into direct competition with the established Everetts, culminating in a public melee after election speeches in June 1844.

As families in the county took sides, the Tutts were supported by the three King brothers: William, Hosea, and James. On the evening of October 9, 1848, a fight in Yellville resulted in the first King casualty (Monks 1907:24). The *Washington Telegraph* reported the incident on October 25:

> A man by the name of Watkins, of the Everett party, shot down Jack King. At the same time Sim Everett fired at Sinclair and missed him. Sinclair returned the shot mortally wounding Everett. King's brother was shot by Bartlett Everett, the ball grazing his shoulder; he in turn shot Bart Everett dead in his tracks. After Sim Everett was shot he gathered a rock and pursued Sinclair, but finding King, who had been shot in the beginning of the fight, he turned on him and mashed his skull in a shocking manner, and expired while in the act.

Not quite a year later, William King, his son Loomis, and nephew Young Bill were shot dead in a road ambush by an "Everett crowd" (Flippin 1958:161). This is the triple homicide that appears in the 1850 census.

A Fully Modern Feud

Given such a pattern of violence, one crucial asset would seem to be male alliances. When the state cannot provide security, self-help often involves reliance on power networks of related men, or what have been called "fraternal interest groups" (Murphy 1957; van Velzen and van Wetering 1960). Such groups are the typical participants in a feud, which may be defined as a series of at least three homicides motivated by revenge (Otterbein 1996:493). Revenge homicides are, in most societies, driven by the desire to preserve the honor of the kin group when the premarital chastity of a female member has been violated (Ericksen and Horton 1992:71–72).

In both the popular and academic literature it has been argued that southerners are especially prone to respond violently to personal slights (e.g., Redfield 2000 [1880]; Nisbett and Cohen 1996; Wyatt-Brown 2001). According to the southern "code of honor," a gentleman was required to demand immediate satisfaction for offense to himself, a loved one, or close friends. Norms that emphasize male competitiveness and the violent defense of masculine honor are argued to have been transmitted to Appalachian and Ozark settlers from their Scottish borderlands ancestors (e.g., Brown 1986; McWhiney 1988; Courtwright 1996; Fischer 1989). As Richard Nisbett and Dov Cohen (1996:4) put it, "the southern preference for violence stems from the fact that much of the South was a lawless, frontier region settled by people whose economy was originally based on herding." An ethos of honor, therefore, was necessary to protect one's livelihood (Nisbett and Cohen 1996:89):

> We believe the southern culture of honor derives from the herding economy brought to the region by the earliest settlers and practiced by them for many decades thereafter.... The hersdman continually faces the possibility of losing his animals through the actions

> of others. The issue of protection is therefore a very serious one and the herdsman cultivates an acquaintance with violence and weapons to deter those who would prey on him. The sensitivity to insult is secondary. The purpose is to preserve the individual's reputation for being willing and able to carry out violence if needed.

The weak link in this argument is the assumption that cultural mores are carried intact across many generations and in quite varied economic, legal, and social environments. What may be more important than cultural heritage is the existing "ecology" of political and economic resources. The penetration of a market economy, in particular, seems to be the driving force behind a set of nineteenth-century Kentucky feuds studied by Keith Otterbein (2000). Participants in these feuds sought to eliminate their rivals for political offices and other strategic positions that provided access to wealth. From Otterbein's (2000:241) perspective, these feuds were caused not by a code of honor but by new opportunities for economic and political gain.

The Tutt-Everett War in northwestern Arkansas seems to have followed a similar pattern. Like the market-driven feuds in Kentucky (Otterbein 2000:238), this conflict involved competition for political offices, making election years particularly volatile: "If one kin group was successful in obtaining such offices, that group became 'the law' and could put opponents in jail or have them executed for retaliatory homicides" (Otterbein 2000:241). In this light, the feuds persisted "because of corrupt government, rather than weak government" (Otterbein 2000:235). In Arkansas, Sheriff Mooney of Marion County was closely allied with the Everett family and helped set up the ambush of the King men (Flippin 1958:160–161).

Otterbein's conception of the Appalachian feud remains conventional in one important respect: he takes kin groups, in the literal sense of extended families, to be the natural units involved in the conflict. Yet how such "kin groups" are constructed is precisely the issue raised by Altina Waller (1988) in her study of the famous Kentucky–West Virginia feud between the Hatfields and McCoys. Like Otterbein, Waller recognizes that Appalachian feuds were driven by a market economy. In particular, "the new externally generated market for timber caused divisiveness and bitter litigation between neighbors and kin" (1988:41). Some 84 percent of the Hatfield supporters "were tied to or dependent upon" Devil Anse, the Hatfield patriarch, "through land purchases or timbering" (Waller 1988:80).

At the same time, Waller's analysis demonstrates that kinship in the literal sense was a surprisingly weak predictor of who supported whom (1988:78):

> If family connections really did determine feud loyalties, then surprisingly few of Devil Anse's relatives appear as his supporters.... Not only were many Hatfields neutral, but on occasion they supported the McCoys.... U.S. census schedules for 1880 reveal that there were thirty-seven Hatfield households in the Tug Valley which did not contribute a single member to the feud. Apparently, family solidarity is not a sufficient explanation for feud alliances.

The widespread notion of "family" feuds, argues Waller, has been perpetuated in both local traditions and official histories. "Blood is thicker than water" is the ideological principle that underlies much of the discourse on human social life (Schneider 1984:165–177; see also Bryant 1981; Ericksen and Horton 1992). From Waller's perspective, such discourse fails to grasp a basic principle of social organization (1988:84–85):

> Like modern nations, the traditional family was a social construction based on geography and ideology—although that ideology tended to be implicit rather than explicit.... Any social conflict in nineteenth-century Appalachia was likely to be expressed as family conflict, not from a lack of alternative community institutions, but because families defined the contours of social, political, even religious organizations.

Waller's formulation suggests that "fraternal interest groups" may be kin groups in name only and that feuds are often waged by political factions with a thin veneer of clannish identity (Verdery 1999; Rodseth and Wrangham 2004).

The propensity to integrate family and kinship ideologies to form political networks, especially for mutual defense, can also be manipulated by authorities. In fact, it was just such a network—the Carroll County militia—that was called out by the Arkansas governor in 1849 to stop the Tutt-Everett War. Two companies were raised from Carroll County, including one under the command of Captain William C. Mitchell. Mitchell's company assembled at William Beller's farm on Crooked Creek before marching northeast to Yellville (Goodspeed Publishing Co. 1889:395). Included in this company were two brothers, John and Alexander Fancher.

Brothers in the Bostons

An idealized image of the fraternal bond has played a crucial role in the construction of modern societies (e.g., Hobsbawm 1965; Carnes 1989; Bullock 1996; Jacob 2006). "Over centuries of European and American history," as

Mary Ann Clawson (1989:5) observes, "fraternalism exerted a persistent appeal, forming the basis for guilds, workers' organizations, political societies, and social groups." Freemasonry in particular provided a model for innumerable organizations that have shaped men's lives in ways both subtle and profound.

Fraternal societies serve a number of purposes. In addition to helping temper and direct the behavior of adolescents and young men, these groups create economic, social, and political bonds among unrelated men (Doyle 1979:184; Clawson 1989:51; Sellers 1991:282; Deloria 1998:48). Secret rituals establish fictive kinship ties that operate, according to one Freemason brother, "with as much force and effect, as the natural relationship of blood" (Clinton in Clawson 1989:371). To legitimize the new kinship ties, "age-old" rituals are invented or embellished, invoking powerful images of death and rebirth (Carnes 1989:54–64; cf. Bloch and Parry 1982). In the case of Freemasonry, a mythic charter was established: "Tracing its origins to the brotherhood of builders who constructed King Solomon's Temple and to operative Masons who carried on the tradition of the craft in medieval and early modern Europe, speculative Freemasonry was a product of early eighteenth-century Britain, from which it spread to the continent and America" (Goodman 1988:9).

Once the rituals become fairly standardized, secret signs, words, and symbols can be recognized by "brothers" everywhere. Thus in Victorian America, "initiation rituals bound the entrant not only to the members of a local lodge, that is, to people immediately available to him, but also to a symbolic union with Pythians, Odd Fellows, or Masons throughout the reaches of a complex and highly stratified society" (Clawson 1989:109). Members were thus assured of "mutual aid," regardless of where they roamed (Sellers 1991:281–282). Masonic lodges tended to grow up along trade routes and attracted men who followed these paths—"merchants, colonial officials, military officers, and other cosmopolitans" (Clawson 1989:113). Masonry, in short, was "irresistible to mobile self-makers" (Sellers 1991:281). Alongside Freemasonry there developed several new fraternities, the most important of which was the Independent Order of Odd Fellows (Clawson 1989:118–123). By the early 1820s some 100,000 men in the United States were Masons (Goodman 1988:3), and there were 44 Masonic lodges in Connecticut alone (Lipson 1977:80).

Membership would plummet, however, between 1826 and 1840, when an anti-Masonic movement swept the northeastern states and nearly drove Freemasonry to extinction (Bullock 1996:277). Beginning as a grassroots movement in western New York, the anti-Masonic crusade portrayed the brotherhood as elitist, anti-Christian, and undemocratic (Cross 1950:114–125; Dumenil 1984:6–7). In the South there was little open hostility to Masonry, but lodge membership dropped off nonetheless (Bullock 1996:310–311). As an organized political movement, anti-Masonry burned itself out in the 1830s, but it would take years for the brotherhood to recover (Cross 1950: 117, 121–122; Goodman 1988:5; Tabbert 2005:61–65).

By midcentury, men's societies were once again popular in America, and Masonic membership tripled between 1850 and 1860 (Dumenil 1984:7). "The rough old male patterns were coming to an end during the 1850s, as the gander pull and the horse race gave way to the more civilized pursuits of commercial farmers and civic leaders" (Faragher 2001:120). Masons in this period tended to be white, Protestant, bourgeois, and ambitious, and many would be attracted to the goldfields of California (Read and Gaines 1949; cf. Roberts 2000).

The Ozarks, like most of the country, had a number of fraternal societies, even before the Civil War (Billingsley 2004:82–83). Due to its positioning along the Arkansas River, Clarksville seems to have attracted an early interest in Freemasonry. The first Clarksville branch was founded sometime before 1845, but this old "Blue Lodge No. 5" was destroyed by fire. The Clarksville contingent united with the Franklin Lodge No. 9, southeast of town (Langford 1921:97). The lodge soon returned to Clarksville, and the restoration was formally celebrated on June 24, 1850.

This event was attended by men from lodges from across the state. According to Langford (1921:99), the ceremonies began as "members formed in line at the lodge room and marched to music furnished by H. L. Wilson and Geo. Basham across the square to the little Methodist Church on the south side where a crowd awaited to witness the installation ceremonies." Prayers and speeches were followed by a supper going for "one dollar per plate." Seven years later a man called Basham—probably George D. Basham—would join a wagon train in Johnson County, only to be lost at Mountain Meadows (Bagley 2002:66).

Meanwhile, north of the Boston Mountains, two Masonic fraternities had been established in 1853. According to local historian Jim Lair (1983:403), "the histories of Yell Lodge Number 64 [in Carrollton] and Ashley Lodge Number 66 [in Berryville] are so closely related that it isn't easy to determine who belonged to which lodge. Many businessmen had interests in both towns." In any case, among the early Masons in the area was at least one by the name of Fancher. A number of Fancher men may well have attended the Yell Lodge, which was located just twelve miles from the original Fancher homestead on Osage Creek (Goodspeed Publishing Co. 1889:392; Larimer and Mahoney 2003).

This lodge came to have special significance for the survivors of Mountain Meadows. In September 1859, when fifteen orphans of the massacre were welcomed back to Arkansas, they spent their first night in Carrollton at the Yell Lodge. The youngest survivors were about three years old, posing a difficult problem for their kith and kin: whose children were they? The community gathered in Carrollton to sort out the orphans, who were then taken in by presumed aunts, uncles, grandparents, and neighbors. Matilda Wilkins (1849–1932), herself just ten years old, "helped prepare a 'dinner on the ground' to honor the surviving children" (Fancher 2006:xiv–xv). Fourteen years later Matilda would marry James Polk Fancher (1849–1939), a nephew of Alexander Fancher. A master storyteller, she was capable into her eightieth year of transfixing an audience of women and men, family and friends, but especially children of the Fancher clan.

Sisters of Civility

Through family history and hero stories, Matilda Wilkins Fancher—affectionately known as "Mattie Ma"—educated the next generation, conveying messages of proper conduct, self-discipline, and middle-class morality. She was acting, in effect, as a civilizing influence and insisted on a high level of decorum, even among the youngest in attendance (Fancher 2006:xv–xvi):

> After the children were arranged about the storyteller, Mattie Ma established the ground rules for all the listeners. There must be absolute quiet. Those who failed to be quiet must go elsewhere. Next, Aunt Margaret [a mulatto servant] passed out the cookies and returned to her seat. Speaking in a strong clear voice, Mattie Ma said, "Today, I am going to tell you the story of Captain Alexander Fancher.... The captain was one of the most charming men who ever passed through Carroll County.... I do not recall anyone ever saying a bad word about him except for the slander heaped upon him by the folks who planned and carried out the massacre."

Though not a professional teacher, Mattie Ma slipped into a role that had been carved out by Victorian reformers such as Catherine Esther Beecher (1800–1878): "Soon, in all parts of our country, in each neglected village, or new settlement, the Christian female teacher will quietly take her station, collecting the ignorant children around her, teaching them the habits of neatness, order and thrift; opening the book of knowledge, inspiring the principles of morality, and awakening the hope of immortality" (Beecher 1846:11–14).

The mid-nineteenth century witnessed a sea change in American education. "Until the 1840s, teachers in the South were not paid or trained well and were not respected members of the community" (Wells 2004:134). By 1850, however, the educational reform movement that had begun in northern cities penetrated the rural South, setting off a struggle for public funds to establish more and better schools for children of all classes. Though this movement was resisted by the planters who could afford private tutors and boarding schools, the professionalization of public education opened a new market for teachers, who fanned out into rural and often impoverished communities (Wells 2004:147). Teaching offered women in particular a rare avenue to a professional career—one of the few ways in which bourgeois women might extend the cult of domesticity beyond their own households.

More generally in this period, women were seen as the purveyors of virtue and compassion in a world increasingly tainted by the cutthroat competition and anonymity of industrial markets (Allured 1988:237): "It was believed that, through their position as wives and mothers, females were the guardians of morality, the saviors of civilization itself. The doctrine of the separate spheres made the home a woman's domain; there she created a haven from the hectic, immoral and corrupting business world for her husband, nurtured Christian values in her children, and gently guided her spouse away from sin and temptation." Across the country the new middle-class values circulated widely in sermons, speeches, tracts, magazines, and textbooks (Wells 2004:42–47). In fact, with the exception of the Bible, school texts were more widely read than any other kind of printed material (Jeffrey 1998: 17). Because such texts were usually written and published in the Northeast, southern schools by default became conduits of bourgeois morality (Knight 1922; Elson 1964; Kleinberg 1999; cf. Wells 2004:128). Even in rural areas of the Deep South the image of women as domestic guardians of piety and virtue was disseminated by schoolteachers, Yankee peddlers, and evangelical preachers alike (Goen 1988; Schantz 1997; Rainer 2005).

What effect did this image have on the social activities and relationships of southern women? On the surface it would seem that these women were quite distinct from their northern counterparts, and indeed many historians have suggested just such a disparity. In the North the cult of domesticity tended to empower women, even within the public realm, as they allied with their clergy to push for social and moral reforms. As a result, even before the Civil War northern women were developing formal, autonomous, and sometimes militant women's organizations (e.g., Cott 1977; Berg 1978;

Smith-Rosenberg 1978, 1979). By contrast, southern women remained embedded in patriarchal kin- and church-centered communities (e.g., Wyatt-Brown 1982, 2001; Heyrman 1997). As Jean Friedman (1986:9) argues, "Male control of evangelical family churches insured a double standard of church discipline which reinforced traditional sexual roles and deterred formation of independent women's organizations."

This longstanding view has been called into question by recent studies that see a profound but subtle change in the early nineteenth century. "Pious women found the 'evangelical boy-preachers' who stormed through the rural South to be lively companions who respected their theological views and affirmed their gifts by arguing that they should speak in public" (Schweiger 2004:44). In this perspective, evangelicalism created not separate spheres but a *meeting ground* for the sexes. Country churches and tent revivals allowed men and women together "to save souls, nurture children, and perform works of benevolence" (Bode 1995:779).

The various "people's churches" had much in common: "Baptists, Methodists, Disciples of Christ, and Cumberland Presbyterians shared a reliance on evangelical, revivalistic methods and a faith in a righteous, caring, and omnipotent God, whose hand was witnessed more often in the miracles of the weather and in the healing of the sick than in the tragedies and failures of Ozark life" (Blevins 2002:58; see also Harrell 1988). An emphasis on healing in particular would have resonated with the women of the congregation, who filled the role of curer and midwife, not just within the family but between households. Health provisioning, in turn, created important social networks for women, who came from near and far to assist in childbirth, provide for the infirm, and prepare the dead for burial (Bolton 1991; Laderman 1996:30).

All this suggests that evangelical religion supported rather than inhibited the development of women's social networks and their vital (though informal) careers in the community. Such a view is elaborated in an important work by Scott M. Stephan (2001), whose results are summarized by Beth Barton Schweiger (2004:48): "Stephan argues that 'the clergy's "official" sanction of [women's] superior piety and virtue in home' gave them 'an informal but wide-ranging power from within the home that ended up expanding their influence beyond it.' It was this informal power—the 'expansive definition of motherly duties'—that historian have missed in their focus on gender roles within formal institutions in this period." In short, the social lives of women in the rural South have remained virtually invisible due to "a religious discourse that affirmed their deference and subordination to men and hid the reality of cooperation between women" (Bode 1995:785).

In this light, it is perhaps unsurprising that relationships among antebellum women in northwestern Arkansas are difficult to discern. In contrast to their fathers, brothers, and husbands, the women of the Ozarks were not known to form their own organizations comparable to the Masons or the Odd Fellows. Moreover, unlike many northern women, those in the southern highlands did not lead reform movements or take on other styles of social activism.

Yet this difference does not imply that Ozark women were unaffected by the social changes taking place, especially the reforms of public education: "Southerners in frontier towns in Mississippi and Arkansas and elsewhere recognized the importance of education to their children's future. Though their gains in the antebellum period were modest, advocates of school reform in the South helped lay the groundwork for the postwar expansion of public schools" (Wells 2004:135). Ella Molloy Langford, an early historian of the Ozarks, recounts how schools were first established in Johnson County (1921:85):

> Wherever there were enough families to furnish fifteen or twenty children of school age, some itinerant teacher found his way into that locality and was welcomed by the people. Sometimes a log dwelling was used for these schools but more often a little church had been built in the neighborhood and these early pedagogues were always welcome to use that.... These transient teachers were nearly always strangers but as a rule they were honest and dependable.

Alongside one-room schools, the first institutions of higher education began to spring up in the Ozarks around 1850. One such institution was the Berryville Academy, founded in 1853, whose meetings were held in a community building that had already served as both a school and a church. The high character of the local community was described in a letter to "Messrs Editors" of an Arkansas newspaper, presumably in Little Rock (quoted in Lair 1983:154–155): "Berryville is a rural village, situated in the midst of an extensive and fine agricultural district; and on account of the low price for boarding, the healthy locality of the town, its enlightened and moral population, its freedom from ostentation, extravagance and vice, and numerous other considerations is peculiarly suited to be the seat of a literary institution, and a nursery for students." The author, identified only as "J. H.," went on to praise the teachers in residence as "ripe scholars," including "a lady of excellent education and rare accomplishments" who assisted in the "female department." After hearing the final examinations, J. H. attended a reception for students and teachers:

> A generous glow of sociality lightened up every countenance and the spirit of friendship appeared to warm and animate all. The gentlemen were companionable, conversable, gay, and gallant; the ladies, God bless them, were just as they should be, bewitching and beautiful. When I first entered the hall, the scene presented was brilliant beyond description. All the ladies in snow white were arrayed on one side; and under the resplendent light of chandeliers seemed a fairy vision.

In this description we glimpse several facets of women's lives at this crucial moment in the rural South. First, there is the clear emergence of at least a few educated women who have taken on the professional task of educating a new generation of young women. Second, the candid observations of J. H. suggest the social evaluation of these women as blessed, beautiful, and pure. ("Bewitching" hints at their sexual potential but also shades it from public view.) Appearing as angelic figures of moral calling, these women embodied the cult of domesticity as it reached into the public domain. Along with the role of healer, that of schoolteacher seemed for a time to offer women a public persona that would not compromise their domestic virtue.

None of the riders on the 1857 train would have attended the Berryville Academy; even the wealthiest among them were unlikely to have moved in such bourgeois circles. Jack and Mary Baker, for example, were themselves illiterate and probably sent their offspring to country schools. In any case, by the time J. H. attended the graduation ceremonies of June 1857, the wagon train was well on its way to Mountain Meadows.

Helpmates

Public events, fraternal societies, and church services helped break up the monotony of rural life, but "sociability remained tied to the work rhythms of the agricultural calendar" (Kelly 2005:115). As a result, especially in frontier areas, women were appreciated especially as wives and helpmates. "This view deemphasized gentility and stressed the desirability of initiative, resourcefulness, and energy" (Jeffrey 1998:78). In general, men took on heavy labor while women were responsible for home, children, and garden. Thus, according to Julie Roy Jeffrey (1998:13), "the basic idea that men and women occupied separate spheres could apply to farm families as well as urban ones."

Though labor on the farm was segregated by age and sex, everyone was subject to the seasons (Faragher 2001:45–47). In the Ozarks, spring meant that it was time to sow the fields and retrieve the cattle from their winter forage in the canebreaks. As the crops matured in the late spring and early summer, a constant vigil of thinning and nurturing was required. By late summer the workload had lightened. Families and communities prepared for an intensive period of labor in the autumn when crops were harvested, animals butchered, and foods processed and stored for winter. This was also the "fever" season, and everyone's health was anxiously monitored for conditions that might interfere with the laborious demands of the harvest (Valenčius 2002:203–204).

The harvest was an especially arduous time for women. In this season, according to Brooks Blevins (2002:51),

> a woman's day started before daybreak, in the kitchen; she may even have had to milk the cow as well. After cooking breakfast and dressing the children, she joined the others in the field. At midday she rushed back to the house to prepare the family's dinner, probably ate little herself, cleaned the kitchen, and returned to the cotton or corn rows to work until she had to cook supper. After supper, she probably worked into the night's darkness washing, mending, or caring for a sick child.

Young wives would have worked alongside their husbands to clear and plow fields, tend animals, butcher livestock, and harvest crops. As the family size increased, however, a woman's attention focused on the household. Daughters helped with "women's work"—milking cows, tending a garden or henhouse, splitting kindling, and minding children.

Men, by contrast, spent most of their waking hours outside the home. In the Ozarks "men planted and cultivated the various crops; cared for work stock, cattle, hogs, and sheep; maintained fences and farm buildings; chopped firewood; supervised harvests; and hunted and fished" (Blevins 2002:50). Boys had their tasks as well; they "mucked out barns, made hay, cleared and gleaned fields, hoed, husked, and plowed, so that by the age of ten or twelve they had assumed most of the working responsibilities of full-grown men" (Faragher 1986:100). Even young sons might join their fathers in the fields, where they were "placed behind a small mule as soon as they were able to grab hold of the plow handles" (Blevins 2002:50). If there were no boys in the home, older girls might be drafted as field hands during the planting season (West 1989:75–77). On a few Ozark farms such family labor would have been supplemented by slaves or hired help.

In most cases, however, extra-domestic labor came not from the market but from an extended network of kith and kin. "Despite the mythology of the lone frontiersman," as Bolton (1993:82) reminds us, "women and children were much in evidence at the edges of expansion, and single males were normally attached to someone's family." In the 1840 census of Arkansas 94 percent of all households included at least one woman. For each of these women, furthermore, there were 1.5 adult males. This figure suggests a significant "surplus" of men in what might be expected to be nuclear family households. "The identity of these men is not given by the census; probably, however, many were relatives of the head of household and his wife" (Bolton 1993:82).

These nephews, cousins, and in-laws offered valuable labor to yeoman farmers who could not afford to hire hands or purchase slaves. But what were the benefits to the young men themselves? Bachelorhood, according to Grob (2002), was a difficult passage for many men on the frontier. By joining the household of a distant kinsman, they gained the services of women who would cook and clean for them. More important, perhaps, laboring for a distant relative enabled a man to marry. Given that single women were at a premium for most of the antebellum period, those men who were not landed could offer their labor to prospective in-laws. What anthropologists call *brideservice*—the (prospective) husband's services to his father-in-law in exchange for rights to the daughter—appears to have been at work in the Ozarks. Typically, for a number of years after marriage, the newlyweds lived in an adjacent "weaner house" until at least one child had been born.[1]

Meanwhile, an ideology of companionate marriage, part of the wider cult of domesticity, was flowing into the rural South from its sources in the urban North. By the last third of the nineteenth century, according to Janet Allured (1988), this ideology was widely disseminated in the Ozarks. In her study of Boone County, Arkansas,[2] Allured finds that by 1870 many women had made a transition, at least in part, to the modern companionate family, "notable for its more loving and equitable relations between spouses, the pre-eminence of motherhood, and the special attention given to children" (1988:233). For her part, Allured attributes the modification of family values to the wide circulation of newspapers and magazines, even in the "backwoods" of the Ozarks.

Such an explanation, as elaborated by Mark Schantz (1997), Jonathan Wells (2004), and others, emphasizes the diffusion of new cultural values from metropolitan centers to the rural periphery. What has not been adequately considered in this context are the changing conditions in the periphery itself and beyond. The gold rush, in particular, seems to have altered the social dynamics of marriage and domestic life. A husband who planned to travel west would have had to negotiate with his wife a suitable arrangement for the management of the household and the farm in his absence. Often this would have involved a transfer of responsibility for many duties from husband to wife and an enhancement of the wife's status as both a helpmate and a full economic partner in the venture. Furthermore, the considerable financial backing required for an overland journey often came from a range of extended kin, including in-laws (Roberts 2000:79). In this light, the prospect of a long separation would have solidified the conjugal bond in both economic and emotional terms.

One vital interest shared by husband and wife, of course, was the welfare of their children. Many overland ventures were undertaken to improve the prospects of the next generation, and absent husbands often wrote home with deep concern for their offspring (Roberts 2000:176). In 1850, for example, William Bedford Temple wrote from the trail to his "wife and little ones" in Osage, Arkansas:

> William you must be a good boy [and] have to learn your Book. If I can send you some money, you must go to school next summer and learn to be a good scholar. If I succeed I expect to educate you at some high school.... Do what you can to promote the happiness of all around you then you will be happy your self. Love your little sister and brother, say no bad words. Always remember you must give an account to god for all evil conduct. For that which is good he will reward you in a nother world. Mary Jane Elizabeth you must not be a bad girl. Love your Mother and brothers. Do all the good acts you can. Do no harm. Boon my little boy, may the good lord watch over you to gether with all my little ones so you may be preserved from all danger with out and with in. Dear children seperated as I am from you and getting farther every day you [must] not for get me. (Temple 1850a)

Temple was traveling to California with his neighbors, John and Alexander Fancher. While he was on the trail, Temple's wife and three children managed the family farm.

Similar companionate sentiments are found in the last will and testament of John Twitty Baker. In April 1857, just before his departure from Beller's Stand, Baker bequeathed his entire estate to his "beloved wife, Mary." Furthermore, he gave special attention to his daughters, willing that "their husbands shall never have any right to dispose of their property or effects." At the same time, Baker appointed a third party as his executor, presumably because Mary Baker, according to the 1850 census, was illiterate. That same year, it should be noted, their young sons and daughters would all attend school.

The Baker children, however, were in the minority, as only a quarter of

Table 5.1. ✦ Literacy and Education of Children in the Core Households, 1850.

HEAD OF HOUSEHOLD	1850 COUNTY	1857 CONTINGENT	NO. ADULTS	NO. ILLITERATE ADULTS	NO. CHILDREN	NO. SCHOOL-AGE CHILDREN ATTENDING SCHOOL
Baker, John T.	Carroll	Northern	2	2	5	5
Baker, George W.	Carroll	Northern	2	0	0	0
Cameron, William	Carroll	Southern	2	2	5	2
Dunlap, Jesse Jr.	Johnson	Northern	2	1	5	5
Dunlap, Lorenzo	Johnson	Northern	2	0	2	2
Fancher, Alexander	[San Diego, CA]	Fancher	2	0	4	0
Fancher, Jane[a]	Carroll	Fancher	2	2	6	6
Jones, John Milum	Johnson	Southern	2	1	0	0
Miller, Josiah	Crawford	Southern	2	2	0	0
Mitchell, William C.[b]	Carroll	Northern	2	0	7	7
Scott, Henry D.	Carroll	Southern	2	1	0	0
Tackitt, Martin	Johnson	Southern	2	0	7	0

Source: U.S. Bureau of the Census 1850, Schedule 1.

[a]Natal household of James and Robert Fancher, killed at Mountain Meadows.

[b]Natal household of Charles and Joel D. Mitchell, killed at Mountain Meadows.

Carroll County's children went to school in 1850. This county, nonetheless, had one of the highest rates of public school attendance in the state of Arkansas (U.S. Bureau of the Census 1850, Schedule 6). Like the rest of the country, the Ozarks witnessed the emergence of a new literate generation in the 1850s. Along with the urban professional class (Wells 2004:14), many rural southerners in this period recognized that education was essential for "advancement and prosperity." Such an outlook seems to have been adopted by a number of the farmers who migrated from the Ozarks in 1857.

Still, the new bourgeois values of domesticity, literacy, and personal improvement seem to have depended on a certain minimum level of affluence. Among the 1857 travelers, as we have seen, there was a marked difference between the families that gathered at Beller's Stand and those that departed from Johnson County to the south. In the southern contingent more of the adults were illiterate and fewer of the children had attended school (Table 5.1). On average, these families were less prosperous than those in the north, and their heavy reliance on children's labor probably limited opportunities for formal schooling (cf. Sellers 1991:394). In the Cameron household, for example, there were five school-aged children in 1850, yet only two of them—both boys—attended school. Similarly, none of Martin and Cynthia Tackitt's seven children attended school in 1850. Interestingly, a lack of formal education did not deter their oldest son, Pleasant Tackitt, from serving as a preacher on the 1857 wagon train, which "held Divine service in one of their large tents" (Bagley 2002:65).

Multitudes of Mishaps

Was life on a wagon train just an extension of the antebellum farmstead, where men took on the danger and women the drudgery? Faragher (2001:66) portrays it as such: "the routines of farm life and the sexual division of farm labor were translated smoothly into the work of the trail." Certainly, in both contexts the physical labor was hard and often injurious to both men and women. Daily life was often accompanied by chronic physical pain (Faragher 1986:99): "Men's hands hardened from gripping plow handles, their legs bowed from tramping over the clods turned up by the plowshare; women's hands cracked, bled, and developed corns from the hard water of the family wash, their knees grew knobby from years of kneeling to grit corn or scrub puncheon floors." According to Daniel Drake, a Kentucky physician who made a comprehensive survey of health and disease in the American interior in the mid-nineteenth century (1971 [1850]:685), farmers were especially vulnerable to "rheumatism of the joints, lumbago, sciatica," and other musculoskeletal disorders.

Along with the physical stress of daily routines, the risk of accidents was ever present on the farm. Though only serious mishaps were likely to be recorded in official documents, the mortality census of 1850 provides some idea of the dangers involved. That year in the Arkansas Ozarks, two men drowned, another was thrown from a horse, two more suffered unspecified fatal accidents, and one was "killed instantly by a log." Though the census reveals no accidental deaths of women, nearly three-fourths of the fatalities were children (Table 5.2). Only four were girls, three of whom were "burnt." Twelve of the children, ranging in age from newborn to sixteen, were boys. Most of these deaths resulted from unspecified "sudden accidents," though one toddler was burned, another succumbed to a snakebite, and one five-year-old froze to death (U.S. Bureau of the Census 1850, Schedule 3). One likely scenario for childhood death is described by West (1989:225): "Given that a girl or boy might spend hundreds of hours a year herding and riding, it is not surprising that many were hurt or killed when they fell from or were kicked by horses."

The overland journey was a respite from some routine tasks, as men in particular turned to the novelties of driving wagons over long distances, driving livestock, and hunting along the trail. Men typically spent most of

Table 5.2. • Accidental Deaths Reported in the Arkansas Ozarks, 1850 ($n = 22$).

SEX	AGE	REPORTED CAUSE	COUNTY
F	8 mo.	Sudden	Franklin
F	2	Burn	Independence
F	5	Burn	Madison
F	12	Burn	Independence
M	0	Sudden	Pope
M	9 mo.	Sudden	Franklin
M	1	Sudden	Washington
M	1	Sudden	Franklin
M	1	Burn	Crawford
M	2	Accident	Izard
M	3	Snakebite	Newton
M	5	Frozen	Crawford
M	6	Sudden	Washington
M	8	Sudden	Pope
M	10	Accident	Madison
M	16	Sudden	Franklin
M	18	Log	Johnson
M	19	Thrown from horse	Benton
M	20	Drown	Washington
M	37	Sudden	Franklin
M	38	Instant	Benton
M	45	Drown	Randolph

Source: U.S. Bureau of the Census 1850, Schedule 3.

their day negotiating some fifteen strenuous miles of trail and river crossings (Faragher 2001:72). At midday and evening breaks the oxen were freed to graze while the men repaired and maintained their wagons and gear. By the end of the day a more leisurely pace set in for most men, except for those few who were rotating through guard duty or taking cattle to find pasture. According to the recollections of Peter C. Campbell, a young drover who accompanied the 1857 wagon train for a time, "When night would come, . . . they drove the cattle into a circle until they had laid down; and then two or three guards were placed around them for the night" (Niswonger 1992:31). Overall, a man's day on the trail was characterized by "a rhythm of long periods of hard work punctuated by periods of rest" (Faragher 2001:75).

By contrast, a woman's daily routine changed little on the trail. Typically, her day began by milking cows and stoking fires to prepare breakfast—all before the men awoke. The midday break required her to lay out a cold lunch that had been prepared the night before. The evening meal absorbed the bulk of women's labor. Once water and fuel had been hauled, dinner prepared, and the masses fed, "beds had to be made up, wagons cleaned out, and provisions taken out to air to prevent mildew" (Faragher 2001:78). Back home, "blue Monday" was set aside for washing laundry, but this chore was sporadic on the trail. Heaps of dirty clothes had to be washed opportunistically.

Cooking, laundry, and other domestic chores would have multiplied on the trail because women were often laboring not only for their own families but for drovers who had hired on for bed and board (Walker 1998). How women felt about their extra burden is suggested by the diary of Amelia Knight, an Iowa emigrant whose household had taken on three hired hands. When they left the train, she was secretly pleased, "as...I shall have three less to wait on" (Knight 1928 [1853]:49). On the 1857 wagon train the northern contingent had attracted a large number of drovers, and women would have absorbed most of the burden of their care. When Peter C. Campbell, Alf Smith, and Tom Farmer became "bored with the slow moving train" and "broke away to take a shortcut" (Niswonger 1992:38), the women who had been taking care of them may well have breathed a sigh of relief.

Under the best of circumstances the trail posed new challenges for parents of young ones (Schlissel 1992:12):

> Children fell out of the wagons. They got lost among the hundreds of families and oxen and sheep. Children suffered all the usual childhood ills—measles, fevers, toothaches, diarrhea. But on the Trail, children who were drenched by days of heavy rains or burned by hot sun could be especially irritable and hard to care for. Free from supervision, older children were full of excitement and mischief. Their mothers worried constantly that Indians would steal them.

The fear of Indians was for the most part unfounded, and children were most likely to be killed or injured when they slipped beneath wagon wheels. In fact, according to Elliott West (1989:213), this type of trail accident "surpassed all others combined." Such accidents were described by Lucena Parsons in her 1850 journal: "a boy...fell from the wagon & broke his leg & died soon after. This is the second child that has broke a leg and died soon after." Other children were luckier and walked away relatively unharmed. In 1852 John Haskins Clark encountered a boy whose head had been rolled over by a wagon the day before. The boy's grandmother explained that it "did not quite kill him...but it made the little rascal holler awfully" (Barry 1942).

In the course of the journey many women would be required to assume traditional male responsibilities—pitching tents, yoking cattle, and loading, unloading, and driving wagons—especially when parties split, drovers quit, or husbands became ill or died (Jeffrey 1998:56). The risk of losing a loved one was real and ever present. As John Unruh (1979:349) vividly illustrates, there were many ways of dying on the trail:

> A great many casualties derived from wagon mishaps and accidents in which draft animals were involved. Children and adults alike fell under moving wheels, were dragged to death after becoming entangled in ropes, and fell off or were kicked by riding animals. At least six emigrants were killed by lightning; four overlanders were crushed to death by a falling oak tree...; one died from overdrinking after a tedious desert crossing; another from an overdose of preventative medicine;...and one traveler was even scalded to death in the boiling spring on the Truckee Desert crossing.

Even these dangers, however, could not match those of the rivers. "One of the most unexpected facts of the 'overland' journey," continues Unruh (1979:346), "was that death by water claimed almost as many victims during the antebellum era as did the much-feared Indians." The vast majority of drowning victims were males (Schlissel 1992:153).

On the 1857 wagon train two women were widowed on the trail. In early August, just north of Salt Lake City, the husband of Malinda Cameron Scott was murdered by someone in their party (Bagley 2002:99). The shock of her husband's death seems to have sent Malinda into labor, for she gave birth to a baby girl the following day (Coates n.d.:11). Malinda's brother-in-law would safely escort her and her children along the northern route to California. Like the majority of overland widows in Lillian Schlissel's study (1992), Malinda would remarry quickly after reaching California.

The fate of the second widow, Saladia Huff, was quite different. Just outside Fort Bridger, in what is now Wyoming, she buried her husband, who had succumbed to the bite of a "venomous creature," according to the *San Jose Pioneer* (21 April 1877). At this point Saladia took control of the wagon, apparently without any outside assistance. The widow pressed on through the Utah Territory with four sons and a four-year-old daughter in tow. All but the daughter, Nancy Saphrona Huff, would leave their bones at Mountain Meadows.

Broken Bones

What can we learn about the victims from the bones they left behind? Specifically, what do these bones tell us about the way the emigrants spent their lives, both in the Ozarks and on the trail? First, we must recognize the

Table 5.3. • Long-Bone Distribution in the Mountain Meadows Sample, by Sex.

		MALE		PROB. MALE		FEMALE		PROB. FEMALE		INDETERMINATE	
ELEMENT	N	RIGHT	LEFT	RIGHT	LEFT	RIGHT	LEFT	RIGHT	LEFT	RIGHT	LEFT
Humerus	46	16 (35%)	12 (26%)	5 (11%)	3 (7%)	1 (2%)	2 (4%)	3 (7%)	2 (4%)		2 (4%)
Ulna	31	11 (35%)	7 (23%)		5 (16%)	3 (10%)	3 (10%)	1 (3%)	1 (3%)		
Radius	29	11 (38%)	9 (31%)		2 (7%)	2 (7%)	1 (3%)	1 (3%)	2 (7%)		
Femur	53	14 (26%)	18 (34%)	3 (6%)	3 (6%)		1 (2%)	2 (4%)	2 (4%)	5 (9%)	5 (9%)
Tibia	36	11 (31%)	13 (36%)	3 (8%)	3 (8%)		1 (3%)	3 (8%)	1 (3%)		1 (3%)
Fibula	33	8 (24%)	11 (33%)	4 (12%)	5 (15%)		3 (9%)	2 (6%)			

limitations of the skeletal sample, especially for purposes of understanding sex differences. Most of those buried at Carleton's cairn were young men. From the reconstruction of crania, we know there were at least two women in the grave. The postcranial remains included ulnae (forearms) from at least three and perhaps four adult females (Table 5.3). In any case, this is a small sample of women to compare with the ten to twenty men in the grave. These limitations notwithstanding, the sample provides some insight into sex differences in both activity and injury patterns.

Previous skeletal studies have shown that long-bone morphology reflects differences in habitual activities. In particular, the robusticity of these bones is affected by patterns of work and physical mobility (e.g., Larsen 1997; Ruff 2000). The emigrant men indeed had robust humeri (upper arms). The right arms, furthermore, were significantly larger than the left.[3] Overall, the degree of robusticity is consistent with what is seen in other antebellum white males (Rathbun and Steckel 2002:216). The female humeri at Mountain Meadows exhibited extensive damage, so it was impossible to draw a comparison with the male sample.

In the case of the femora (upper legs), such a comparison yielded an interesting result. Like other white males in the antebellum period, the men who died at Mountain Meadows had femora with round midshafts. Their upper leg bones, in other words, appear in cross section as circular rather than oval-shaped. This is significant because oval-shaped midshafts are associated with habitual walking and running whereas round midshafts are consistent with reduced pedestrian mobility (Ruff 2000:80). The women, by contrast, have significantly more elongated femoral diaphyses, suggesting that they were spending considerably more time walking.[4] Again, because only two women's femora could be assessed, these results should be considered tentative. Nevertheless, this sex difference probably reflects an asymmetry in mobility patterns, as women were walking extensively on the hilly landscape while men were riding horses.

In fact, horseback riding is likely to account for another distinct pattern in the leg bones—lateral bowing or curvature of the men's tibiae (lower legs). More than one-third (36 percent) of the tibiae in the sample exhibited such bowing. Although rickets or healed fractures can sometimes produce bowed bones (Roberts and Manchester 2005; Lewis 2007), the condition observed in this sample was clearly caused by mechanical stress over the life course. When horseback riding and other strenuous activities are undertaken by children, the morphological changes begin early, altering the shape of the developing bones. Just such a pattern is described by West (1989:87) in his study of childhood on the frontier:

> So many cowboys and ranchers claimed to have started their saddle education when barely out of diapers that the modern reader is tempted to suspect exaggeration; but evidence for the claim is remarkably consistent. "I was raised on horse's back; never did learn to walk good," one recalled. Bill Dobbs was riding when he was too small to reach the stirrups as he stood beside his horse, by five he was riding herd, by twelve working roundups.

Another morphological effect of strenuous activity is the degeneration of the spine and joints. Osteoarthritis is characterized by the destruction of cartilage-covered joints, resulting in the formation of bone spurs (osteophytes) and pits (porosis). Over time the disease leads to erosion and polishing (eburnation) of the joint surfaces (Mann and Murphy 1990; Roberts and Manchester 2005). The condition is associated with both advancing age and strenuous activities. Since most of the emigrants were young (Figure 5.1), it is not surprising that only a few of the vertebrae and joints exhibited degenerative changes (Table 5.4). At the same time, most of the joint surfaces were damaged or consumed by carnivores (Figure 5.2), making it difficult to assess the extent of degenerative disease in the sample.

Many healed injuries were clearly evident in the Arkansans' skeletal remains. Such trauma ranged from bumps on the shin (the most common form of injury) to serious fractures (Table 5.5). Some degree of healing could be observed in all these cases. After a hard-tissue injury, patches of woven bone

Figure 5.1. ◆ Glenoid fossa (shoulder joint) of a subadult right scapula. Photo by Laurel Casjens.

Table 5.4. ◆ Degenerative Joint Disease in the Mountain Meadows Sample.

ELEMENT	SURFACE	CONDITION	LOCATION	SEVERITY
Osteophyte Formation				
Scapula	Glenoid fossa	Fragmentary	Margin	Mild
Scapula	Glenoid fossa	Fragmentary	Margin	Mild
Cervical vertebra	Facet	Complete	Margin	Mild
Cervical vertebra	Facet	Complete	Margin	Mild
Cervical vertebra	Centrum	Fragmentary	Margin	Mild
Cervical vertebra	Centrum	Fragmentary	Margin	Mild
Thoracic vertebra	Centrum	Complete	Margin	Mild
Porosity				
Scapula	Glenoid fossa	Fragmentary	Margin	Mild
Thoracic vertebra	Facet	Complete	Surface	Mild
Thoracic vertebra	Facet	Fragmentary	Surface	Mild

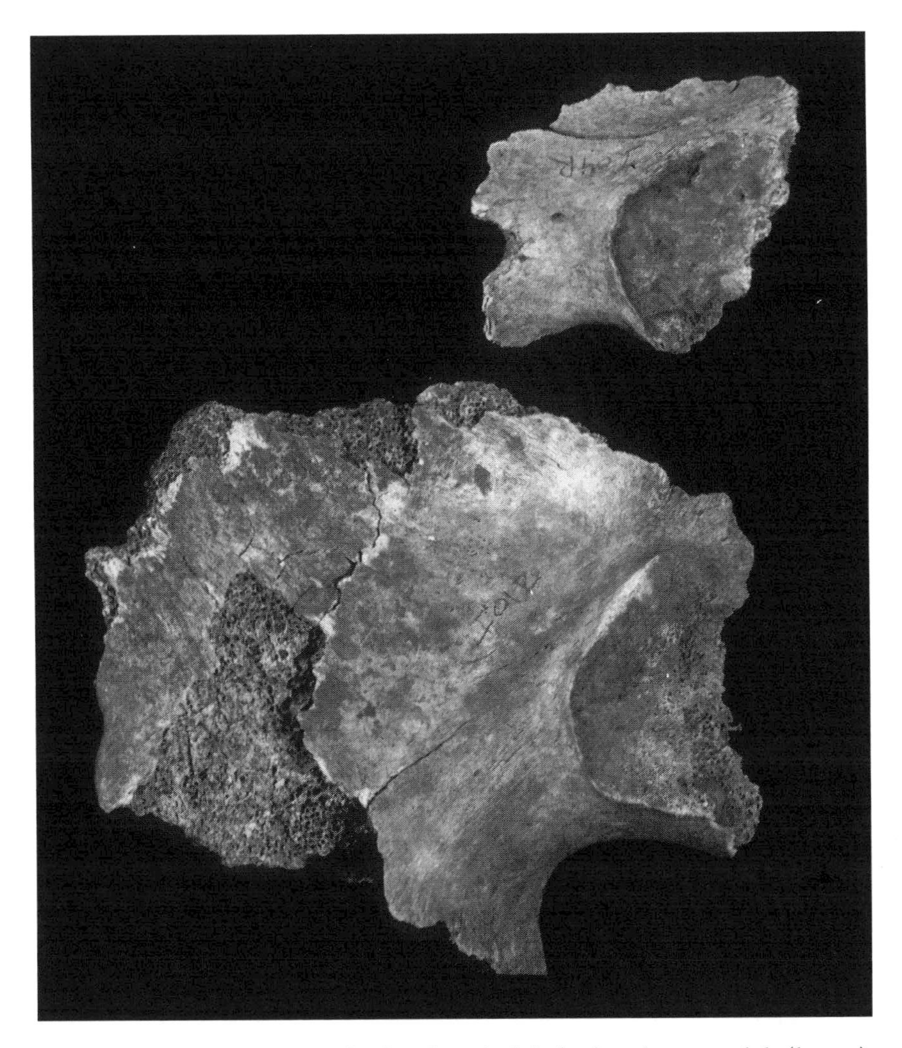

Figure 5.2. • Fragmentary right ilia of a subadult (*top*) and young adult (*bottom*). Photo by Laurel Casjens.

(periostitis) begin to repair the trauma. Over days and weeks these irregular surfaces are replaced by smoother, more mature bone. Healing can take months or years, depending on the patient's age and health as well as the severity of the wound (Ortner and Putschar 1981). As a result, the age at which the injury occurred can be only roughly estimated.

The vast majority of healed wounds in the skeletal sample appear as discrete, asymmetrical patches of periostitis on the long bones. This asymmetrical pattern suggests traumatic injury rather than infectious disease, which tends to cause bilateral inflammation. Nine long bones—primarily the lower legs—displayed periostitis. In fact, of the right tibiae in the grave,

Table 5.5. • Antemortem Trauma in the Mountain Meadows Sample.

ELEMENT	AGE	SEX	CONDITION	SEVERITY	STATE
Cranial					
R. Parietal[a]	YA	Male	Fracture	Ectocranial	Healed
L. Parietal	YA	Male	Fracture	Ectocranial & endocranial	Healed
Frontal	3.5–4.5	Ind.	Fracture	Ectocranial	Healed
Postcranial					
R. Clavicle[a]	YA	Male	Fracture	Complete	Healed
R. Rib[a]	YA	Prob. male	Fracture	Complete	Healed
R. Humerus[a]	YA	Male	Fracture	Complete	Healed
L. Humerus	OA	Female	Periostitis	Mild	Healed
R. Humerus	YA	Prob. female	Periostitis	Mild	Healed
L. Ulna	OA	Male	Periostitis	Mild	Active
L. Femur	YA	Male	Periostitis	Mild	Healed
L. Tibia	OA	Male	Periostitis	Mild	Healed
R. Tibia	YA	Male	Periostitis	Mild	Healed
R. Tibia	YA	Male	Periostitis	Moderate	Active
R. Tibia	YA	Prob. male	Periostitis	Mild	Active
R. Tibia	OA	Prob. female	Periostitis	Mild	Healed

Note: YA = young adult; OA = old adult; Ind. = indeterminate.
[a]Same individual from a sort.

nearly a quarter (24 percent) had some degree of inflammation (Figure 5.3). Tibiae are especially at risk for injury because the shin has little soft tissue to protect the bone (Goodman and Martin 2002:34–35). A simple cut, scrape, or contusion on this surface is enough to damage the periosteum—the osteogenic sheath that surrounds the bone—which triggers the formation of "woven" bone.

Most of the affected tibiae were those of young adult males, the same cohort that had activity-related bowing in these bones. The lower right leg of males, in particular, seems to have been prone to trauma, most likely from the stress and strain of daily labor. Two-thirds of the long-bone lesions were well healed, indicating that most of the emigrants' injuries appear to have happened *prior* to the overland trek. One old adult male and two young adult males had active periostitis, indicating that they likely received injuries on the journey.

Although many of the accidents associated with this level of periostitis may have gone virtually unnoticed, a few of the emigrants experienced

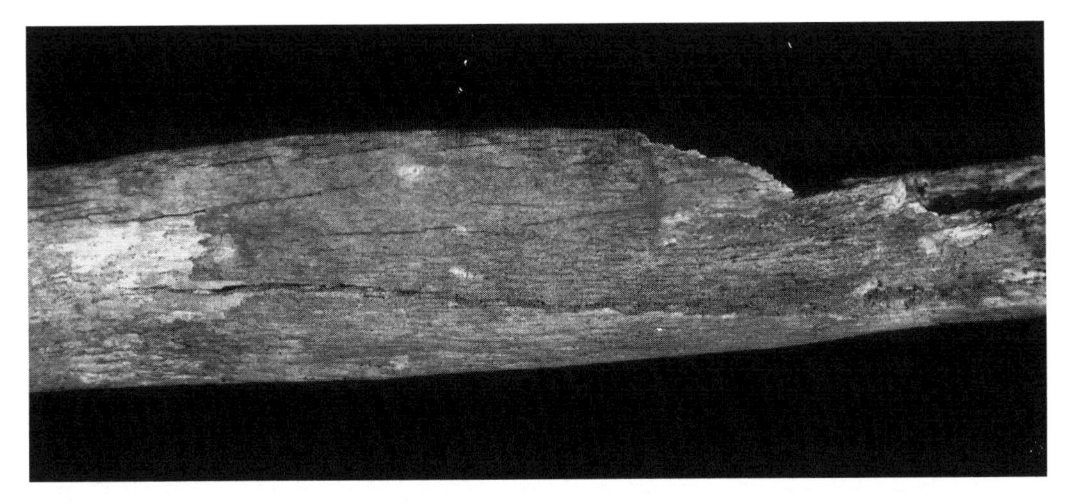

Figure 5.3. ✦ Active periostitis on the left tibia of an old adult male. Photo by Laurel Casjens.

more severe and destructive injuries. A four-year-old (Cranium 14) from the mass grave, for example, had a small depression fracture in the forehead. This lesion was so well healed, however, that the concavity was barely palpable. Because of the accelerated rate of healing in young children, such a wound could have occurred before migration or in the early months on the trail.

In contrast, a young adult male in the grave had multiple bone fractures that were extensively remodeled, suggesting that the trauma must have occurred years before the 1857 migration. This young man had severe fractures in the right clavicle, humerus, and rib that had not been set properly.[5] The humerus was completely severed near the neck (Figure 5.4), and as the bone healed, the shoulder joint was displaced. This would have resulted in shortening of the arm. The right clavicle had been fractured into two parts and was also misaligned when it healed (Figure 5.5). These irregularities, however, apparently did not impede the young man's use of his arm, as there was no evidence of atrophy and his muscle attachments were well developed. This pattern of injuries, when combined with a healed fracture in a mid-right rib, is consistent with a serious fall in which the young man landed on his right shoulder and torso.[6] The degree of healing and extensive remodeling of the bone suggests that his injuries occurred some years before his death.

In another young man (Cranium 1) two well-healed depression fractures were present in the cranial vault. One of these fractures caused an elliptical lesion on the side of his skull, just behind the right ear (Figure 5.6). The impact would have been quite severe as the fracture penetrated the skull's interior (endocranium). The second facture was located on the opposite side of

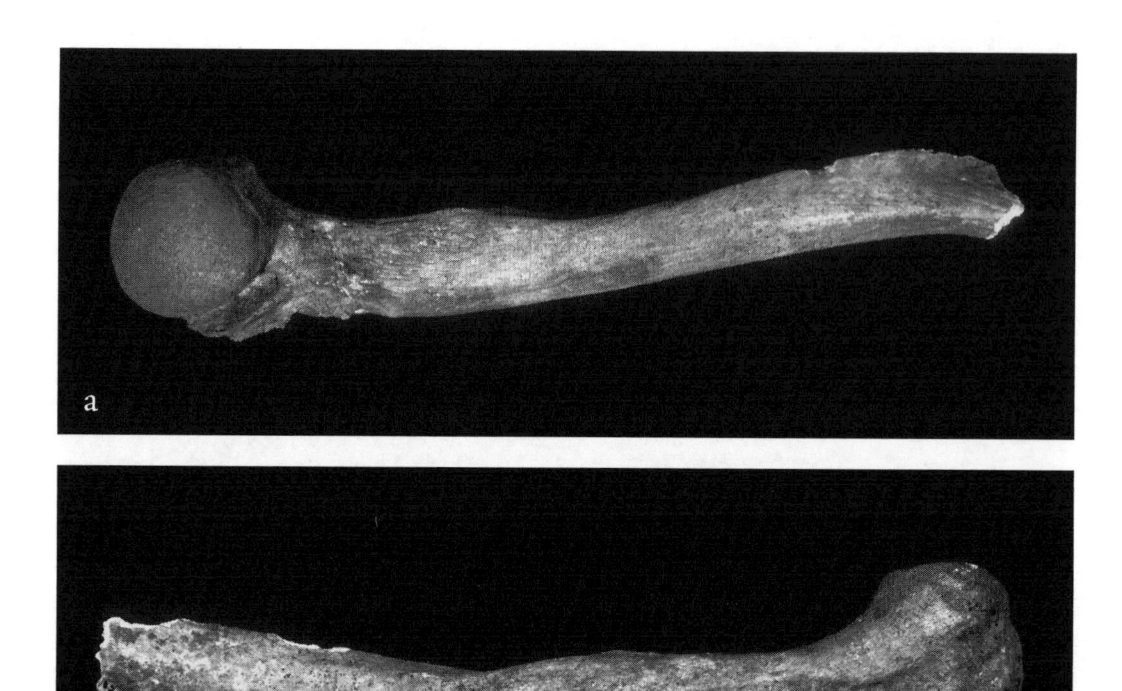

Figure 5.4. ◆ Medial (*a*) and lateral (*b*) views of a well-healed fracture in the humerus of a young adult male. Photo by Laurel Casjens.

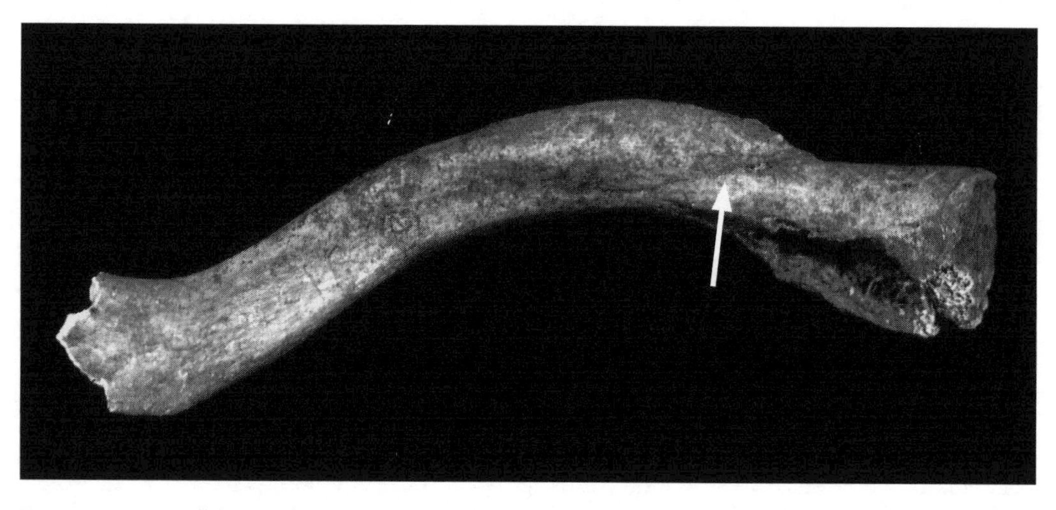

Figure 5.5. ◆ Well-healed fracture in the clavicle of a young adult male. Photo by Laurel Casjens.

Figure 5.6. ◆ Well-healed depression fracture in the right parietal of a young adult male. Photo by Laurel Casjens.

the head, just above the left ear. This trauma, by contrast, was long and linear but less severe, as the lesion was shallow and did not penetrate the endocranium.

While such wounds might have been caused by any number of accidents on the farm or the trail, another etiology must be considered—violent assault. Blows to the head might well account for lesions of this kind, though it is impossible specify the weapon involved or the nature of the attack. Nevertheless, we should be wary of the popular assumption that life in the hills or on the frontier was chronically violent and lawless (cf. Gill 1994; Crist 2006). Even on the trail, as we shall see, there were subtle but usually effective mechanisms to prevent quarrels from escalating into violent fights.

Band and Bond

One source of social friction on the trail was the assignment of duties and the common perception that some travelers were working harder than others. "In our own little company of five," one emigrant reminisced about his 1850 journey, "there were occasional angry debates while the various burdens were being adjusted" (Brooks 1902:805). Similar confrontations were observed in other companies, where "bloody fisticuffs were invariably the outcome of disputes over divisions of labor" (Brooks 1902:805). Disputes that escalated to homicide, according to John Phillip Reid (1997a:86), usually occurred "between men who knew each other and had been getting on one another's nerves for weeks" (see also Mattes 1969; Unruh 1979). Yet violent fights were exceptional. "Even those who, on the trail, did what they had never done at home—fought with their companions once, twice, or several times on the trip—did not as a general rule draw weapons, and did not wound, or cripple, or kill" (Reid 1997a:89).

Contributing to such disputes was the exaggerated sociality of overland travel. In contrast to the farmstead, where most labor was routine and negotiated among close kin, the trail required people to perform in novel and communal settings. The performance, furthermore, was frequently quite public. Though the family wagon might provide some respite from the public gaze, daily activities were under constant scrutiny. As a result, families on the trail contended with some of the same problems found in a foraging band, which usually amounts to a small mobile party of several households.

Thus, like hunter-gatherers in the Arctic or the Kalahari, overland migrants were subject to continuous monitoring and social sanctioning by their fellow travelers. This summary description of life in a foraging band might well apply to a company on the overland trail (Wilson 1988:27):

> Living under such intense intimacy can conceivably be a strain: other people's idiosyncrasies grate more easily and trivialities become more magnified.... Marjorie Shostak notes that the !Kung dread the prospect of tempers flaring out of control (1981:306), and so, too, do the Inuit Eskimos (Briggs 1982). Though open and intimate, camp life is not without its tensions, and occasionally these erupt into open conflict and fighting (see Turnbull 1982:122–24; Lee 1979:382).

One factor that tended to ameliorate conflict and fighting on the trail was the presence of women, who purportedly had a "civilizing" effect on otherwise rowdy companies. One man who had traveled overland in both 1850 and 1852 marveled at how different the experience could be when women joined the train (Udell 1856, quoted in Reid 1997a:14):

> [On my second journey], I realized more vividly than I ever did before, the influence of women upon my own sex. There were one or more ladies in nearly every company, and the conduct of the men presented as great a contrast to that of those whom I fell in with during my former trip, as perfect civilization does to a state of savage rudeness. Few of us are aware of the mighty influence women [*sic*] exerts over man in all his actions.

In some cases the introduction of just one woman to an all-male company seems to have had a significant impact. "How strange!" proclaimed one man. "Our whole camp is quieter, obscene & improper language not heard just because a woman is in camp.... This is the refining influence of woman, without society men almost become desperadoes, *men care not for men*" (Decker 1849, quoted in Reid 1997a:14).

Yet many men did enjoy the masculine company of the trail. When they were not driving wagons or tending to their conjugal families, men spent much of their time mingling with other men, especially on the hunt. Hunting was "a central aspect of male identity" on both the farm and the trail and "had a strong ego-supporting function for men" in general (Faragher 2001:50, 99). Again, as in a foraging band, hunting on the trail provided an opportunity for men to show off and to solidify their "fraternal" bonds (Rodseth and Novak 2000; Rodseth and Wrangham 2004).

The potential for competitive displays was exaggerated during overland migration because of the opportunity to hunt buffalo. "A true test of manhood," emphasizes Faragher (2001:99), "was to bring down a species of big game." Such a kill could elevate a man's status in the fluid wagon-train hierarchy. Under such a hierarchy, captains were deposed frequently; their authority was weak and shifted with the popular will. At the same time, because buffalo hunts were cooperative, they helped solidify and mend strained relationships. The hunt, like the overland journey itself, required emigrants to reconcile two competing nineteenth-century civic values: "the national tolerance of extreme individualism" and "the felt need and necessity for collective social defense" (Reid 1997a:102). As a result, both leadership and punishment on the overland trail were designed to minimize conflict within the group by maintaining democratic ideals.

Serious transgressions were punished by consensus of the company as a whole. Under these circumstances, according to John Phillip Reid (1997a: 208), the collective acted swiftly to ensure order, deter antisocial behavior, and enforce "rules of social behavior that the emigrants had long respected as 'law.'" On the trail the point of punishment was not simply to make the culprit suffer. "Far more important was to heal the body politic and keep it whole" (Reid 1997a:212). When this "body" became too large to be effectively managed, troublesome individuals or entire families might be expelled (Reid 1997a:171).

Traveling in smaller parties helped temper conflict within the group, but it also had the effect of reducing the company's defensive capability. Emigrants thus faced the problem of adjusting party size so as to minimize internal strife while maintaining an adequate collective defense against real or perceived threats. In particular, the ideology of fraternalism was engaged to solidify alliances among real or imagined brothers.

Signs of Distress

The wagon train that camped at Mountain Meadows contained at least fifteen pairs of adult brothers, in the biological sense. It is quite likely, furthermore, that some of these men were members of fraternal organizations, providing them with countless other "brothers" on the trail. Although the total number of Freemasons who traveled west is unknown, the ubiquity of Masonic symbols on trailside graves suggests that fraternalism was a firmly established, quasi-religious tradition among many emigrants (cf. Read and Gaines 1949:213). Overland journals often refer to the "five points of fellowship" and the "Lodge in the Wilderness." Many such references are found in the papers of J. Goldsborough Bruff (1804–1889), a devout Mason and member of the Federal Lodge in Washington, D.C. Bruff pointed out the special appeal of Masonry to those planning an overland trek (Read and Gaines 1949:xxx):

> The Masonic Lodges all over the Union were set to work like so many mills running at their full capacity in grinding out Masons to meet the demand for human sympathy and brotherhood that might be required for mutual aid and assistance on their journey.... Human kindness and the simple modes of recognition among Brethren were deemed of more importance than proficiency in the knowledge of the ritual of the degrees.

The crucial Masonic virtue, especially on the overland trail, was not esoteric wisdom but an ability to recognize and help fellow Masons. To summon obligatory aid, a brother was taught to use King Solomon's "grand hailing sign of distress" (Homer 1994:18).

Well before the gold rush, such a sign would have been familiar to many American men, including the founding members of the Mormon Church. In 1842 the Mormon prophet, Joseph Smith Jr. (1805–1844), became a Master Mason in the lodge that his older brother, Hyrum Smith (1800–1844), had helped organize in Nauvoo, Illinois (Homer 1994:28). Another devout Mormon, John D. Lee, also joined the Nauvoo Lodge, where he served as the librarian of the order (Bishop 2001 [1877]:149).

All three of these Mormon patriarchs, in fear for their lives, would look to their Masonic brethren for deliverance. In early 1842 Lee set out from Illinois for the hills of Tennessee to preach the Mormon gospel and baptize converts. Near Murfreesborough, according to Lee's account, two visiting Missourians had raised a mob of some twenty-five men "determined to tar and feather me if I preached again" (Bishop 2001 [1877]:141). On this occasion Lee was protected by women in the audience, who formed a circle around the pulpit. "While thus surrounded," Lee recalled, "I continued my sermon." The following Sunday, however, he was confronted by a still larger mob, including several drunken roughnecks (Bishop 2001 [1877]:142):

> I had just commenced speaking, when one of these men began to swear and use indecent language, and made a rush for me with his fist drawn. I at once made a Masonic sign of distress, when, to my relief and yet to my surprise, a planter rushed to my aid.... He took the drunken men and led them out of the crowd, and sat by me during the rest of my sermon, thus giving me full protection. That man was a stranger to me, but he was a good man and a true Mason. His action put an end to mob rule at that place. After the meeting, I baptized some ten persons.

Two years later Joseph and Hyrum Smith were not nearly so fortunate. Besieged by a mob in Carthage, Illinois, Joseph is said to have signaled for help using Masonic cries and gestures (*Times and Seasons*, 15 July 1844). Though several in the mob—some disguised in blackface—were in fact Masons (Homer 1994:32), they took no mercy on the Smith brothers. Joseph and Hyrum were shot to death and their corpses carted back to Nauvoo. "After [the Mormons made] a show of burying them publicly, the bodies were hidden and guarded in fear of desecration" (Arrington and Bitton 1992:82).

When the Mormons migrated to Utah in 1847, the church hierarchy was filled with Master Masons (Homer 1994:97). Though it is unclear how many of the early settlers continued to practice the craft, at least one prominent pioneer was both a Mormon and a Mason. John D. Lee settled in the Salt Lake Valley in autumn 1848; just two years later he was ordered by Brigham Young to spearhead the Mormon colonization of southern Utah. In the course of the 1850s Lee helped build several settlements north and east of Mountain Meadows. By September 1857 he would have had personal experience with many caravans on their way to California.

Yet Lee, on the killing fields of Mountain Meadows, had no sympathy for the distress signs of his "brothers." The Arkansas emigrants, several of whom were Masons, had been pinned down by Lee and his confederates for three days when they desperately "drew up a paper addressed to the Masons, Odd Fellows, Baptists, and Methodists of the States, and to all good people everywhere," and implored help "if there was time; if not, justice" (Brooks 1962:99). The three Arkansans carrying the message—possibly Abel Baker, Jesse or Lorenzo Dunlap, and John Milum Jones—never made it out of Utah. They were purportedly tracked by a group of Indians led by Mormon interpreter Ira Hatch, and "killed, one by one" (Bigler 1998:171; see also Bagley 2002: 141–142). Their fate was unknown to the emigrants who remained at Mountain Meadows.

On September 11, 1857, John D. Lee was allowed to enter the train and negotiate with the emigrants, "probably using his government position and Masonic signs to win their trust" (Bagley 2002:145). What he found was a grim circle of survivors. A number of men had been killed during the siege, and the rest of the party was "famished from thirst" (Evans 1897). In the course of his negotiations Lee personally witnessed the burial of two "men of note" (Bishop 2001 [1877]:245). Ten more, he was told, had already been laid to rest, their bodies wrapped in buffalo robes.

EPITAPH

Nothing is dead:
men feign themselves dead,
and endure mock funerals and mournful obituaries,
and there they stand looking out of the window, sound and well,
in some new and strange disguise.

— RALPH WALDO EMERSON, "NOMINALIST AND REALIST," 1844

Revolutions and riots often begin with a funeral.

— GAIL HOLST-WARHAFT, *THE CUE FOR PASSION: GRIEF AND ITS POLITICAL USES*, 2000

Death was much on the minds of antebellum Americans. Images of the dead and dying were woven into novels, poetry, correspondence, public events, and daily discourse (e.g., Reiss 2001; Stern 2003). By the 1850s, according to James Farrell (1980:35–36), "most Americans approached the issues of life and death from a religious perspective colored by sixty years of successful evangelicalism." The Great Revival, which had begun around 1800, reached a new pitch in the 1830s, when evangelical figures such as Charles Finney (1792–1875) advanced a message of salvation through self-improvement and personal responsibility. "Because of their greater belief in human agency, Christians of the evangelical era encouraged preparation for death" (Farrell 1980:36)—a rational, responsible approach, reflecting a more general attitude toward business, family, and society at large.

In fact, the ideology of death was being reshaped by the same market forces that had transformed gender and class relations in the early nineteenth century (Sellers 1991). Thus the cult of domesticity found its counterpart in the cult of death, a Victorian obsession with "mourning clothing, adornment of the home of the deceased with funeral crepe and wreaths, erection of elaborate grave markers, and encouragement of decorative arts commemorating death, or memento mori" (Little et al. 1992:411). Like the notion of the home or the countryside as a haven from the industrial city, the image of the cemetery provided a "safety valve" for capitalist culture (Farrell 1980:32). In the Northeast many graveyards were transformed into parks, idyllic settings where families could gather, remember, and socialize (e.g., French 1975; Linden-Ward 1992; Connors 2003). "The Victorian cult of death had a significant effect upon urban American cemeteries, particularly expressed in the compartmentalization of the cemetery into family grave plots, in new designs for arrangement of graves, and in the profusion of elaborate grave-markers" (Jeane 1992:119).

Yet this movement was slow to penetrate small towns (Wells 2000), rural farms (Little et al. 1992), and much of the South (Farrell 1980:14–15). In such contexts there were no specialists in bereavement, no hospitals or almshouses where the terminally ill could be sent to die. In fact, in most of the country, death remained an intimate process that was managed at home by family and friends (Laderman 1996:29):

> Preparing the body was a duty for the close living relations of the deceased, and they rarely hesitated to participate in these activities. The intimacy that survivors maintained with the corpse preserved it, at least until the actual interment, as evidence of a valuable, and vital, social relation. Although the body had lost the spark that animated it, deeply rooted social conventions demanded that it be given proper respect and care from the living. Its uncertain status—as an empty container for the newly departed spirit, as an evocative representative of the lost loved one, as a highly charged object of reflection and remembrance, and as a decomposing, unstable cadaver—also contributed to the deliberate, careful handling by the living survivors.

After the body was washed—usually by women as part of their domestic duties—it was wrapped in a shroud and placed in a hexagon-shaped ("toe-pincher") coffin for viewing. Final respects were paid while the family kept a vigil over the body. To make the corpse more presentable, coins were placed on the eyes and a cloth might be used to tie the mouth shut. Rags soaked in alum or vinegar were placed intermittently on the face to slow decomposition (Farrell 1980:147; Laderman 1996:31). Depending on the rate of decay, the period of mourning was adjusted, even if this meant an abbreviated viewing. In the antebellum South "men ordinarily attended the coffin in procession to the grave site, leaving the women to prepare the feast at home" (Wyatt-Brown 1982:275).

In most rural areas, graves clustered in small plots on the periphery of the farmstead, preferably on a knoll. These "folk cemeteries" were scattered across the landscape, each accommodating just a few families who were related by blood or marriage. Grave markers were also simple and expedient—just two pieces of fieldstone, the larger at the head and the smaller at the foot. Though less grand than the centralized cemeteries emerging in the Northeast, rural graveyards also served as gathering places for extended families. Especially in the South, a special day in late summer or early fall was set aside for the maintenance of both graves and family relationships. This was a festive occasion, culminating in a communal meal at midday, followed by sermons and song. "Young folks often courted, and some recall that the menfolk might conduct a bit of horse trading or even discreet drinking and gambling" (Jeane 1992:115).

By the 1850s certain aspects of the cult of death had become common around the country, though many others were too expensive or impractical to be adopted in rural areas. Keeping a braided lock of the deceased's hair, donning a black ribbon, or inking black borders on stationary or a diary struck a compromise between fashion and function. Many cemeteries, even in the "Upland South," were beginning to see changes as well. Although elaborate spires and romantic cenotaphs were still rare, family plots might be delineated and set apart from the "grassed interspaces" (Jeane 1992:116). In northwest Arkansas the town of Clarksville established a centralized graveyard as early as 1848, when land was deeded for this purpose to the Methodist Church (Langford 1921:76). Outside the city centers, however, most graves were still marked by simple fieldstones.

Several riders on the 1857 wagon train had lost close family members not long before the trek. Manerva Beller had lost three, all in the winter of 1849–1850. Her mother and infant sister had died first, possibly from complications of childbirth. A few weeks later her father died of smallpox (U.S. Bureau of the Census 1850, Schedule 3). Having served as postmaster and county treasurer, he had left a sizable estate of land, livestock, and slaves (Logan 1998:12). Manerva herself was eighteen years old and newly married to George Washington Baker. When the wagons assembled at Beller's Stand, they were near the spot where Manerva's family had been interred. Unlike most families in the area, the Bellers had been able to commision a crypt.

Martin Tackitt, by contrast, would have had a quite humble burial. When he died in the early 1850s, his widow, Cynthia, was left to manage a large family on a small farm. The precise location of Martin's grave is unknown, but

Figure 6.1. • Nineteenth-century cemetery on Basham Creek, Johnson County. Photo by Shannon A. Novak.

it is probably in the foothills near his farm on Basham Creek (Figure 6.1). When she decided to move west in 1857, Cynthia Tackitt would leave the care of her husband's grave to others. She could take comfort in the fact that his body had been properly interred near his home, and not on the overland trail amid thousands of anonymous dead.

Grave Terrors

Although Victorians in general were "fatalistic about the inevitability of death," they "were deeply affected by its uncertainties" (Fischer 1989:699). One of their greatest fears was to die alone. A "good death" took place at home in the presence of loved ones, while a "bad death" was lonely and terrifying, especially at the hands of a murderer (Schlissel 1992:131; Isenberg and Burstein 2003:5). Close relatives and companions of the dying were expected to witness, as both a duty and a privilege, the moment of passing. The deathbed was thus a powerful site of social performance. "Indeed, to an almost unnerving degree, the imagination, emotion and memory of humble America hovered about that sacrosanct place" (Saum 1975:41).

Another terror that surrounded death was the possibility of the body's desecration, especially in the absence of a proper funeral. Such a terror is vividly illustrated in "Roger Malvin's Burial," a short story published by Nathaniel Hawthorne in 1832. The tale begins with two men lying on a boulder in the forest, each of them wounded by an Indian bullet. Roger Malvin is seriously injured and insists that Reuben carry on without him. At first, Reuben offers to stay by his friend's side and bear witness to his "parting words." To save his own life, however, Reuben eventually agrees to leave. All that Roger asks is for his friend to come back and bury his bones. Reuben vows to do so and receives this blessing from the dying man: "Heaven grant you long and happy days, and may your children's children stand round your death bed!" (1882 [1832]:389). Yet Reuben fails to keep his promise. Roger's bones remain exposed to the elements, and Reuben is haunted by the image of "an unburied corpse...calling to him out of the wilderness" (Hawthorne 1882 [1832]:394).

Migrants on the overland trail had especially deep anxieties about the circumstances of their deaths. Dying in the wilderness, without witnesses or proper burial, became an obsessive fear. In April 1857 Jack Baker prepared for the worst: "I, John T. Baker, of the County of Carroll and State of Arkansas, as being this day sound in mind and body and my recollection being good, but knowing the uncertainty of life and the certainty of death and not knowing the time of my dissolution do make known and declare the following to be my last will and testament." Baker's immediate purpose was to ensure his proper interment: "First, I will at my death my body a decent burial in the bosom of it's [*sic*] mother Earth and my spirit to the God who gave it." Like many emigrants, Baker dreaded the thought of his bones left unburied and exposed to the sun, the wind, and the wolves.

To reduce their anxiety, many overlanders practiced a kind of "postmortem witnessing." By noting the deaths of strangers, they hoped to ensure that their own deaths would not go unnoticed. Thus a standard part of the emigrant experience seems to have been counting graves and recording names and inscriptions from the makeshift headstones (Mattes 1977:76). Such observations varied by gender. According to Schlissel's (1992) study of overland diaries, men seem to have been more interested in cumulative death counts whereas women were inclined to record each and every grave they passed, often noting whether it was old or new and who had taken in orphaned children (see especially Schlissel 1992:111–115). Of special interest was the cause of death. "Cholera, illness, accident—these were central facts in the minds of the women who were the ritual caretakers of the dying and the dead" (Schlissel 1992:154).

There were attempts to practice funerary rituals on the trail, but as the journey progressed, such practices became more austere. Though a few travelers brought their own coffins with them, most would resort to miscellaneous materials—boxes, wagon boards, scavenged wood—to construct makeshift caskets (Mattes 1977:76). Graves were marked by headboards or stones, with little or no inscription. Occasionally, there was a cenotaph, and in a number of cases Masonic symbols were used to identify a fraternity brother. Other commemorations were limited to a paper note, whose sentiments faded quickly. Services, if they occurred at all, were simple. Sometimes a minister or preacher was available to preside.

Lemuel Herbert, for example, was a Methodist minister on the trail near St. Joseph, Missouri. In May 1850 he delivered a eulogy for the only child of a young Ohio couple. In their tent Herbert found that the "little corps[e] was enclosed in a little box made of rough boards, for they could get no coffin" (quoted in Rieck 1991:21). A large procession made its way to a hilltop, where the minister presided over the service.

> I stood by the mouth of the little grave and preached from Ecles. 7... 'It is better to go to the house of mourning, than to go to the house of feasting.' We had a very interesting time burying our dead in the wilderness. After preaching, we deposited the little corps[e] in the grave to sleep until the morning of the resurrection day. We then dismissed the congregation with a benediction. Thus we parted to meet no more on earth. The parents of the child were terribly afflicted as they went away from the grave, not knowing but that the little flesh of their darling might be food for the ravening wolves.

To avoid such desecration, some kept the corpse of a loved one for days, even as they continued on the trail. In 1862, for example, young George Millington had died of dysentery in a remote section of the Plains. According to his twelve-year-old sister, Ada, the family had "used spirits of camphor very freely on George's clothes" in order to "take his body on at least another day" (Schlissel 1992:131). They "couldn't bear the thought," Ada explained, "of leaving his little body among the sands of this wilderness surrounded by Indians and wolves."

Though most children would survive the trek, stories of untimely deaths tended to fuel their imaginations and inflame their fears of dying or being orphaned (West 1989:40–41):

> For all its wonders, there was something nightmarish about the passage as a child perceived it, a quality usually found only in the most

> frightening fairy tales. With no warning, these youngest pioneers were plunged into a space without the security of limits, a land of baby-stealers, slavering animals, and storms that tore at the earth, a place where mothers were taken away and children were abandoned forever, put alone into the ground as a portion for wolves.

Parents might exacerbate the problem by using frightening imagery to keep the children close to camp and on their best behavior. Sometimes these tales were confirmed, however, when "emigrants were greeted, not only with scattered bones, buttons, and bits of clothing, but hands, feet, and various other parts of the human anatomy in varying stages of decomposition" (Mattes 1969:88). Such images filled the diaries and reminiscences of children and adults alike. On reaching California, forty-niner Elisha D. Perkins exclaimed, "The grave has more terrors than I ever before felt" (quoted in Saum 1975:42).

Bereaved travelers were faced with a dilemma: should a loved one's grave be commemorated and marked, or should evidence of the burial be obliterated to prevent disturbance by the dreaded wolves and Indians? A number appear to have chosen the latter, believing "that the greatest service they could do the deceased was to *hide* the gravesite" (Mattes 1977:76). In many cases great lengths were taken to conceal a grave. The disturbed soils were covered with vegetation, or wagons and animals were driven across the burial site.

Sometimes, however, what appeared to be a grave was a cache in disguise. As loads became cumbersome or as robbery became an imminent danger, valuables might be deposited in a pit and then marked with a headstone. Captain Howard Stansbury (1853), for example, reported that an apparent grave, "instead of containing the mortal remains of a human being, had been a safe receptacle for divers casks of brandy." Yet such receptacles were hardly safe. Mormon pioneers, among others, formed scavenging parties to retrieve goods discarded or buried by overland travelers. Such pioneers, according to one Mormon observer, "being somewhat inclined to marvelous deeds...gave resurrection to many bodies even before dissolution" (Unruh 1979:305).

One "picking-up expedition," led by John D. Lee, set out from Salt Lake City in July 1849. Riding east into Wyoming, Lee was specifically in search of a stove. "About thirty miles before he reached Devil's Gate he found one to his liking, a fine large Premium Range No. 3 which would have cost more than fifty dollars to purchase. On the way back he started loading up with powder and lead, cooking utensils, tobacco, nails, tools, bacon, coffee, sugar, trunks of clothing, axes, and harness" (Brooks 1992 [1972]:148). Yet Lee's most valuable find was buried near the grave of his fifth wife, Abigail, who had died of mountain fever on the way to Zion. Here, in the Wind River Range, Lee "'reserected' a deposit which he said weighed almost five hundred pounds and consisted mostly of medicines" (Brooks 1992 [1972]:149).

A few weeks later, in the same region of Wyoming, J. Goldsborough Bruff recorded this entry in his journal (Read and Gaines 1949:66): "Told of a grave, in the rear, inscribed with the death of a 'Dr. —— of St. Louis, died of Cholera.'—it seems that this was a *càche*,—and where the aforesaid Doctor, had deposited $500 worth of Medicines, on his way to the [Salt] Lake Settlement.—Had sent a mormon wagon out for it, but found, on reaching it, that some knowing one had abstracted about $200 worth, and left a note to that effect." Whether the note was left by John D. Lee or some other "knowing one" is an intriguing question. In any case, eight years later, Lee and his confederates at Mountain Meadows would strip the possessions of men, women, and children, stealing whatever remained of an "overburdened" company.

The Indian Problem

The most ominous threat on the trail was thought to be Indians. Routinely accused of stealing livestock, robbing graves, and murdering women and children, Native Americans were seen as savages to be eluded, appeased, or eliminated. During her journey to California in 1849, Luzen Wilson recognized the tension between her observations of the natives and the tales of horror that filled her imagination (quoted in Levy 1990:40):

> I had read and heard whole volumes of their bloody deeds, the massacre of harmless white men, torturing helpless women, carrying away captive innocent babes. I felt my children the most precious in the wide world, and I lived in an agony of dread that first night. The Indians were friendly, of course...but I, in the most tragic-comic manner, sheltered my babies with my own body, and felt imaginary arrows pierce my flesh a hundred times during the night.

Much of this imagery emerged from stories in the popular press, creating an especially edgy group of travelers (Unruh 1979:177): "Reports of depredations, whether accurate or not, combined with the guidebook advice, predisposed overlanders toward treating all Indians with suspicion and distrust. Further, since the major tragedies and mythical massacres occurred almost exclusively during the post-1849 period, it was during the 1850s that overlanders were most uneasy as they launched out onto the plains." In general, Indian encounters were much less of a threat than emigrants had imagined. In the antebellum period, according to Unruh (1979:408), fewer than four hundred emigrants were killed by Native Americans—perhaps 4 percent of an estimated ten thousand deaths. By far the most common cause of mortality on the trail was not Indian assault but disease (Rieck 1991:15). In any case, violent encounters with Indians were rarely pitched battles but tended to be small skirmishes or ambushes. Emigrants were most likely to be assaulted "while out hunting, or when otherwise absent from their train, when on guard duty, when small emigrant parties tracked Indians in an attempt to retrieve stolen stock, in sudden flare-ups at toll bridges, or when tribute payments were refused" (Unruh 1979:189).

Many acts that were presumed to be Indian depredations would turn out instead to be the work of white bandits or looters. In 1850, on his first trip to California, Alexander Fancher had two of his steers stolen near the Kansas-Nebraska border. When Fancher and his traveling companion, William Bedford Temple, went in search of the cattle, they found the animals being herded by a white man. Temple elaborated on this experience in a letter to his family: "I am now over 475 miles from home in the midst of the savage Indians have not seen one yet[.] [T]hey are afraid to come near the road...I would here remark near all the stealing and killing is done by the Whites following the Trains" (Temple 1850b). Such "white Indians," as Reid (1997a:55) points out, "were more desperate, better disciplined, better armed, and... may have been more cruel" than the "red savages" who induced such anxiety and loathing among overland migrants.

In 1854 Brigham Young warned that travelers through the Utah Territory could be robbed or murdered by "a numerous and well organized band of *white* highwaymen, painted and disguised as Indians" (*Deseret News*, 13 July). At the same time, many emigrants suspected that the Mormons themselves were involved—as organizers, participants, or both—in many so-called Indian attacks. Such accusations cropped up first in California newspapers and soon made their way into the national consciousness. By the mid-1850s even the eastern press was bombarded with "irate letters from former overlanders recalling their own sufferings among the Saints" (Unruh 1979:336). According to Unruh, in fact, "the travail of the overlanders while in the Mormon mecca" played a major role in ratcheting up the social and political tensions between Utah and the U.S. government.

In public discourse, at least, these tensions came to center on the issue of polygamy. In Nauvoo, Illinois, some two years before his death, Joseph Smith had received the "Revelation on Celestial Marriage," which declares polygamy to be an "everlasting covenant" by which all Saints must abide. "At the time of the revelation in 1843, and for almost ten years afterward, polygamy remained secret, revealed to a few trusted Church leaders and the women who married Smith and his closest advisers" (Gordon 2002:23). Only in 1852, five years after the Mormon exodus to Utah, was plural marriage revealed as an official doctrine of the church. Now polygamy became the focus of anti-Mormon sentiment, not only in Washington D.C. but across the northern states. By the mid-1850s Mormon marriage was being described as a form of "white slavery," allowing antipolygamists to join forces with abolitionists (Gordon 2002:55–57):

> At the first Republican national convention in 1856, the new party adopted a radical reformist platform. Included was an explicit connection between polygamy and slavery—a call for the abolition of the "twin relics of barbarism" in the territories.... As Republicans learned quickly, the identification of slavery with Mormon polygamy allowed opponents of both to claim that the patriarchs of Utah and those of the slaveholding states and territories violated Christian mandates.... And although it was easier to condemn polygamy than to condemn slavery, action against polygamy was understood by all concerned as an opening wedge in the protective shield around states' rights, and the South's "peculiar domestic institution."

For their part, Mormons were used to being condemned by their tormentors in the East. What they were not accustomed to was being lumped together with slave owners in the South. Most early Mormon converts were of New England stock (Rust 2004) and had been viewed by many in the Midwest as "strange Yankees" with "suspected abolitionist proclivities" (Sellers 1991:223). Now ensconced in the Great Basin, the Mormons had begun to take on a new identity (O'Dea 1954, 1957; May 1980; Moore 1986; Davies 1989). No longer linked to their Yankee ancestors, they were emerging as a separate people with their own "peculiar domestic institution."

Viewed from the East, Utah was a monolithic theocracy. By 1856, however, the solidarity of the Saints had been undermined by a series of internal crises that threatened to discredit the leadership of Brigham Young. Polygamy itself was a major source of internal conflict. "Especially during the 1850s, Young's fiery sermons goaded faithful men to marry multiple wives, and faithful women to encourage their husbands' polygamy" (Gordon 2002: 27). Yet the practice had always been controversial within the Mormon rank and file. In the fall of 1856 a number of plural wives who were discontent in their marital arrangements petitioned the church to grant them divorces.

This push came at an especially awkward time for Young. A few months earlier his second bid for Utah statehood had been rebuffed in Washington and was never even considered by Congress. Meanwhile, Young received news that some one thousand Mormon emigrants had been trapped by early winter storms in Wyoming as they attempted to pull their handcarts to Zion (Bigler 1998:118). The starving and ragged survivors who began to arrive in Salt Lake City would be stark reminders of the inability of the church to guarantee safe passage for new converts. As 1856 drew to a close, Mormon leaders faced an unprecedented challenge to their legitimacy.

In response to the crisis, Young pressed his people to recapture and restore the original millennial spirit of Mormonism. In September 1856—exactly one year before the massacre at Mountain Meadows—he had called for a "great reformation," a spiritual "cleansing" that would "merit divine favor in the inevitable confrontation with the American Republic" (Bigler 1998:121). As part of this revitalization movement (Wallace 1956), the Saints were required to repent their sins, undergo a new baptism, and renew their covenants. Mormons were told to "repent and wash themselves, cleanse their premises, their houses, back houses, and everything else about them, and then get the Holy Ghost and go from house to house and purify the whole city." Such housecleaning was necessary, according to Jedediah Morgan Grant—leader of the crusade and the "sledgehammer of Brigham"—because "the wrath of God burns against us, owing to the filth and abomination" (Bishops' Meetings, 30 September 1856; quoted in Sessions 1982:219). Hannah Tapfield King, a forty-year-old English convert, recorded these details of the Mormon "catechism" (8 October 1856; quoted in Bigler 1998:128): "Every Bishop had the 'cue' given to him and he rose up and lashed the people as with a cat-o-nine tails. The people shrunk, shivered, wept, groaned like whipped children. They were told to get up in meeting and confess their sins. They did so 'till it was sickening, and brought disease." Grant's sudden death from typhoid on December 1 seemed to signal the end of the Great Reformation. After two weeks of mourning, however, "other Mormon leaders put their full weight behind the crusade for reform and the spiritual flames leaped even higher in Utah settlements" (Bigler 1998:129).

Throughout the winter, tensions between Utah and the U.S. government sharply escalated. "If Brigham Young did not intentionally provoke a war with the United States, by early 1857 he was busily preparing for it" (Bagley 2002:77). In January the Utah legislature voted to reorganize the territorial militia along the lines of the Nauvoo Legion. In March the Mormons began to manufacture imitation Colt revolvers and were soon producing twenty guns per week. In April, Young and more than a hundred other officials from around the Utah territory traveled north to Fort Limhi, a Mormon outpost at the mouth of a strategic pass in the Bitterroot Mountains. Though Young described it as a mere "pleasure ride," the excursion was actually a daring reconnaissance of possible escape routes over the Continental Divide to a location along the Missouri River. The company included Col. William Dame, Major Isaac Haight, and other militiamen from the new Mormon settlements in Iron and Washington counties, hundreds of miles to the south. Also accompanying the expedition was Chief Arapene of the Utes, "a noted leader of the Great Basin tribes who came to represent his hosts favorably to his counterparts in Oregon Territory" (Bigler 1998:144).

Meanwhile, the eastern press was filled with calls for President Buchanan to put down the "Utah rebellion." By July 1857 a U.S. Army detachment of some 2,500 troops was en route to replace Brigham Young with a non-Mormon governor and to quell any further resistance. "Incredibly, the administration seems to have believed that the Mormon people would hail the army as saviors, especially, they believed, women oppressed by polygamous marriages and those who feared for their lives from Destroying Angels" (Alexander 2003:125). Also known as Danites, the Destroying Angels were an order of secret police originally organized by Joseph Smith in 1838. "Although the formal Danite organization lasted only a few weeks, it created an enduring belief that the Mormons sponsored a secret brotherhood of religious terrorists" (Bagley 2002:11).

Secret brotherhood or not, the Mormons were preparing for war. Thus when the Arkansas emigrants arrived in Utah, goods and ammunition had been cached in the foothills, plans had been drawn up to demolish settlements and make the land barren for the invading army, and military units were activated in every settlement in the territory (Arrington and Bitton 1992:166–167). Orders had come down that "no supplies shall be furnished emigrants or others bound for California" (Brooks 1962:21). In fact, the Mormons were looking to the overland traffic to bolster their own lagging supplies. Franklin D. Richards, a brigadier general in the Nauvoo Legion, instructed his officers: "The opportunities that occur of obtaining arms & ammunition from passing emigrants should not escape your carefull attention" (Brooks 1962:21). Although the Saints had stockpiled plenty of lead ore to make bullets, their armory contained only 150 pounds of gunpowder (Bagley 2002:77, 90).

Mormon Utah was little prepared for an assault by the U.S. Army. To buy time, it would seem, Brigham Young threatened in 1857 to close the overland trail—not by his own initiative, but by "turning loose" the natives: "If the United States send their army here and war commences, the travel must stop; your trains must not cross this continent back and forth. To accomplish this I need only say a word to the [tribes,] for the Indians will use them up unless I continually strive to restrain them. I will say no more to the Indians, let them alone, but do as you please. And what is that? It is to use them up; and they will do it" (quoted in Bagley 2002:91). On September 12, the day after the Mountain Meadows massacre, Young wrote a letter to the U.S. superintendent of Indian Affairs. News of the army's advance, he claimed, had incited Indian raids on cattle herds. "The blood and nerves of an Indian," in Young's opinion, are quickened by "the sound of war" (Bagley 2002:137).

Execution

Most of the Arkansas emigrants passed through Salt Lake City in early August 1857. From here they "disappeared into a historical maze built of lies, folklore, popular myth, justifications, and a few facts" (Bagley 2002:99). Some of the Arkansans, such as Basil Parker, the Scott and Poteet families, and the drovers Farmer, Campbell, and Smith, would break away to take an alternate path, but the majority would travel the so-called Mormon Corridor—the southern route that passed through a string of outlying settlements before intersecting with the Spanish Trail.

On their way south the emigrants met a Mormon patriarch, Jacob Hamblin, who was heading to Salt Lake City. Hamblin later testified that while camped at Corn Creek with apostle George A. Smith and a group of Indians, he conversed at some length with one of the Arkansas riders whose party had settled for the evening about forty yards away (Bagley 2002:106). His characterization of the company is especially interesting: "They remarked that this one train was made up near Salt Lake City of several trains that had crossed plains separately; and being southern people had preferred to take the southern rout[e]" (Carleton 1995 [1859]:12). Hamblin advised the emigrants to rest at Mountain Meadows, which was just four miles beyond his own farmstead. This little oasis, he explained, would be "the best point to recruit their animals before they entered upon the desert."

Some two weeks later the Arkansans did indeed camp at the Meadows. Their choice of location, however, would have been based on Fancher's previous overland experience rather than Hamblin's advice. The spring-fed pasture was nestled in the parched juniper-covered hills, a welcome sight for man and beast. Arriving after sunset and exhausted by the late summer heat, the emigrants settled down to sleep near the little ravine of Magotsu Creek. Now on the final leg of their journey, many were anticipating reunions with loved ones, friends, and former neighbors who had already started new lives in California. Within days they expected to be through the Mojave Desert and approaching the great Central Valley.

Instead, just before daybreak on September 7, the company was fired on by an unknown enemy concealed in the nearby creek bed (Bigler 1998:169;

Bagley 2002:123). This assault killed or wounded at least ten men. Faced with return fire from the surviving emigrants, the assailants retreated into the hills and continued the siege for four days. By September 11 the emigrants were dehydrated, low on ammunition, and demoralized. With bodies of their loved ones still unburied, the emigrants allowed two local militiamen to enter the wagon train.

John D. Lee and William Bateman tried to convince the emigrants that they were being attacked by Indians. If they would surrender and "put their arms in the wagon, so as not to arouse the animosity of the Indians," the militia would escort them to safety (Lee 2001 [1877]:246). Clearly, the Arkansans were suspicious, as it took nearly two hours to come to an agreement. The circumstances of the surrender are still somewhat mysterious (Brooks 1992:215): "Had Captain Fancher been killed in the first attack? Or did he give the Masonic signal of distress and receive an answering promise? Some have argued that he otherwise would never have consented to this arrangement."

In any case, the Arkansans were disarmed and Lee "hurried up the people," segregating them by age and sex (Lee 2001 [1877]:246). Children under the age of six were placed in a wagon that led the procession across the Meadows. A second wagon carried two or three wounded men and a woman; at some distance, the other women and older children followed on foot. A few hundred yards behind, each emigrant man was escorted by a militiaman. Some eighteen months later Brevet Major James H. Carleton (1995 [1859]:36) would be haunted by the spectacle:

> The idea of the melancholy procession of that great number of women and children—followed at a distance by their husbands and brothers, after all their suffering, their watching, their anxiety and grief, for so many gloomy days and dismal nights at the corral; thus moving slowly and sadly up to the point where the Mormons and Indians lay in wait to murder them; these doomed and unhappy people literally going to their own funeral.

After marching the men to an open space in the Meadows, the order was given by Major John Higbee to "DO YOUR DUTY" (Lee 2001 [1877]:243). Each militiaman is said to have shot the man he was escorting, while "the Indians" rushed out of the brush to bludgeon the women and children (Brooks 1962:75; Bigler 1998:172). Amid the corpses, some fifty perpetrators swore "most binding oaths to stand by each other, and to always insist that the massacre was committed by Indians alone" (Lee 2001 [1877]:251).

News of the massacre reached California within three weeks and the cities in the East within two months (Brooks 1962:118; Bagley 2002:188). Despite the efforts of church leaders to portray the event as an Indian massacre, suspicion immediately fell upon the Mormons. In San Bernardino, where the church had established a colony in 1851, the many defectors from the faith "pronounced it a Mormon act and no Indian affair at all" (Bagley 2002:189).

Bare Bones

Within weeks of the massacre the historical maze of conflicting interpretations was already under construction. For decades, it would grow and turn in on itself, convincing many observers that one could never know what "really happened" at Mountain Meadows. Then, in the summer of 1999, there seemed to be a break in the maze—a shortcut back to the victims themselves, whose bones might be able to "tell their story," purified of all the lies, folklore, justifications, and innuendo.

So what can be told from the human remains? In many respects the pattern of skeletal trauma corroborates the basic historical accounts. Men, women, and children were certainly killed at Mountain Meadows. Most of the victims in the mass grave were young adult males who had been shot. Most of the women and children had been bludgeoned to death. At the same time, the skeletal findings do not support historical accounts of "scalping" or other claims of specifically "Indian" atrocities.

In fact, the only *material* evidence for "Indians" at Mountain Meadows consists of three teeth. Although "race" cannot be determined from a single anatomical trait, dental morphology provides some indication of biological ancestry.[1] In particular, the incisors (front teeth) of Native Americans tend to be heavily enameled on the lingual ("toward the tongue") surface. The enamel buildup results in a "shovel-shaped" tooth as opposed to the "spatulate" incisor that is characteristic of Europeans and Euro-Americans (Carbonell 1963; Hillson 1996). Not surprisingly, most of the victims in the mass grave had typically European dental morphology. The three shoveled incisors, however, suggest some degree of Native American ancestry for at least two of the victims.[2] One shoveled tooth was an unerupted incisor from a juvenile of indeterminate sex. The crown of the tooth had completely developed, but the root had just started to grow (Figure 6.2). This stage of development indicates a child approximately six years of age.[3] The other two shoveled incisors, fully developed and slightly worn from use, belonged to a young adult.

The Native American traits in the skeletal remains seem mysterious until they are considered in a genealogical light. For almost fifty years (*c.* 1780–1828), the Ozarks served as a refuge for Cherokees fleeing political

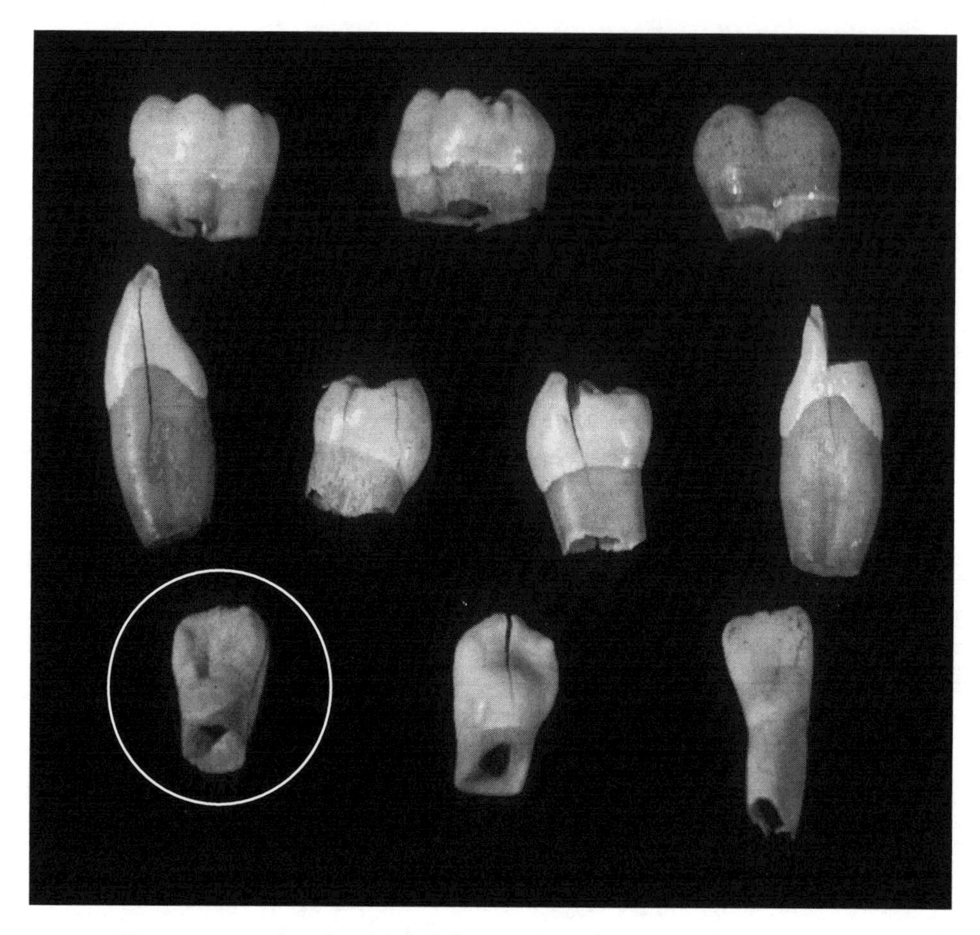

Figure 6.2. ◆ Sample of subadult teeth in various stages of development. Circle identifies the shoveled incisor of child, approximately 6 years of age. Photo by Laurel Casjens.

conflict and persecution in the southern Appalachians (Bolton 1998:73–74; Blevins 2002:17). Most of the white settlers who subsequently flooded into Arkansas and Missouri had themselves passed through the Cherokee homeland. As a result, Arkansas "hill folks" can usually claim at least one Native American ancestor, either in the Ozarks or back in Appalachia. Any such claim, of course, must be taken with a grain of salt: "While it is possible and even likely that some of the Appalachian settlers in the [Ozark] region had intermarried with the Cherokee or other tribes, it is unlikely that it was as common as eager genealogists would have us believe" (Blevins 2002:277 n. 19).

Of those on the 1857 train, only two families—the Bakers and the Millers—are known to have had Indian ancestry. John Twitty Baker had a Cherokee grandmother, making him "one-quarter" Native American (Baker 1982: 160). The typically Indian trait of shoveled incisors may have been passed down from Baker to any of his offspring, including George Washington Baker, Sarah Baker Mitchell, and Abel Baker, all young adults on the 1857 train. In the next generation, only Mary Levina Baker—the seven-year-old daughter of George Washington Baker—fits the profile of the juvenile whose shoveled incisor was recovered from the mass grave. Though this does not prove that the teeth in question were from the Baker line, it offers a possible explanation for the Native American traits in the victims' remains.

A similar account may be given for the Miller family. Two adult riders on the train, Josiah Miller and Armilda Miller Tackitt, were descended from Hugh Miller, who was purportedly Cherokee (Elisa Rawlinson, personal communication, 2007). Josiah was Hugh Miller's son and thirty years old when he was killed at Mountain Meadows. Armilda, a granddaughter of Hugh Miller, was twenty-two. Either of these young adults, given their Cherokee ancestry, may have had shovel-shaped incisors.[4]

If the ancestry of the victims remains an open question, there is little doubt about how they died. The most common injury observed in the skeletal sample was a single gunshot wound to the head.[5] The pattern of trauma is consistent with point-blank, execution-style shooting as opposed to long-distance killing under battlefield conditions (e.g., Gill 1994). In a pitched battle or firefight, bullet wounds are likely to be found in various anatomical locations, not just in the head, and tend to be quite irregular in shape and severity (e.g., Willey and Scott 1991; Scott et al. 1998). These wounds, by comparison, seem to have resulted from precise firing at close range, a pattern consistent with Lee's account of the massacre (2001 [1877]:250–251): "When I reached the place where the dead men lay, I was told how the orders had been obeyed. Major Higbee said, 'The boys have acted admirably, they took good aim, and all of the d——d Gentiles but two or three fell at the *first fire*.'" Eleven distinct gunshots can be accounted for in the reconstructed crania and cranial fragments (Table 6.1). Seven of the reconstructed crania had unambiguous gunshot lesions (six entrance and two exit wounds),[6] and there were four partial exit wounds in the unsorted fragments. Only a single young adult male (Individual 9) exhibited both entrance and exit wounds in the same skull.

The locations of the gunshot wounds indicate that the assailants shot their victims either from behind or while face-to-face (Figure 6.3). Bullets entering the back of the head (Figure 6.4) are likely to have exited through the face, which would explain much of the trauma to small facial bones and teeth (Figure 6.5). Frontal assaults are indicated by exit wounds in the back

Table 6.1. • Perimortem Trauma in Reconstructed Crania in the Mountain Meadows Sample.

DISTINCT INDIVIDUALS (N = 18)			TRAUMA			
INDIVIDUAL	SEX	AGE (YR)	RAD FX	GSW-ENT	GSW-EXIT	BLUNT
1	Male	20–34	1	1		
2	Male	16–22	1			1
3	Male	16–22	1			
4	Male	25–34	1	1		
5	Male	16–22	1			1
6	Indeterminate	10–15	1	1		
7	Male	30–39	1			
8	Probable male	20–34	1		1	
9	Male	29–34	1	1	1	
10	Male	45–54				
11	Female	35–44	1			
12	Male	18–24	1	1		
13	Probable male	18–22	1			
14	Indeterminate	3.5–4.5	1			1
15	Indeterminate	6.5–7.5	1			1
16	Indeterminate	8.5–9.5	1			1
Fro06C	Female	48–54	1			1
Occ02	Male	20–34	1	1		
			N (%) 17 (94)	*N* (%) 6 (33)	*N* (%) 2 (11)	*N* (%) 6 (33)
Fragments with Identifiable Trauma						
Occ03R	Indeterminate	Adult	1		1	
Occ04R	Indeterminate	Adult	1		1	
Occ05R	Indeterminate	Adult	1		1	
Par08L	Indeterminate	Adult	1		1	
Man04C	Male	18–22				1

Note: Rad FX = radiating fracture, GSW-ent = gunshot wound entrance, GSW-exit = gunshot wound exit.

of five heads (Figure 6.6), plus a single entrance wound in the forehead of a young adult male (Figure 6.7). Such a killing is described by John D. Lee: one of the wounded men was grabbed by the hair so the killer could "look into his face; the man shut his eyes, and Joe shot him in the head." Joe, according to Lee (2001 [1877]:249), was an "Indian from Cedar City."

All the gunshot wounds were identified in males,[7] with the exception of one entrance wound in a subadult of indeterminate sex (Individual 6). In this case the ten- to fifteen-year-old victim was shot in the top of the head (Fig-

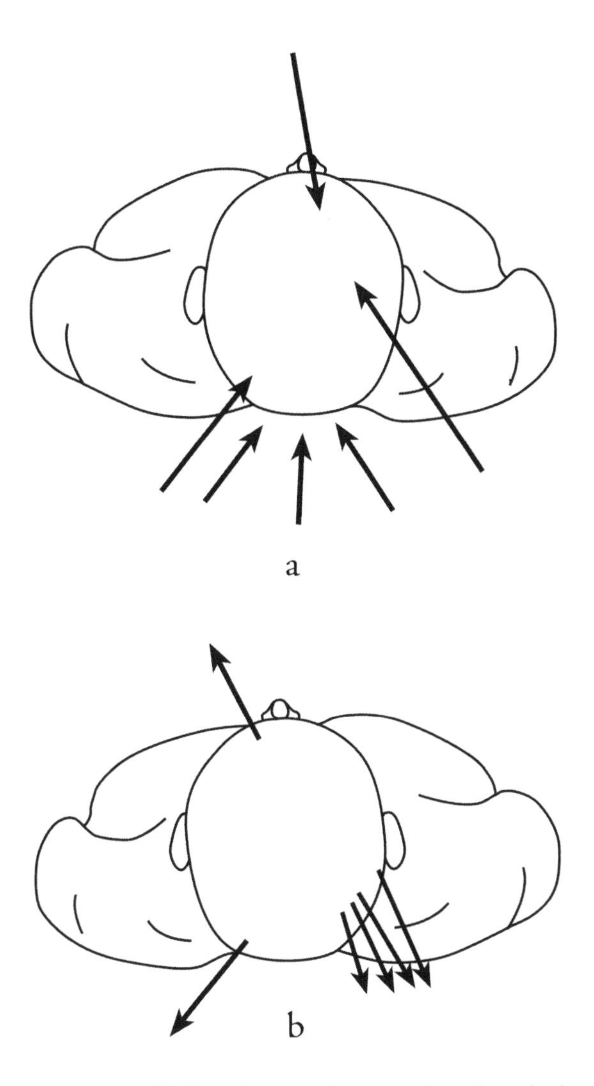

Figure 6.3. • Trajectory of bullets through the crania based on the location of gunshot entrance wounds (a) and exit wounds (b). Reprinted from *Historical Archaeology* 37(2) by permission of The Society for Historical Archaeology.

ure 6.8).[8] The elongated "keyhole" shape of this entrance wound indicates that the assailant was holding the gun above and behind the victim's right side. The execution of an adolescent girl is described by survivor Nancy Huff (Cates 1875:3): "At the close of the massacre there was eighteen children still alive, one girl, some ten or twelve years old, they said was too big and could tell, so they killed her, leaving seventeen." Given that Nancy was only four years old at the time of the massacre, her testimony must be approached with caution. An independent source, however, also reports that a "last girl"

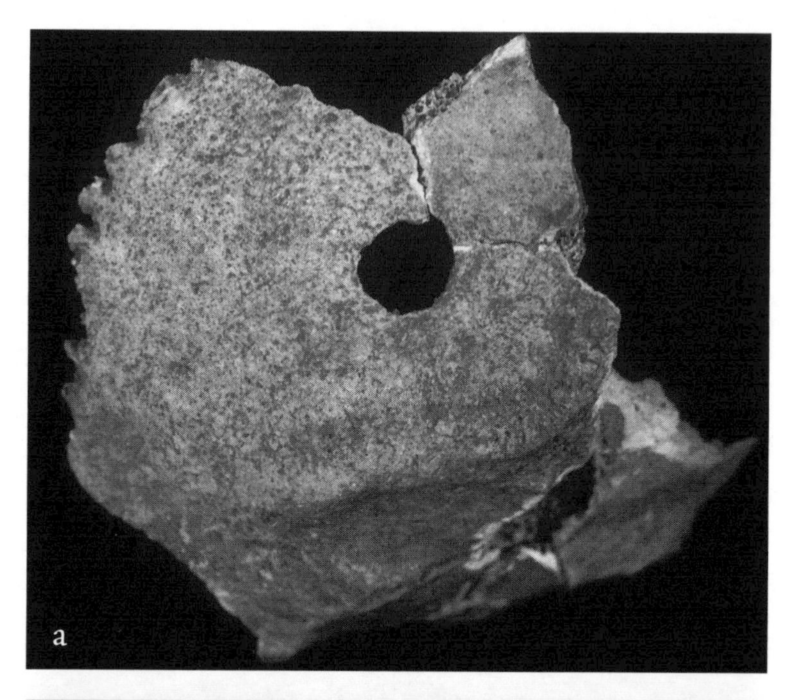

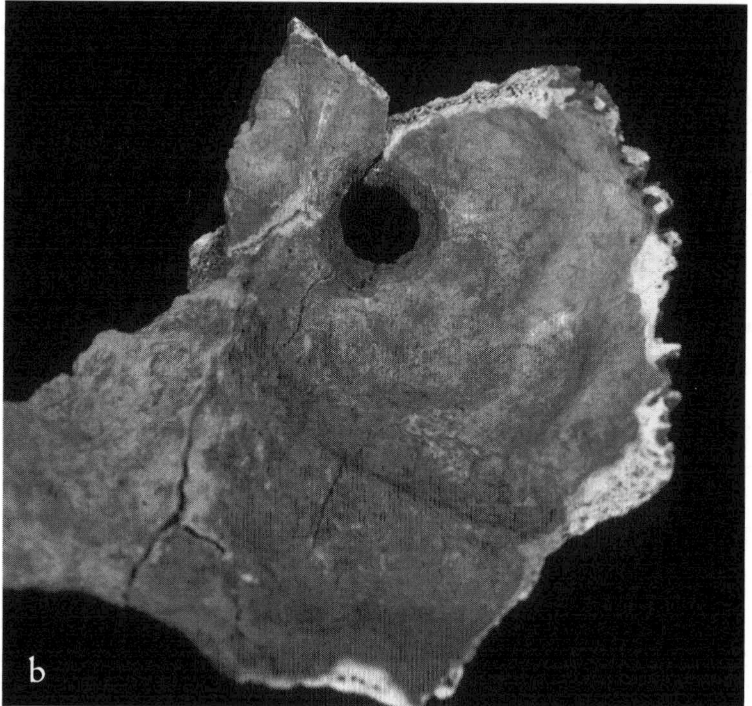

Figure 6.4. ✦ Ectocranial (*a*) and endocranial (*b*) views of a gunshot entrance wound in the occipital of young adult male (Cranium 17). Photo by Laurel Casjens. Reprinted from *Historical Archaeology* 37(2) by permission of The Society for Historical Archaeology.

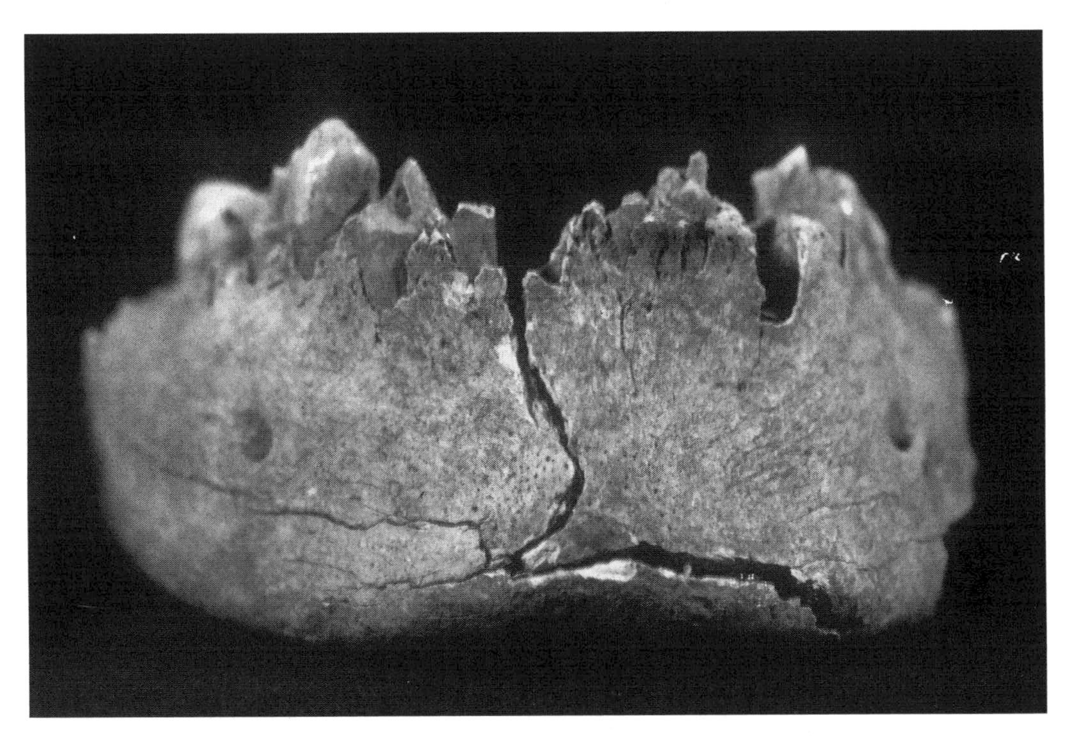

Figure 6.5. • Perimortem trauma in the mandible and dentition of a young adult male (Man04C). Photo by Laurel Casjens.

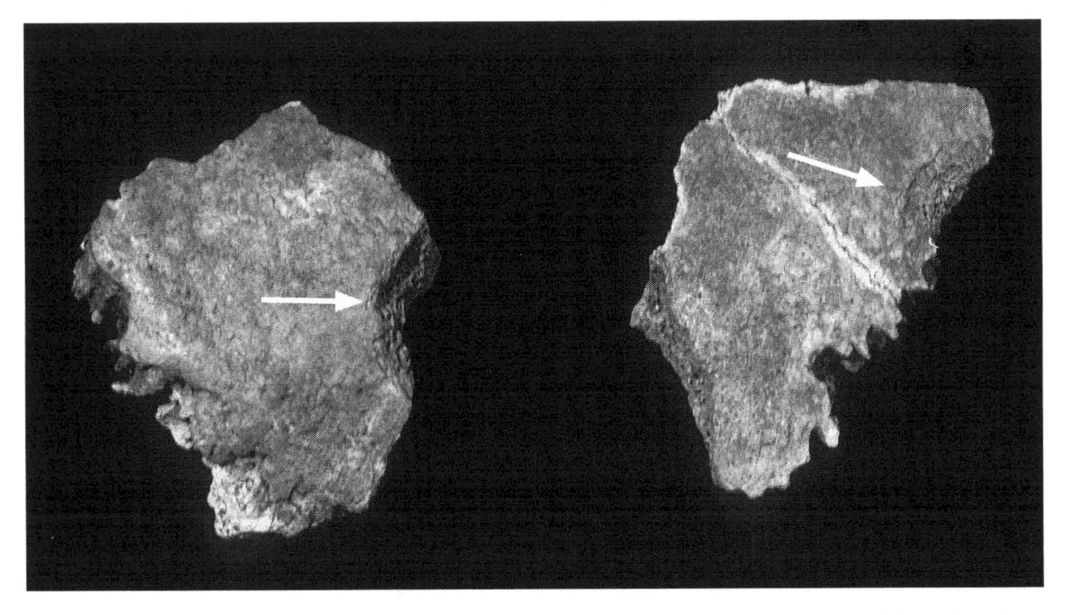

Figure 6.6. • Fragmentary gunshot exit wounds in cranial fragments from two probable males. Photo by Laurel Casjens.

Figure 6.7. • Ectocranial (*a*) and endocranial (*b*) views of a gunshot entrance wound in the frontal of a young adult male (Cranium 9). Photo by Laurel Casjens.

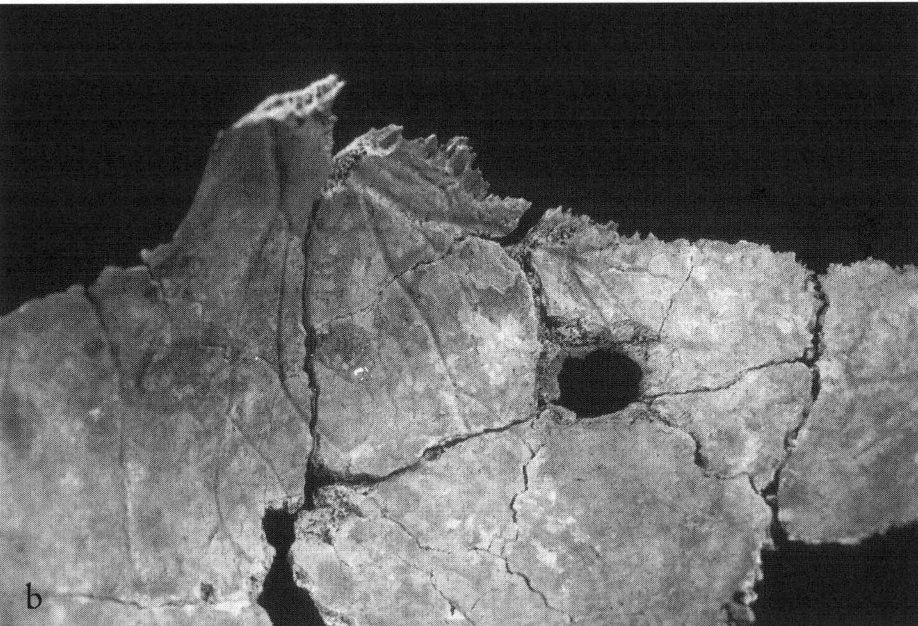

Figure 6.8. ✦ Ectocranial (*a*) and endocranial (*b*) views of a gunshot entrance wound in the superior right parietal of a subadult (Cranium 6). Photo by Laurel Casjens. Reprinted from *Historical Archaeology* 37(2) by permission of The Society for Historical Archaeology.

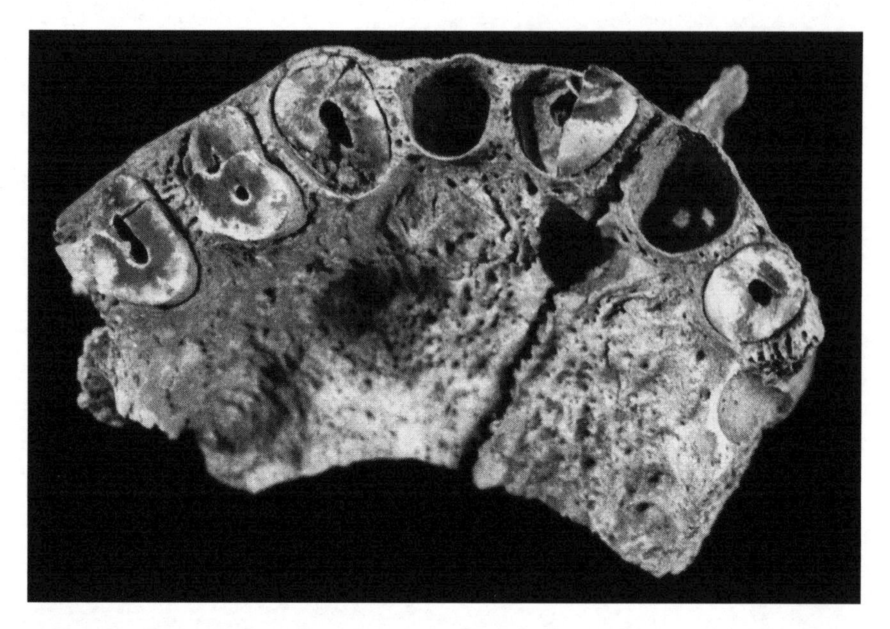

Figure 6.9. • Perimortem fractures in the maxillae and dentition of a young adult female. Photo by Laurel Casjens. Reprinted from *Historical Archaeology* 37(2) by permission of The Society for Historical Archaeology.

was executed. John D. Lee's son, Joseph Lee, claimed that his father refused to perform the deed, so another militiaman, Harrison Pearce, carried out the murder (Bagley 2002:150).

In addition to skulls with distinct gunshot wounds, other bones from the mass grave had fracture patterns indicative of projectile trauma. Such a pattern was especially evident in the case of a young adult female. Her facial bones had large radiating fractures running through the palate, and the crowns of her teeth were broken and had a blackened, polished appearance (Figure 6.9). This kind of trauma is consistent with the extensive damage left by a bullet entering or exiting the face. The shooting of at least one woman was alluded to in the trial of John D. Lee (2001 [1877]:342).[9] According to the testimony of militiaman Samuel McMurdy, "Lee had his gun to his shoulder, and when the gun had exploded I saw, I think it was a woman, fall backwards.... He must have hit her in the back of the head." Possibly a second case was described by Nancy Huff (Cates 1875:3), who recalled seeing her mother, Saladia, shot in the forehead.

Bludgeoning was evident in six of the reconstructed heads: one old adult female, two young adult males, and three children (Table 6.2). The children's heads had extensive crushing (Figures 6.10–6.12), indicating blows that were delivered with great force (Gurdjian 1975; Galloway 1999).[10] Although

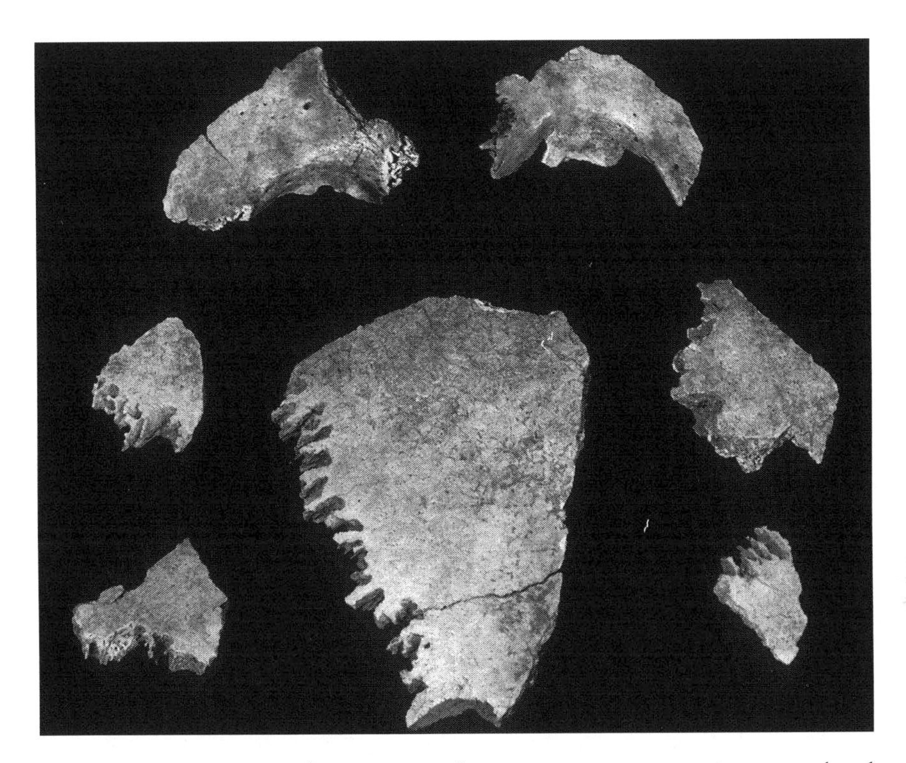

Figure 6.10. ✦ Extensive fragmentation from perimortem trauma in unsorted and unreconstructed cranial fragments of children. Photo by Laurel Casjens.

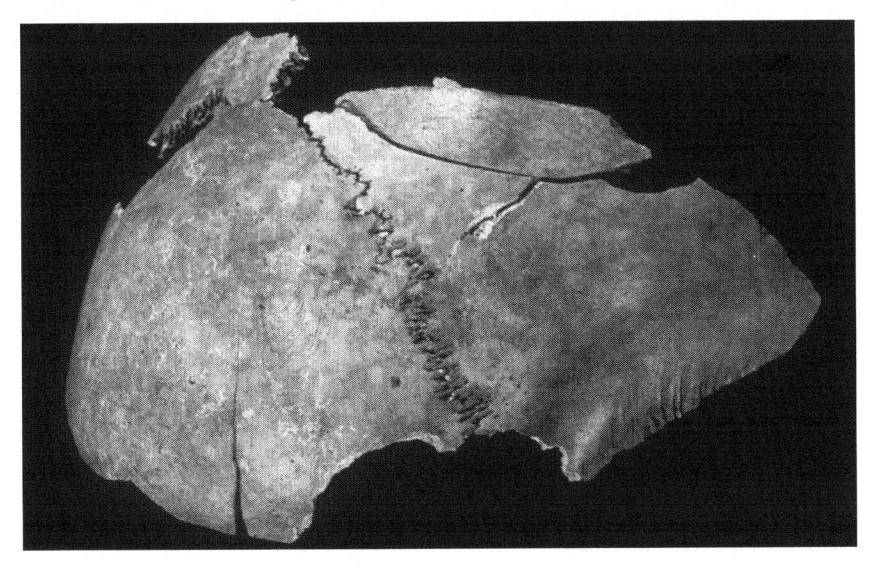

Figure 6.11. ✦ Concentric and radiating fractures in the vault of a child (Cranium 16). Left lateral profile of the vault with the frontal bone facing left. Photo by Laurel Casjens. Reprinted from *Historical Archaeology* 37(2) by permission of The Society for Historical Archaeology.

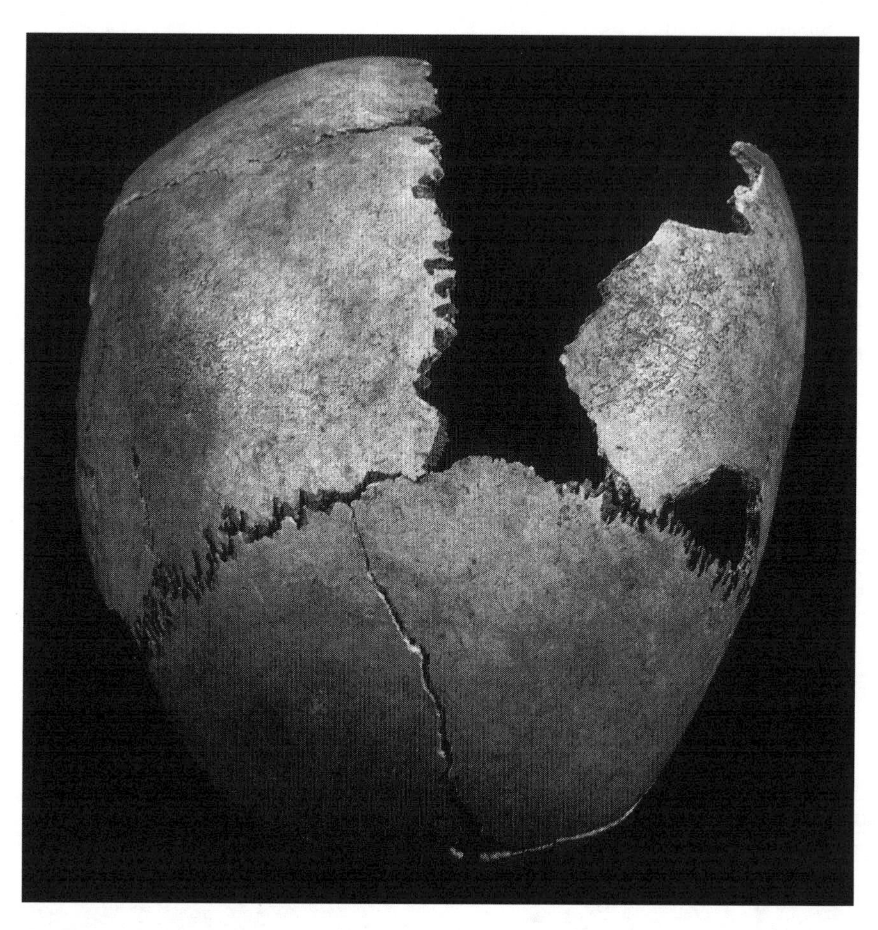

Figure 6.12. ♦ Superior view of blunt force trauma in the posterior vault of a child (Cranium 14). Photo by Laurel Casjens.

Table 6.2 ♦ Blunt Force Trauma and Angle of Attack in the Mountain Meadows Sample.

ELEMENT/INDIVIDUAL	AGE (YR)	SEX	ANGLE OF ATTACK
2	16–22	Male	Anterior and posterior
5	16–22	Male	Anterior
14	4.5–5.5	Indeterminate	Posterior-superior
15	6.5–7.5	Indeterminate	Posterior-superior
16	8.5–9.5	Indeterminate	Superior left lateral
Fr06C	48–54	Female	Anterior
Man04C	20–34	Male	Anterior

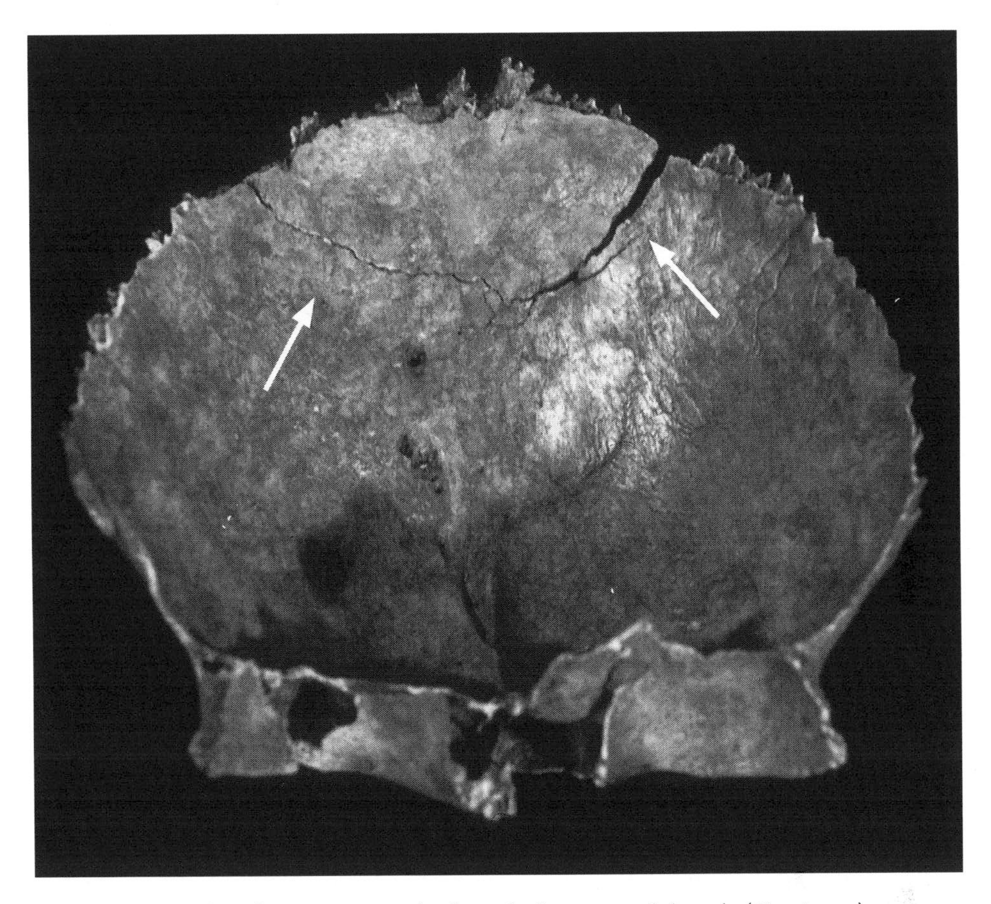

Figure 6.13. ✦ Blunt force trauma in the frontal of a young adult male (Cranium 5). Photo by Laurel Casjens.

most of the militiamen denied killing children, William Stewart and George Adair purportedly bragged about such murders. Stewart claimed he held "the d——d Gentile babies by the heels and cracked their skulls over the wagon tires," while Adair attempted to "imitate the pitiful, crushing sound" (quoted in Bagley 2002:148–149).

The older woman and two young men experienced more localized blunt-force impacts to their foreheads. The resulting bony lesions were fairly nondescript (Figures 6.13, 6.14), although one male (Individual 2) had an impact site that was well defined. Here a linear blunt object struck the left side of his forehead, causing a fracture that removed a rectangular piece of bone (Figure 6.15). Another blow from this same type of weapon was directed at the back of his head. Lee describes the case of a boy, about fourteen years old, who was assaulted in a manner that could have produced such a wound. The boy, according to Lee (2001 [1877]:249), was running to a wagon when Samuel

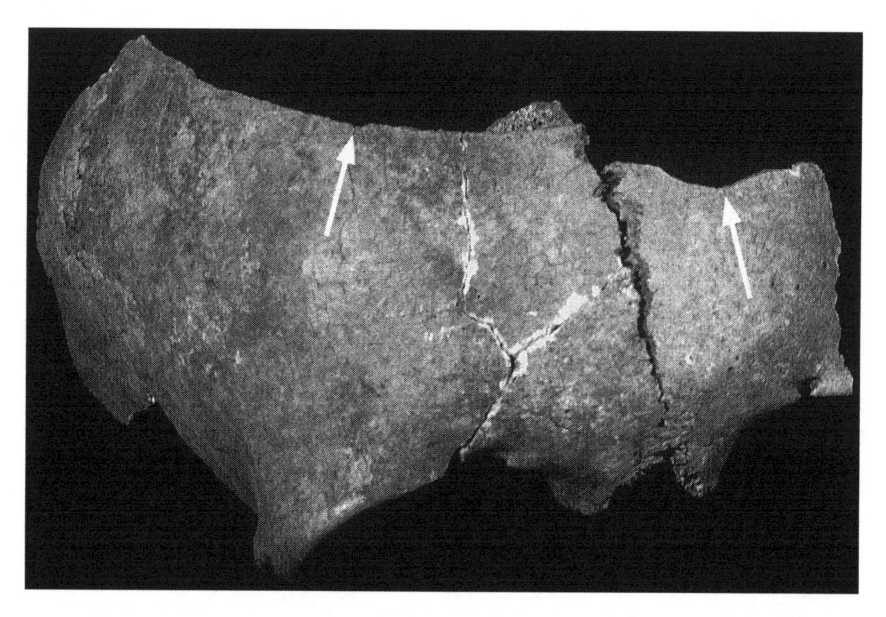

Figure 6.14. • Blunt force trauma in the frontal of an old adult female (Fr06C). Photo by Laurel Casjens.

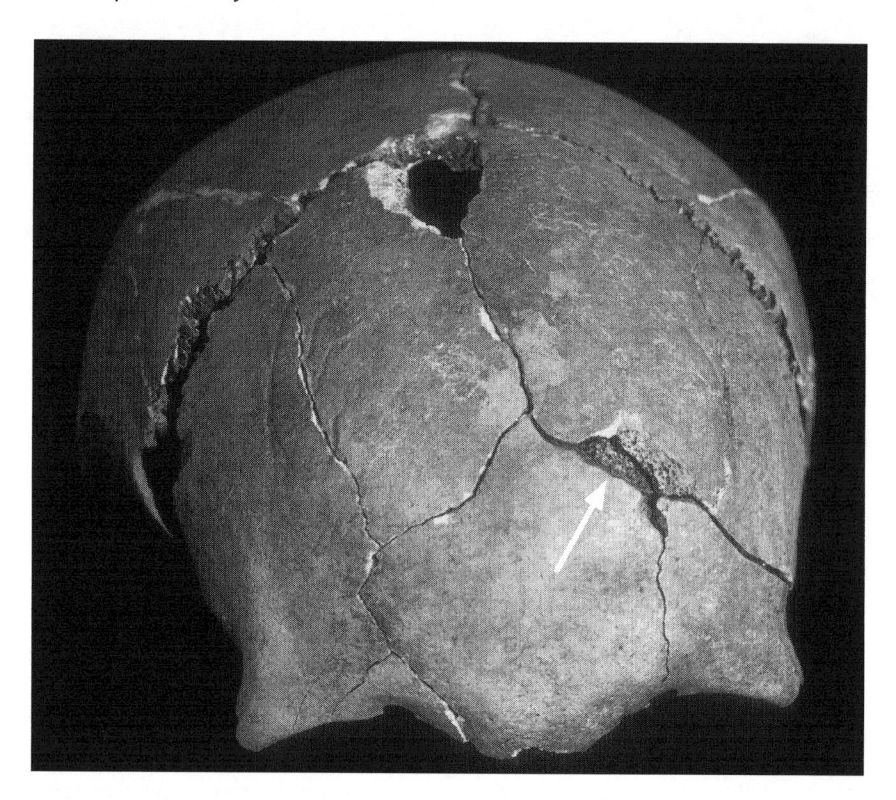

Figure 6.15. • Linear blunt force trauma in the frontal of a young adult male (Cranium 2). Note that the hole near bregma is the result of postmortem damage. Photo by Laurel Casjens. Reprinted from *Historical Archaeology* 37(2) by permission of The Society for Historical Archaeology.

Knight, one of the Mormon wagon drivers, "struck him on the head with the butt end of his gun, and crushed his skull." Similarly, Nancy Huff recalled the assailants clubbing the women and eventually "beating out their brains" (Cates 1875:3).

Some historical accounts, however, were not supported by the skeletal findings. In particular, there was no evidence for the use of knives to scalp, behead, or cut the throats of the victims (cf. Carleton 1995 [1859]:6; Drewer 1859; Lee 2001 [1877]:251; Brooks 1962:75). Evidence was also lacking for projectile trauma from arrows.[11] Yet images of Indian weaponry are deeply woven into many of the massacre narratives, including those of the surviving children. One of these children, John Calvin Miller, remembered being near his mother—Matilda Cameron Miller—when she was wounded, and pulling "the arrows from her back until she was dead" (Carleton 1995 [1859]:33). Forty years after the massacre Rebecca Dunlap provided her version of the story to the *Fort Smith Elevator* (Evans 1897). Here she claimed that Mormons and Indians had shot "men, women and children, then pierced them with bows and arrows, then cut their throats with knives." Similarly, at age eighty-five, Sarah Baker recalled "the screaming of the other children and the agonized shrieks of women being hacked to death with tomahawks" (Mitchell 1940). All such "memories," however, are suspect. John Calvin Miller, for example, was only six at the time of the massacre and could not remember his own surname when he was retrieved by federal officials some eighteen months later. Though he described his mother as being riddled with arrows, Miller also claimed to have seen John D. Lee "shoot my mother" (Cradlebaugh 1863:20)—presumably with a rifle or a pistol rather than a bow.

Many accounts provided by adults are hardly more reliable. In 1858 Mormon apostle George A. Smith reported that "a large number of the dead were killed with arrows; the residue with bullets, the Indians being armed with guns and bows" (Brooks 1962:244). Not surprisingly, the Southern Paiutes, the Indians who lived in the area, used bows, and by the mid-1850s they were tipping their arrows with metallic heads fashioned from salvaged bits of axle and other wagon-train debris (Knack 2001:44). Although such projectiles might have been used against the emigrants, the skeletons recovered from the mass grave showed no trace of arrow wounds of any kind.

Of course, the gunshot wounds in the skeletal sample might have been inflicted by Indians. After all, skeletal evidence alone cannot determine the shooter's ethnic or racial identity. Yet the Southern Paiutes are especially unlikely to have wielded firearms on such a large scale. Carleton (1995 [1859]:30) reported that Jacob Hamblin, "himself their Agent, informed me that to his certain knowledge in '55 there were but three guns in the whole tribe. I doubt if they had many more in '57." Indeed, the Paiutes at the time were known to "possess few firearms and little skill at using them" (Bigler 1998:169).

In Euro-American fantasies about Indian weaponry a special place was granted to the tomahawk. The Southern Paiutes would have undoubtedly acquired knives and even hatchets from Mormon settlers or other emigrants passing through the area, but the tomahawk is typical of groups living in the woodlands rather than the Great Basin. Nonetheless, this "Indian" weapon came to symbolize native atrocities and to carry a powerful implicit message. In a letter dated September 12, 1857, such symbolism was invoked by Brigham Young himself. If President Buchanan did not concede, he wrote, "the war cry will resound.... It [will be] peace and rights...or the knife and tomahawk—let Uncle Sam choose" (Bagley 2002:139).

War Paint

Young's warning reflected a fundamental doctrine of Mormon theology: the belief in a close genealogical link between Latter-day Saints and Native Americans, a link that destined the two races to unite against their "Gentile" adversaries. According to the Book of Mormon, American Indians are descended from ancient Hebrews who sailed under divine guidance to the Western Hemisphere. Here they came to practice "an advanced form of Christianity," having been visited by Jesus Christ after his crucifixion (Arrington and Bitton 1992:145). Yet one clan, the Lamanites, fell from the faith, destroyed their righteous cousins, and were cursed with dark skin. Only in the Last Days would the descendants of the Lamanites ally with the Saints against the Gentiles (Bigler 1998:64). In returning to the faith of their fathers, the Lamanites would again become a "white and delightsome people" (*Book of Mormon*, 2 Nephi 30:6).[12]

Based on these scriptural premises, American Indians could be construed as "both a cursed and a chosen people" (Holt 1992:22). And indeed, from the earliest Mormon missions to the Ohio frontier, Indians were seen as benighted "children of the forest" who were nonetheless junior partners in the epic struggle to restore Zion. The prospect of a Mormon-Indian alliance spread alarm among the Gentiles in the Midwest (Arrington and Bitton 1992:146):

> One of the factors causing the Mormon expulsion from Missouri in 1833 and 1839 was the fear on the part of other settlers that the Mormons might give the Indians a false sense of power and importance. The Mormons were accused of "keeping up a constant communication with the Indian tribes of our frontier, ...[of] declaring, even

> from the pulpit, that the Indians are a part of God's chosen people, and are destined, by heaven, to inherit this land, in common with themselves."

In this light, a blurring of Mormon and Indian identities would come naturally to most nineteenth-century Americans, who associated the Mormons with what William McNeill (1992:22) calls a "neo-barbarian style of frontier life."

"Savage Indians," according to Philip Deloria (1998:3), "served Americans as oppositional figures against whom one might imagine a civilized national Self." The Mormons, it may be argued, served a similar purpose. Like Indians, Mormons were "beyond the pale" (literally, *outside the boundary*)—set apart by the barbarism of polygamy, their clannish communities, and their mysterious rituals of baptism and communion with the dead.

At the same time, from the beginnings of the LDS Church, Mormons were able to capitalize on their outsider status—their reputation as a "peculiar people." Perhaps because his followers *were* Americans, Joseph Smith seems to have realized that he had something to gain by making his claims as outrageous as possible—indeed, that his movement "had no chance of going anywhere without opposition, both real and imagined" (Moore 1986:34). As Deloria (1998:21) argues: "We construct identity by finding ourselves in relation to an array of people and objects who are not ourselves. Every person and thing is Other to us. We situate some Others quite closely to the Selves we are calling into being; others, we place so far away as to make them utterly inhuman." Such oppositional thinking—who one is not—seems to be at the root of both religious movements and many ethnic and nationalist ideologies (e.g., Gerlach and Hine 1970; Said 1978; Anderson 1991; Smith 2003). By tapping this root, Smith was trying to vitalize not just a church but a nation. The Mormon mission, in short, was *to become a people* (Moore 1986).

In this light, the Mormons were reenacting the process by which their colonial ancestors had separated themselves from their European homeland and staked a claim to a new national identity. It is worth remembering in this context that rebellious colonists in Boston donned Indian dress to carry out one of the most dramatic demonstrations of resistance to British rule—the Boston Tea Party. Why did the colonists dress like Indians? As disguise, their costumes were hardly very effective, and the identities of most of the participants were well known (Labaree 1964). Instead, according to Deloria (1998), the real significance of the Indian attire was to redraw the boundary between "us" and "them"—to set off the colonists as *Americans* rather than Englishmen or Europeans. In short, "as England became a them for colonists, Indians became an us" (Deloria 1998:22). At this dramatic moment of ethnogenesis, Native Americans were construed not as exotic others but, on the contrary, as potent symbols of the selves that the rebels were "calling into being."

Like their revolutionary ancestors, Mormons would "play Indian" as part of an attempt to construct a new identity, separate from their nation of origin. At Mountain Meadows a number of the militiamen painted their faces and donned Indian garb before carrying out the massacre (Carleton 1995 [1859]; Prince 1859; Rogers 1860; Higbee 1894). Years later Nephi Johnson admitted that some of the "Indians" who attacked the women and children "were Mormons in disguise" and that "white men did most of the killing" (Quinn 1997:252; Bagley 2002:147, 151). A number of the surviving children reported seeing men wash paint from their faces (e.g., Evans 1897; Terry 1938). In 1859 Christopher Carson Fancher explained to a playmate, "My father was killed by Indians; when they washed their faces they were white men" (Bagley 2002:154).

Mountain Meadows, furthermore, was not the only case of violence by Mormons in disguise (e.g., Parshall 2005). Just weeks after the massacre, another company of emigrants passing through southern Utah reported to the *San Francisco Bulletin* that they had been assaulted and robbed by "painted Indians" (Bagley 2002:168):

> The emigrants noted a striking peculiarity in the Paiutes surrounding their wagons.... Some of the "painted Indians had blue, gray, and different colored eyes; they had straight, curly, and fine hair, differing materially from the other Indians in this respect," George Davis wrote. He noticed many of them had streaks and spots of white in the creases round their eyes. Around their ears "the skin of the white man was quite apparent. The painted *whites* were shy; they did not act with the same freedom and boldness as the aborigines did."

By itself, a case like this would seem to have a simple explanation. Criminals often seek to disguise their identities to avoid capture and punishment. As we have seen, however, "playing Indian" may have had deeper implications, especially for the Mormons at Mountain Meadows.

"Misleading dress," as Deloria (1998:34) remarks, "possesses a surprising degree of power, conferring upon its wearer a doubled consciousness, the physical equivalent of metaphoric language." More generally, play is powerful, for it not only makes meanings but makes them tangible to a wider audience (Deloria 1998:184): "The donning of Indian clothes moved ideas from brains to bodies, from the realm of abstraction to the physical world of concrete experience. There, identity was not so much imagined as it was performed, materialized through one's body and through the witness and recognition of others."

To the militiamen at Mountain Meadows, whose identities had been formed by both real and imagined persecution, their performance must have been liberating. For the moment, they *did* "act with the same freedom and boldness" that seemed to come naturally to the "aborigines." Wild Indianness, after all, had always been attractive as well as repulsive, a way of crossing the boundaries of civilized behavior to engage in the most dramatic kind of political theater. If the American revolutionaries had made a point—both economic and political—by dumping tea into Boston Harbor, the Mormons at Mountain Meadows sent their own message by leaving bodies in the wilderness.

Message in a Body

Immediately following the massacre, the corpses were searched for valuables. After what Lee described as a good night's sleep, he and his accomplices returned to the Meadows to bury the dead. On his arrival, he reported "the bodies of men, women and children had been stripped entirely naked, making the scene one of the most...loathsome and ghastly that can be imagined" (Lee 2001 [1877]:252). Some of the "brethren" made a feeble attempt to bury the corpses. "They piled the dead bodies up in heaps in little gullies, and threw dirt over them. The bodies were only lightly covered, for the ground was hard, and the brethren did not have sufficient tools to dig with" (Lee 2001 [1877]:253).

Though other wagon trains passed near the massacre site over the next few days, Mormon escorts either diverted them around the Meadows or led them through the area under cover of darkness. One of the earliest descriptions of the killing field was provided by a young emigrant, John Aiken, approximately one week after the massacre. In an affidavit filed in San Bernardino, California, he reported seeing "about twenty wolves feasting upon the carcasses of the murdered," and went on to note that "women and children were more generally eaten by the wild beasts than were the men" (Aiken 1857).

It would be eighteen months after the massacre before U.S. military personnel were dispatched from Los Angeles with orders to bury the victims. In May 1859 Major Carleton arrived at the Meadows to find Captain Reuben P. Campbell of the Second Dragoons encamped there with his troops. Some of the victims had already been interred under Campbell's supervision. According to Dr. Charles Brewer, the U.S. Army surgeon on the scene, 18 people had been buried in one grave, 12 in another, and 6 in the smallest plot

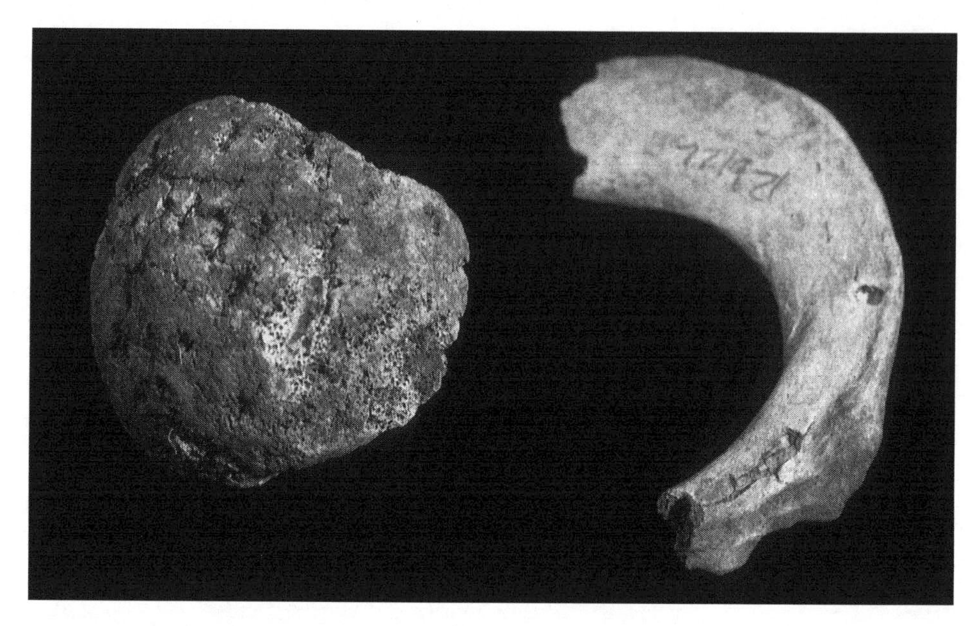

Figure 6.16. • Pits from carnivore activity in the proximal epiphysis of a femur (*left*) and a left rib (*right*). Photo by Laurel Casjens. Reprinted from *Historical Archaeology* 37(2) by permission of The Society for Historical Archaeology.

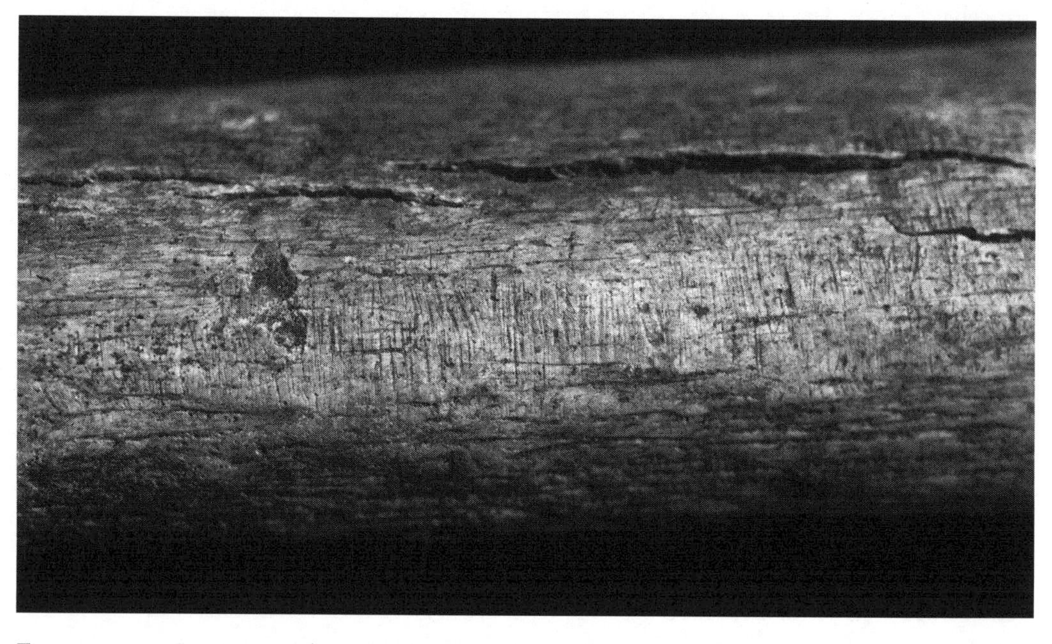

Figure 6.17. • Carnivore tooth scoring that is split by weathering on a right femora shaft of a young adult male. Photo by Laurel Casjens.

(Carleton 1995 [1859]:35). Carleton ordered his troops to make a systematic search of the site. The remains of approximately 34 more individuals were widely scattered across the Meadows:

> Women's hair, in detached locks and masses, hung to the sage brushes and was strewn over the ground in many places. Parts of little children's dresses and of female costume dangled from the shrubbery or lay scattered about; and among these, here and there, on every hand, for at least a mile in the direction of the road, by two miles east and west, there gleamed, bleached white by the weather, the skulls and other bones of those who had suffered. (Carleton 1995 [1859]:36)

The historical accounts of both Aiken and Carleton are supported by the findings of the skeletal analysis (Novak and Kopp 2003). Clearly, the bodies were subject to feeding and disarticulation by carnivores, after which the scattered bones remained exposed on the surface for many months. Experimental studies of canid scavenging (Lyman 1994; Fisher 1995) indicate that feeding usually begins around the neck and moves to the ventral abdomen until the arms are removed from the rest of the body (Haglund 1997:368). After a few months the legs are removed, leaving only the vertebral column, the cranium, and assorted elements and fragments. Depending on the time of exposure, as little as 20 percent of a body may be left for recovery. Given that the victims had been stripped of their clothing, this process would have been accelerated.

The mass grave contained very few small bones of the hands, feet, and vertebrae. Also underrepresented were the joint surfaces, as these spongy bone centers are preferred chewing surfaces for canids (Figure 6.16). Carnivore teeth leave four distinct signatures on the surface of a bone: punctures, pits, scoring, and furrows (Haynes 1980; Binford 1981). All four signatures were present in the victim's remains. Furthermore, many of these marks were bisected by splits in the shafts caused by weathering (Figure 6.17). This pattern indicates that the bodies were subject to heavy carnivore feeding followed by exposure to the extreme climate of the high desert.

In short, "it was not much of a burial," as Lee (2001 [1877]:254) admitted. Such callous treatment would have been significant in itself. Indeed, the effective abandonment of the bodies may have been a deliberate attempt to warn and intimidate any challengers to Mormon sovereignty. Posted messages on the overland trail, as Reid (1997a:201) points out, were often intended "to establish justification, validity, legitimacy, and legality for punishments—especially executions." These messages could be shockingly blunt. Near Fort Laramie, Wyoming, in 1852, a murderer was left "hanging in the tree and there was a board put up saying fresh meat for sale" (Eaton 1974:150–151). Similar cases involved the exposure or shallow burial of a corpse so that the "body should become the prey of wolves & other animals" (Reid 1997a:205). Such images, according to Reid, were intended "to impress passing emigrants with the awesomeness of punishment on the overland trail."[13]

In some cases, overlanders felt compelled to bury or rebury human remains. On his way to California, J. Goldsborough Bruff came across a new grave with a headboard reading: "The remains of a dead person, dug up by wolves, and reburied, by the San Francisco Company, Octr 7th—1849" (Read and Gaines 1949:181). Corpses on the trail, like the travelers themselves, were in a liminal state—neither here nor there. Improvised funerals provided some semblance of the civilized state that had been left behind. By putting death—or at least its material evidence—in proper order, the travelers might hope to gain some control over the wilderness.

Before they departed Mountain Meadows, Carleton and his troops collected the widely scattered bones and arranged them in a trench that had been dug by the emigrants themselves during the initial standoff. It was spring in the high desert valley. The winter's golden grass had already given way to new shoots and wildflowers. Carleton was determined to give the emigrants he had never met a proper burial: "Around and above this grave I caused to be built of loose granite stones, hauled from the neighboring hills, a rude monument, conical in form, and fifty feet in circumference at the base and twelve feet in height" (1995 [1859]:35–36). Among the simple family plots of the Arkansas highlands, such a monument would have seemed especially grand. Here it stood alone in the Meadows, a single headstone on a vast and sprawling grave.

Yet Carleton was not finished. He had the cairn topped off with a red cedar cross, some 24 feet tall. "On the transverse part of the cross," he reported (1995 [1859]:35), "facing towards the north, is an inscription carved deeply in the wood:—VENGEANCE IS MINE! I WILL REPAY, SAITH THE LORD." At the base of the cairn, and again facing north, was this inscription on a granite slab:

HERE
120 MEN, WOMEN AND CHILDREN
WERE MASSACRED IN COLD BLOOD EARLY
IN SEPT. 1857
THEY WERE FROM ARKANSAS.

NOTES

Introduction: Perspectives

1. See Briggs 2006 for a defense of the use of such testimony in historical reconstruction (cf. Bagley et al. 2007, Briggs 2007).
2. Standard procedures were employed to determine the demographic profile of the remains and the minimum number of individuals (MNI). These methods are detailed in Novak and Kopp 2003:88–92.

Chapter 1. Streams

1. Bagley (2002:63) mistakenly has Nancy Mitchell married to Lorenzo Dunlap. Rather, Nancy Dunlap married William C. Mitchell in Tennessee and migrated to Arkansas with him. Nancy's brothers, Lorenzo and Jesse Jr., followed later and married sisters in Madison County (Judy Farris, personal communication, 2003).
2. According to Franz Boas (1894a:761), the American continent was uniquely suited to study changes in morphology, fertility, and stature that had resulted from a "process of slow amalgamation between three distinct races."
3. Family genealogies compiled by Ima Jean Baker Young and kindly provided to me in 2003 by Roy Lee Baker Jr. indicate that Jack's parent were born in North Carolina, their first child was born in Tennessee, their second and third in Kentucky, and the last three children in Alabama. In addition, the 1850 census lists Jack's place of birth as Kentucky (U.S. Bureau of the Census 1850, Schedule 1). Baker (1982:160) and Bagley (2002:63), however, report that Jack was born in North Carolina.
4. Baker (1982:161) recalls six children, but the genealogy compiled by Ima Jean Baker Young (see n. 3) indicates that Mary and John would have had eight children when they left Alabama.
5. Calculated from seven households listed before and seven households listed after the Fancher households (nos. 96 and 97; U.S. Bureau of the Census 1850, Schedule 1, California, County of San Diego, pp. 279 and 280). It is important to note that this census took place in March 1851.

Chapter 2: Confluence

1. Most of the names and ages I use in the demographic analysis are taken from a list compiled by Roger Logan of Harrison, Arkansas. This list was used to inscribe a monument placed near the massacre site in 1990 (see Bagley 2002:370, 374, Appendix). I supplement this list with U.S. census statistics and family genealogies, especially in my assessment of kinship relations.
2. Newspaper reports written after the massacre portray Beller's Stand as the meeting place for all the families on the wagon train (for example, the *Arkansas State Gazette*

and Democrat, 27 February 1858). The Johnson County contingent, however, traveled along the Arkansas River valley and met with the Beller's Stand group in Indian country (Thurston 1877). In addition, it is unlikely that the Benton County group (Alexander Fancher and Huff families) backtracked; instead, they probably waited for the Beller's Stand party to catch up with them on the trail.

3. Calculations are based on age at death. When the wagon train left in April, all individuals would have been five months younger.
4. Malinda Cameron Scott Thurston remembers leaving the Clarksville area on March 29, 1857.
5. Although some confusion exists about the family unit associated with Malinda Cameron and H. D. Scott (see Bagley 2002:65), depositions from Malinda, her son Joel, and brother-in-law George T. Scott seem to clarify the relations (Thurston 1877; Thurston et al. 1911).
6. There seems to be no support for Denton's (2003:98) suggestion that the "Camerons of Carroll County" were "perhaps the wealthiest family" on the wagon train.
7. Unlike Smith and Farmer, Campbell is not listed among the names of those associated with the wagon train (Bagley 2002:388). Campbell's inclusion here is based on oral family histories that have been collected in *Histories of Newton County* (Niswonger 1992).

Chapter 3. Nourishment

1. In his highland sample Bolton (1993:43) also includes the Ouachita Mountains to the south of the Arkansas River.
2. A surprising number of forty-niners tried to bring slaves to work the goldfields. Indeed, some argued that Africans were especially suited to the western landscape. In 1850, for example, Jefferson Davis claimed that "the European races now engaged in working the mines of California sink under the burning heat and sudden changes of the climate, to which the African race are altogether better adapted" (Richards 2007:103).
3. A weaning age of 20 months is consistent with an interbirth interval of 2.3 years, which was calculated for the women on the wagon train from the birth dates of their children.

Chapter 4. Constitution

1. Temple himself apparently died of cholera near Scott's Bluff, Nebraska.
2. Those children with one to three siblings had a 10.3 percent nonsurvival rate; four or more siblings increased nonsurvival to 17.4 percent (Steckel 1988:340).
3. Ideally, the location of the linear enamel defect would be measured and the age of the stress could be calculated (Goodman and Rose 1990; FitzGerald and Rose 2000). In this case the expedited reinterment precluded such measurements and analysis.
4. In general, LDS officials preached that all Christian nations, including England and the United States, sanctioned "whoredoms" by prohibiting plural marriage (see Hardy 2007).

Chapter 5. Domains

1. *Weaner house* (or *weaning house*) is a term that continues to be used in the Ozarks. As defined by one Arkansas native, it is a small house on the family farm that was

occupied by the newlyweds for a number of years while they "weaned" themselves from their parents before moving on to start an independent household.

2. Boone County was carved out of a portion of Carroll County in 1869.
3. $t = -2.08$, $df = 20$, $p = < 0.05$.
4. $t = -2.97$, $df = 22$, $p < 0.01$.
5. These elements were all identified from a sort and associated with a single young adult male based on color, bone density, and morphology. Because the clavicle epiphysis was open, this person would have been younger than 23 years at the time of death (see Figure 5.5).
6. It is important to note that these injuries did not necessarily happen all at the same time. The wounds do have a similar state of healing, however, and the surrounding bone has remodeled to adapt to the change in morphology.

Chapter 6. Epitaph

1. The fragmentary nature of the facial elements precluded use of the preferred multivariate metric assessment of race in the MMM series (Gill and Rhine 1986; Krogman and Iscan 1986; Gill 1998).
2. Platymeria, or the medial-lateral elongation of the proximal femur shaft, was observed in 11 elements. This measurement classified femurs with an index less than 84.9 as platymeric. Native Americans are characterized by platymeric indices of approximately 74 whereas individuals with Caucasian ancestry tend to exhibit a rounder diaphysis and have an index in the mid-80s (Bass 1995). A large degree of interpopulation variation has been found in the expression of platymeria, however, and both mobility and activity patterns can influence the shape of the femur (Ruff 1992).
3. Maxillary second (lateral) incisors at a growth stage of root initial are not included in the standards developed by Moorrees et al. (1963a, b). The crown of this tooth, however, completes development at 5.8 years, and one-fourth of the root has formed by 6.7 years. The stage of root initial was calculated as the mean of these two stages at 6.2 years. Harris and McKee (1990) developed a schedule of tooth calcification that does include maxillary incisors. The stage of root initial, by their standards, corresponds to a mean age of 6.5 years in white males and 5.9 years in white females (s.d. 1.22).
4. In 1896 Hugh Miller's grandson and great-grandson, along with thirty-two of his other descendants, applied to the Cherokee Roll (John Sroka, personal communication, 2007). Their claims to Native American ancestry were based on some degree of relatedness to Hugh, who died in Carroll County, Arkansas, in 1852.
5. For detailed analysis techniques and interpretation of such wounds, see Novak and Kopp 2003.
6. Individual 7 exhibited radiating fractures that suggest a probable gunshot wound, but because of incomplete reconstruction, there was no clearly delineated entry or exit wound. Therefore, this individual is not included in this count.
7. The fragments with identifiable exit wounds were too small to assign age and sex with any confidence, although the density and thickness of the vault fragments suggested that these were most likely adult males.
8. In a survey of historic gunshot victims, Thomas Crist (2006:123) points out that this individual is the only subadult gunshot fatality reported in the archaeological literature.

9. In 1874 Lee was indicted and arrested for his participation in the massacre. His trial began a year later but ended with a hung jury: the eight Mormon jurors voted to acquit, while the four non-Mormons voted to convict. Lee's second trial was held in 1877, and a unanimous jury found him guilty. At the age of 64, Lee was executed by firing squad on March 23, 1877, at Mountain Meadows.
10. Cranial reconstruction was interrupted by the expedited reinterment, and the exact locations of impact were not delineated in these children. The pattern of concentric and linear radiating fractures was useful, however, in determining the general impact locations.
11. There may be a number of reasons for the absence of blade or arrow wounds. First, these weapons may not have been used in the massacre, or they were simply not used to attack any of the individuals in the mass grave. Second, knives and arrows may have been used, but they did not penetrate to the bone (Milner 2005). Finally, carnivore activity and other postmortem factors may have resulted in the loss of skeletal elements that manifest such wounds.
12. Bigler (1998:64 n. 2) points out that this phrase has been recently changed to "pure and delightsome." In fact, this revision was originally made by Joseph Smith in 1840 as he prepared the third American edition of the Book of Mormon for publication; this edition, however, was not adopted by the LDS Church until 1981 (Hugh Stocks, personal communication, 2005).
13. On the prevalence of lynching in the West, especially as it was used against minorities, see Gonzales-Day 2006.

BIBLIOGRAPHY

Tax, Census, and Land Records

Tax records, Arkansas. Microfilm. Family and Church History Department, Church of Jesus Christ of Latter-day Saints, Salt Lake City, Utah.

Benton County, 1855, 1856, 1857.

Carroll County, 1840, 1855, 1856.

Johnson County, 1855, 1856.

Marion County, 1855, 1856.

U.S. Bureau of the Census

1840 Sixth Census. Arkansas, Madison County: Bowen township. Microfilm. Family and Church History Department, Church of Jesus Christ of Latter-day Saints, Salt Lake City, Utah.

1850 Seventh Census.

Schedule 1: Free Inhabitants. Arkansas, Carroll County: Carrollton, Crooked Creek, and Osage townships; Crawford County: Mountain township; and Johnson County: Mulberry and Spadra townships. California, County of San Diego. Microfilm. Family and Church History Department, Church of Jesus Christ of Latter-day Saints, Salt Lake City, Utah.

Schedule 2: Slave Inhabitants. Arkansas. Carroll County Historical Society, http://www.rootsweb.com/~arcchs/Census/1850/1850slaves.html

Schedule 3: Statistics of Mortality. Arkansas. In *1850 Mortality Schedules of Arkansas*, ed. Bobbie Jones (Mrs. Gerald B.) McLane and Capitola Hensley Glazner. Hot Springs National Park, Arkansas.

Schedule 4: Agriculture. Arkansas, Carroll County: Carrollton, Crooked Creek, and Osage townships; Johnson County: Mulberry and Spadra townships. Microfilm. University of Arkansas Library, Fayetteville.

Schedule 6: Social Statistics. Arkansas. In Bureau of the Census Library, *The Seventh Census of the United States, 1850: An Appendix*. Washington, D.C.: Robert Armstrong, Public Printer, 1853.

U.S. Bureau of Land Management. General Land Office Records. Land patents, Benton County, Arkansas, November 15, 1854. Documents 6766 and 7574 (Peter Huff); 6620, 6621, 6622, and 6623 (Alexander Fancher). http://www.glorecords.blm.gov/PatentSearch/.

Works Cited

Abbott, Simon B.

1844 *The Southern Botanic Physician*. Charleston, S.C.: Burges and James.

Aegerter, Ernest E., and John A. Kirkpatrick

1975 *Orthopedic Diseases: Physiology, Pathology, Radiology*. 4th ed. Philadelphia: W. B. Saunders.

Aiken, John

1857 Affidavit Made before Marcus Kate, Notary Public, November 24. San Bernardino, Calif.

Alexander, Thomas G.

2003 *Utah: The Right Place*. Rev. ed. Salt Lake City: Gibbs Smith.

Allured, Janet

1988 Ozark Women and the Companionate Family in the Arkansas Hills, 1879–1910. *Arkansas Historical Quarterly* 47:230–256.

Anderson, Benedict

1991 *Imagined Communities: Reflections on the Origin and Spread of Nationalism*. New York: Verso.

Arnold, Morris S.

2002 Indians and Immigrants in the Arkansas Colonial Era. In *Arkansas: A Narrative History*, ed. Jeannie M. Whayne, Thomas A. DeBlack, George Sabo III, and Morris S. Arnold, pp. 46–74. Fayetteville: University of Arkansas Press.

Arrington, Leonard J., and Davis Bitton

1992 *The Mormon Experience: A History of the Latter-day Saints*. Chicago: University of Illinois Press.

Aufderheide, Arthur C., and Conrado Rodríguez-Martín

1998 *The Cambridge Encyclopedia of Human Paleopathology*. Cambridge: Cambridge University Press.

Bagley, Will

2002 *Blood of the Prophets: Brigham Young and the Massacre at Mountain Meadows*. Norman: University of Oklahoma Press.

In press *"A Long, Rugged, and Weary Road": Life on the Oregon and California Trails, 1840 to 1870*. Washington, D.C.: National Park Service.

Bagley, Will, Polly Aird, John R Alley, David Bigler, Ed Firmage, Ronald L. Holt, Jeffrey Nichols, Shannon A. Novak, W. L. Rusho, and Douglas Seefeldt

2007 Letter to the Editor in Response to Robert H. Briggs 2006. *Utah Historical Quarterly* 75(3):292.

Bailey, Garrick A.

1973 *Changes in Osage Social Organization, 1673–1906*. University of Oregon Anthropological Papers No. 5. Eugene: University of Oregon Press.

Baird, David W.

1980 *The Quapaw Indians: A History of the Downstream People*. Norman: University of Oklahoma Press.

Baker, Roy

1982 One of the Baker Families of Carroll (Boone) County Arkansas. Transcription of taped interview of Jack Baker Holt. *Boone County Historian* 5:160–166.

Baker, Shane A., Richard K. Talbot, and Lane D. Richens

2003 Archaeological Remote Sensing Studies and Emergency Data Recovery at

42WS2504, Washington County, Utah. Brigham Young University Museum of Peoples and Cultures, Technical Series No. 03-8. Provo, Utah: Office of Public Archaeology.

Bancroft, Hubert Howe
1889 *History of Utah, 1540–1886*. San Francisco: History Co.

Barry, Louise (ed.)
1942 Overland to the Goldfields of California in 1852. *Kansas Historical Journal* 11: 255–256.

Bass, William M.
1995 *Human Osteology: A Laboratory and Field Manual*. 4th ed. Columbia: Missouri Archaeological Society.

Battershell, Gary
1999 The Socioeconomic Role of Slavery in the Arkansas Upcountry. *Arkansas Historical Quarterly* 58:45–60.

Beadle, John Hanson
1870 *Life in Utah; or, the Mysteries and Crimes of Mormonism, Being an Exposé of the Secret Rites and Ceremonies of the Latter-day Saints, with a Full and Authentic History of Polygamy and the Mormon Sect from Its Origin to the Present Time*. Philadelphia: National Publishing Co.

Bean, Lee L., Geraldine P. Mineau, and Douglas L. Anderton
1992 High Risk Childbearing: Fertility and Infant Morality on the American Frontier. *Social Science History* 16:337–364.

Beecher, Catharine
1846 *The Evils Suffered by American Women and American Children: The Causes and the Remedy*. New York: Harper and Brothers.

Beidleman, Richard G.
1954 The 1818–1820 Arkansas Journey of Thomas Nuttall. *Arkansas Historical Quarterly* 15:249–259.

Benedict, Russell W.
1951 Story of an Early Settlement in Central Arkansas. Edited by Ted R. Worley. *Arkansas Historical Quarterly* 10:117–137.

Bennett, Swannee
1980 Inventory of an Arkansas Household, 1850–1860. *Ozark Historical Review* 9:1–10.

Berg, Barbara J.
1978 *The Remembered Gate: Origins of American Feminism*. New York: Oxford University Press.

Bigler, David L.
1998 *Forgotten Kingdom: The Mormon Theocracy in the American West, 1847–1896*. Logan: Utah State University Press.

Billingsley, Carolyn Earle
2004 *Communities of Kinship: Antebellum Families and the Settlement of the Cotton Frontier*. Athens: University of Georgia Press.

Billington, Ray Allen
1967 *Westward Expansion: A History of the American Frontier*. 3rd ed. New York: Macmillan.

Binford, Lewis R.
1981 *Bones: Ancient Men and Modern Myths*. New York: Academic Press.

Bishop, William (ed.)
2001 [1877] *Mormonism Unveiled; or, The Life and Confessions of the Late Mormon Bishop, John D. Lee*. Albuquerque, N.M.: Fierra Blanca Publications.
Blevins, Brooks
2002 *Hill Folks: A History of Arkansas Ozarkers and Their Image*. Chapel Hill: University of North Carolina Press.
Bloch, Maurice
1974 Symbols, Song, Dance, and Features of Articulation: Is Religion an Extreme Form of Traditional Authority? *European Journal of Sociology* 15:55–81.
1992 *Prey into Hunter: The Politics of Religious Experience*. Cambridge: Cambridge University Press.
Bloch, Maurice, and Jonathan Perry (eds.)
1982 *Death and the Regeneration of Life*. Cambridge: Cambridge University Press.
Boas, Franz
1894a The Half-Blood Indian: An Anthropometric Study. *Popular Science Monthly* 45:761–763.
1894b Human Faculty as Determined by Race. *Proceedings of the American Association for the Advancement of Science* 43:301–327. Reprinted in *A Franz Boas Reader: The Shaping of American Anthropology, 1883–1911*, ed. George W. Stocking Jr., pp. 221–242. Chicago: University of Chicago Press, 1974.
Bode, Frederick A.
1995 A Common Sphere: White Evangelicals and Gender in Antebellum Georgia. *Georgia Historical Quarterly* 79:775–809.
Bolton, Conevery A.
1991 "A sister's consolations": Women, Health, and Community in Early Arkansas, 1810–1860. *Arkansas Historical Quarterly* 50:271–291.
Bolton, S. Charles
1984 Economic Inequality in the Arkansas Territory. *Journal of Interdisciplinary History* 14:619–633.
1993 *Territorial Ambitions: Land and Society in Arkansas, 1800–1840*. Fayetteville: University of Arkansas Press.
1998 *Arkansas, 1800–1860: Remote and Restless*. Fayetteville: University of Arkansas Press.
2005 Jeffersonian Indian Removal and the Emergence of Arkansas Territory. In *A Whole Country in Commotion: The Louisiana Purchase and the American Southwest*, ed. Patrick G. Williams, S. Charles Bolton, and Jeannie M. Whayne, pp. 77–90. Fayetteville: University of Arkansas Press.
Bordin, Ruth
1981 *Woman and Temperance: The Quest for Power and Liberty, 1873–1900*. Philadelphia: Temple University Press.
Briggs, Robert H.
2006 The Mountain Meadows Massacre: An Analytical Narrative Based on Participant Confessions. *Utah Historical Quarterly* 74(4):313–333.
2007 Letter to the Editor in Response to Will Bagley et al. 2007. *Utah Historical Quarterly* 75(3):293–295.
Brinkley, Garland L.
1997 The Decline in Southern Agricultural Output, 1860–1880. *Journal of Economic History* 57:116–138.

Brooks, Juanita
1962 *The Mountain Meadows Massacre*. Reprint. Norman: University of Oklahoma Press. Originally published by Stanford University Press, 1950.
1992 [1972] *John Doyle Lee: Zealot, Pioneer Builder, Scapegoat*. Logan: Utah State University Press.
Brooks, Noah
1902 The Plains Across. *Century Magazine* 63 (April 1902): 803–820.
Brown, Keith M.
1986 *Bloodfeud in Scotland, 1573–1625: Violence, Justice, and Politics in an Early Modern Society*. Edinburgh: John Donald Publishers.
Bryant, F. Carlene
1981 *We're All Kin: A Cultural Study of a Mountain Neighborhood*. Knoxville: University of Tennessee Press.
Bullock, Steven C.
1996 *Revolutionary Brotherhood: Freemasonry and the Transformation of the American Social Order, 1730–1840*. Chapel Hill: University of North Carolina Press.
Campbell, Randolph B.
1987 Planters and Plain Folks: The Social Structure of the Antebellum South. In *Interpreting Southern History: Historiographical Essays in Honor of Sanford W. Higginbotham*, ed. John B. Boles and Evelyn Thomas Nolen, pp. 48–77. Baton Rouge: Louisiana State University Press.
Carbonell, V. M.
1963 Variations in the Frequency of Shovel-Shaped Incisors in Different Populations. In *Dental Anthropology*, ed. D. R. Brothwell, pp. 211–234. London: Pergamon Press.
Carey, Anthony Gene
2001 Frank L. Owsley's *Plain Folk of the Old South* after Fifty Years. In *Reading Southern History: Essays on Interpreters and Interpretations*, ed. Glenn Feldman, pp. 49–60. Tuscaloosa: University of Alabama Press.
Carleton, James Henry
1943 [1845] *The Prairie Logbooks*. Edited by Louis Pelzer. Chicago: Caxton Club.
1995 [1859] *Special Report on the Mountain Meadows Massacre*. 57th Cong., 1st sess., H. Doc. 605. Washington, D.C. Spokane, Wash.: Arthur H. Clark.
Carnes, Mark C.
1989 *Secret Ritual and Manhood in Victorian America*. New Haven, Conn.: Yale University Press.
Carter, Clarence Edwin (ed.)
1948 Account of Indian Tribes. 29 September. In *The Territorial Papers of the United States*, vol. 13. Washington, D.C.: U.S. Government Printing Office.
Cates, Nancy Huff
1875 Letter. In "The Mountain Meadow Massacre: Statement of One of the Few Survivors." *Daily Arkansas Gazette*, 1 September.
Chambers, J. S.
1938 *The Conquest of Cholera: America's Greatest Scourge*. New York: Macmillan.
Clawson, Mary Ann
1989 *Constructing Brotherhood: Class, Gender, and Fraternalism*. Princeton, N.J.: Princeton University Press.

Clifford, James

1997 *Routes: Travel and Translation in the Late Twentieth Century.* Cambridge, Mass.: Harvard University Press.

Coates, Lawrence G.

n.d. The Fancher-Baker Train: From Salt Lake to Mountain Meadows. Ms. on file, Special Collections, Browning Library, Dixie College, St. George, Utah.

Coelho, Philip R. P., and Robert A. McGuire

1998 An Exploratory Essay on the Impact of Diseases upon the Interpretation of American Slavery. In *The Biological Standard of Living in Comparative Perspective,* ed. John Komlos and Joerg Baten, pp. 181–189. Stuttgart: Steiner.

Cohen, Daniel A.

1993 *Pillars of Salt, Monuments of Grace: New England Crime Literature and the Origins of American Popular Culture, 1674–1860.* New York: Oxford University Press.

2003 Blood Will Out: Sensationalism, Horror, and the Roots of American Crime Literature. In *Mortal Remains: Death in Early America,* ed. Nancy Isenberg and Andrew Burstein, pp. 31–55. Philadelphia: University of Pennsylvania Press.

Coleman, James S.

1990 *Foundations of Social Theory.* Cambridge, Mass.: Harvard University Press.

Colton, Calvin

1844 *Junius Tracts, VII: Capital and Labor.* New York.

Condon, K., J. L. Becker, J. R. Hoffman, and C. Condon

1994 Dental and Skeletal Indicators of a Congenital Treponematosis. *American Journal of Physical Anthropology,* Supplement 17:73.

Condran, Gretchin, and Eileen Crimmins

1979 A Description and Evaluation of Mortality Data in the Federal Census: 1850–1900. *Historical Methods* 12:1-23.

Connors, Thomas G.

2003 The Romantic Landscape: Washington Irving, Sleepy Hollow, and the Rural Cemetery Movement. In *Mortal Remains: Death in Early America,* ed. Nancy Isenberg and Andrew Burstein, pp. 187–203. Philadelphia: University of Pennsylvania Press.

Cott, Nancy F.

1977 *The Bonds of Womanhood: "Women's Sphere" in New England, 1780–1835.* New Haven, Conn.: Yale University Press.

Courtwright, David T.

1991 Disease, Death, and Disorder on the American Frontier. *Journal of the History of Medicine* 46:457–492.

1996 *Violent Land: Single Men and Social Disorder from the Frontier to the Inner City.* Cambridge, Mass.: Harvard University Press.

Craddock, Susan

1995 Sewers and Scapegoats: Spatial Metaphors of Smallpox in Nineteenth Century San Francisco. *Social Science and Medicine* 41:957–968.

Cradlebaugh, John

1863 Utah and the Mormons: Speech of Hon. John Cradlebaugh, of Nevada, on the Admissions of Utah as a State. Delivered in the House of Representatives, 7 February 1863. Privately printed.

Crist, Thomas A.
2006 The Good, the Bad, and the Ugly: Bioarchaeology and the Modern Gun Culture Debate. *Historical Archaeology* 40:109–130.
Cross, Whitney R.
1950 *The Burned-Over District: The Social and Intellectual History of Enthusiastic Religion in Western New York, 1800–1850*. New York: Harper and Row.
Cummings, Richard D.
1941 *The American and His Food: A History of Food Habits in the United States*. Chicago: University of Chicago Press.
Cutress, T. W., and G. W. Suckling
1982 The Assessment of Non-carious Defects of Enamel. *International Dental Journal* 32:117–122.
Daily Alta California
1857*a* The Immigrant Massacre. 17 October.
1857*b* Letter from Angel's Camp. 1 November.
Davidson, James M., Jerome C. Rose, Myron P. Gutmann, Michael R. Haines, Keith Condon, and Cindy Condon
2002 The Quality of African-American Life in the Old Southwest near the Turn of the Twentieth Century. In *The Backbone of History: Health and Nutrition in the Western Hemisphere*, ed. Richard H. Steckel and Jerome C. Rose, pp. 226–277. Cambridge: Cambridge University Press.
Davies, Douglas
1989 Mormon History, Identity, and Faith Community. In *History and Ethnicity*, ed. Elizabeth Tonkin, Maryon McDonald, and Malcolm Chapman, pp. 168–182. London: Routledge.
DeBlack, Thomas A.
2002 Prosperity and Peril: Arkansas in the Late Antebellum Period. In *Arkansas: A Narrative History*, ed. Jeannie M. Whayne, Thomas A. DeBlack, George Sabo III, and Morris S. Arnold, pp. 135–165. Fayetteville: University of Arkansas Press.
DeBow, James D. B.
1854 *Statistical View of the United States,... Being a Compendium of the Seventh Census*. Washington, D.C.: A.O.P Nicholson.
Deloria, Philip J.
1998 *Playing Indian*. New Haven, Conn.: Yale University Press.
Denton, Sally
2003 *American Massacre: The Tragedy at Mountain Meadows, September 1857*. New York: Alfred A. Knopf.
Dickinson, Everard B.
1850 Letter, North Fork, Arkansas, to Mr. and Mrs. Philo Dickinson, Springfield, Mass., 21 June 1850, box 1, file 54. Heiskell Small Manuscripts, University of Arkansas, Little Rock.
Din, Gilbert C.
1995 Between a Rock and a Hard Place: The Indian Trade in Spanish Arkansas. In *Cultural Encounters in the Early South: Indians and Europeans in Arkansas*, ed. Jeannie Whayne, pp. 112–130. Fayetteville: University of Arkansas Press.

Dorn, Michael L.
2000 (In)temperate Zones: Daniel Drake's Medico-Moral Geographies of Urban Life in the Trans-Appalachian American West. *Journal of the History of Medicine* 55:256–291.
Doyle, Don Harrison
1979 The *Social Order of a Frontier Community: Jacksonville, Illinois, 1825–1870*. Urbana: University of Illinois Press.
Drake, Daniel
1832 A *Practical Treatise on the History, Prevention, and Treatment of Epidemic Cholera*. Cincinnati: Corey and Fairbank.
1948 [1870] *Pioneer Life in Kentucky, 1785–1800*. New York: Henry Schuman.
1971 [1850] *A Systematic Treatise, Historical, Etiological, and Practical, on the Principal Diseases of the Interior Valley of North America*. New York: Lenox Hill.
Drewer, Thomas
1859 Letter to Dr. Abram Clauds, Camp Floyd, 31 March. Partial transcription "of the Contents of a Letter from Camp Floyd Utah Territory" in Paul C. Rohloff Mormon Collection. Copy in Caroline Parry Woolley Collection. Special Collections, Gerald R. Sherratt Library, Southern Utah University, Cedar City.
Duffy, John
1971 Social Impact of Disease in the Late 19th Century. *Bulletin of the New York Academy of Medicine* 47:797–811.
Dumenil, Lynn
1984 *Freemasonry and American Culture, 1880–1930*. Princeton, N.J.: Princeton University Press.
Dunn, F. L.
1965 On the Antiquity of Malaria in the Western Hemisphere. *Human Biology* 37:385–393.
Duval, Kathleen
2005 Could Louisiana Have Become an Hispano-Indian Republic? In *A Whole Country in Commotion: The Louisiana Purchase and the American Southwest*, ed. Patrick G. Williams, S. Charles Bolton, and Jeannie M. Whayne, pp. 41–55. Fayetteville: University of Arkansas Press.
Eaton, Herbert
1974 *The Overland Trail to California in 1852*. New York: G. P. Putnam's Sons.
Elson, Ruth Miller
1964 *Guardians of Tradition: American Schoolbooks of the Nineteenth Century*. Lincoln: University of Nebraska Press.
Ericksen, Karen Paige, and Heather Horton
1992 Blood Feuds: Cross-cultural Variation in Kin Group Vengeance. *Behavioral Science Research* 26:57–85.
Etting, John
1993 Hookworm Disease. In *The Cambridge World History of Human Disease*, ed. Kenneth F. Kiple, pp. 784–788. New York: Cambridge University Press.
Evans, Rebecca Dunlap
1897 Mountain Meadows Massacre...Related by One of the Survivors. *Fort Smith Elevator*, 20 August.

Fancher, Burr

1999 *Westward with the Sun*. Albany, Ore.: Fancher & Associates.

2006 *Captain Alexander Fancher: Adventurer, Drover, Wagon Master and Victim of the Mountain Meadows Massacre*. Portland, Ore.: Inkwater Press.

Fancher, Lynn-Marie

2005 Mariah Sneed Fancher...the Lady under the Tree. *Carroll County Historical Quarterly* 50:25–27.

Faragher, John Mack

1986 *Sugar Creek: Life on the Illinois Prairie*. New Haven, Conn.: Yale University Press.

2001 *Women and Men on the Overland Trail*. 2nd ed. New Haven, Conn.: Yale University Press.

Farrell, James J.

1980 *Inventing the American Way of Death, 1830–1920*. Philadelphia: Temple University Press.

Ferreira, L. F., A. J. G. de Araújo, and U. E. C. Confalonieri

1983 The Finding of Helminth Eggs in a Brazilian Mummy. *Transactions of the Royal Society of Tropical Medicine and Hygiene* 77:565–566.

Ferreira, L. F., A. J. G. de Araújo, U. Confalonieri, M. Chamee, and R. M. Ribeiro

1987 Encontro de ovos de ancilostomideos en coprolitos humano datados de 7230 ± 80 anos, Piaui, Brasil. *Ánales Académia Brasileira de Ciéncials* 59:280–281.

Finger, John R.

2001 *Tennessee Frontiers: Three Regions in Transition*. Bloomington: Indiana University Press.

Fischer, David Hackett

1989 *Albion's Seed: Four British Folkways in America*. New York: Oxford University Press.

Fischer, David Hackett, and James C. Kelly

2000 *Bound Away: Virginia and the Westward Movement*. Charlottesville: University Press of Virginia.

Fisher, J.

1995 Bone Surface Modification in Zooarchaeology. *Journal of Archaeological Method and Theory* 2:7–68.

FitzGerald, Charles M., and Jerome C. Rose

2000 Reading between the Lines: Dental Development and Subadult Age Assessment Using the Microstructural Growth Markers of Teeth. In *Biological Anthropology of the Human Skeleton*, ed. M. A. Katzenberg and S. R. Saunders, pp. 163–186. New York: Wiley-Liss.

Flanner, Henry Beeson

1843 Henry Beeson Flanner Family Correspondence. Indiana Historical Society, Indianapolis.

Flint, Timothy

1828 *A Condensed Geography and History of the Western States or the Mississippi Valley*. Cincinnati: W. M. and O. Farnsworth.

Flippin, W. B.

1958 The Tutt and Everett War in Marion County. *Arkansas Historical Quarterly* 17: 155–163.

Flyvbjerg, Bent

2001 *Making Social Science Matter: Why Social Inquiry Fails and How It Can Succeed Again.* Cambridge: Cambridge University Press.

French, Stanley

1975 The Cemetery as Cultural Institution: The Establishment of Mount Auburn and the "Rural Cemetery" Movement. In *Death in America*, ed. David E. Stannard, pp. 69–91. Philadelphia: University of Pennsylvania Press.

Friedman, Jean E.

1986 *The Enclosed Garden: Women in the Evangelical South.* Chapel Hill: University of North Carolina Press.

Galloway, Alison (ed.)

1999 *Broken Bones: Anthropological Analysis of Blunt Force Trauma.* Springfield, Ill.: Charles C. Thomas.

Gerhard, W. W.

1842 *Lectures on the Diagnosis, Pathology, and Treatment of Disease of the Chest.* Philadelphia.

Gerlach, Luther P., and Virginia H. Hine

1970 *People, Power, and Change: Movements of Social Transformation.* Indianapolis.

Gibbs, Josiah

1910 *The Mountain Meadows Massacre.* Salt Lake City: Salt Lake Tribune Publishing Co.

Gill, George W.

1994 Skeletal Injuries of Pioneers. In *Skeletal Biology in the Great Plains: Migration, Warfare, Health, and Subsistence*, ed. Douglas W. Owsley and Richard L. Jantz, pp. 159–172. Washington, D.C.: Smithsonian Institution Press.

1998 Craniofacial Criteria in the Skeletal Attribution of Race. In *Forensic Osteology*, 2nd ed., ed. K. J. Reichs, pp. 293–315. Springfield, Ill.: Charles C. Thomas.

Gill, George W., and J. S. Rhine (eds.)

1986 *Skeletal Race Identification: New Approaches in Forensic Anthropology.* Albuquerque, N.M.: Maxwell Museum.

Goen, Clarence C.

1988 Scenario for Secession: Denominational Schisms and the Coming of the Civil War. In *Varieties of Southern Religious Experience*, ed. Samuel S. Hill, pp. 11–23. Baton Rouge: Louisiana State University Press.

Goodman, Alan H., and Debra L. Martin

2002 Reconstructing Health Profiles from Skeletal Remains. In *The Backbone of History: Health and Nutrition in the Western Hemisphere*, ed. Richard H. Steckel and Jerome C. Rose, pp. 11–60. Cambridge: Cambridge University Press.

Goodman, Alan H., and Jerome C. Rose

1990 Assessment of Systemic Physiological Perturbation from Dental Enamel Hypoplasias and Associated Histological Structures. *Year Book of Physical Anthropology* 33:59–110.

Goodman, Paul

1988 *Towards a Christian Republic: Antimasonry and the Great Transition in New England, 1826–1836.* New York: Oxford University Press.

Goodspeed Publishing Co.
1889 *The Goodspeed Biographical and Historical Memoirs of Northwestern Arkansas.* Chicago: Goodspeed Publishing Co.
Gonzales-Day, Ken
2006 *Lynching in the West, 1850–1935.* Durham, N.C.: Duke University Press.
Gordon, Sarah Barringer
2002 *The Mormon Question: Polygamy and Constitutional Conflict in Nineteenth-Century America.* Chapel Hill: University of North Carolina Press.
Graustein, Jeannette E.
1967 *Thomas Nuttall, Naturalist: Explorations in America, 1801–1841.* Cambridge, Mass.: Harvard University Press.
Grob, Gerald N.
2002 *The Deadly Truth: A History of Disease in America.* Cambridge, Mass.: Harvard University Press.
Gunn, John
1986 [1830] *Gunn's Domestic Medicine.* Knoxville: University of Tennessee Press.
Gunnison, John W.
1856 The *Mormons, or, Latter-Day Saints, in the Valley of the Great Salt Lake.* Philadelphia.
Gurdjian, E. S.
1975 *Impact Head Injury: Mechanistic, Clinical, and Preventive Correlations.* Springfield, Ill.: Charles C. Thomas.
Haglund, William D.
1997 Dogs and Coyotes: Postmortem Involvement with Human Remains. In *Forensic Taphonomy: The Postmortem Fate of Human Remains,* ed. W. D. Haglund and M. H. Sorg, pp. 367–382. Boca Raton, Fla.: CRC Press.
Haines, Michael R.
1979 The Use of Model Life Tables to Estimate Mortality for the United States in the Late Nineteenth Century. *Demography* 16:289–312.
1998 Health, Height, Nutrition, and Mortality: Evidence on the "Antebellum Puzzle" from Union Army Recruits for New York State and the United States. In *The Biological Standard of Living in Comparative Perspective,* ed. John Komlos and Joerg Baten, pp. 155–180. Stuttgart: Steiner.
Haines, Michael R., Lee A. Craig, and Thomas Weiss
2003 The Short and the Dead: Nutrition, Mortality, and the "Antebellum Puzzle" in the United States. *Journal of Economic History* 63:382–413.
Haller, John S., Jr.
1994 *Medical Protestants: The Eclectics in American Medicine, 1825–1939.* Carbondale: Southern Illinois University Press.
Hannerz, Ulf
1990 Cosmopolitans and Locals in World Culture. *Theory, Culture, and Society* 7: 237–251.
Hardy, B. Carmon (ed.)
2007 *The Works of Abraham: Mormon Polygamy; Sources on Its Origin, Thought, and Practice.* Norman, Okla.: Arthur H. Clark.

Harkins, Anthony
2004 *Hillbilly: A Cultural History of an American Icon*. New York: Oxford University Press.
Harrell, David Edwin, Jr.
1988 The Evolution of Plain-Folk Religion in the South, 1835–1920. In *Varieties of Southern Religious Experience*, ed. Samuel S. Hill, pp. 24–51. Baton Rouge: Louisiana State University Press.
Harris, Edward F., and Joy H. McKee
1990 Tooth Mineralization Standards for Blacks and Whites from the Middle Southern United States. *Journal of Forensic Sciences* 34:859–872.
Hatfield, Gabrielle
2004 *Encyclopedia of Folk Medicine: Old World and New World Traditions*. Santa Barbara, Calif.: ABC-CLIO.
Hawthorne, Nathaniel
1882 [1832] *The Complete Works of Nathaniel Hawthorne: Mosses from an Old Manse*. Boston: Houghton Mifflin.
Haynes, G.
1980 Prey Bones and Predators: Potential Ecological Information from Analysis of Bone Sites. *Ossa* 7:75–97.
Hays, J. N.
1998 *The Burden of Disease: Epidemics and Human Response in Western History*. New Brunswick, N.J.: Rutgers University Press.
Helms, Mary W.
1988 *Ulysses' Sail: An Ethnographic Odyssey of Power, Knowledge, and Geographical Distance*. Princeton, N.J.: Princeton University Press.
Herdt, Gilbert
2003 *Secrecy and Cultural Reality: Utopian Ideologies of the New Guinea Men's House*. Ann Arbor: University of Michigan Press.
Heyrman, Christine Leigh
1997 *Southern Cross: The Beginnings of the Bible Belt*. New York: Alfred A. Knopf.
Higbee, John M.
1894 Higbee Statements. Mountain Meadows File, LDS Archives, Salt Lake City, Utah.
Higgins, Rosanne L., Michael R. Haines, Lorena Walsh, and Joyce E. Sirianni
2002 The Poor in the Mid-Nineteenth-Century Northeastern United States: Evidence from the Monroe County Almshouse, Rochester, New York. In *The Backbone of History: Health and Nutrition in the Western Hemisphere*, ed. Richard H. Steckel and Jerome C. Rose, pp. 162–184. Cambridge: Cambridge University Press.
Hilliard, Sam Bowers
1972 *Hog Meat and Hoecake: Food Supply in the Old South, 1840–1860*. Carbondale: Southern Illinois University Press.
Hillson, Simon
1996 *Dental Anthropology*. Cambridge: Cambridge University Press.
Hobsbawm, Eric J.
1965 *Primitive Rebels*. New York: Norton.

Hofstadter, Richard
1973 *America in 1750: A Social Portrait.* New York: Vintage.
Holt, Jack Baker
1982 One of the Baker Families of Carroll (Boone) County Arkansas. Edited transcript of an interview conducted by Roy L. Baker Jr. *Boone County Historian* 5(3):160–166.
Holt, Ronald L.
1992 *Beneath These Red Cliffs: An Ethnohistory of the Utah Paiutes.* Albuquerque: University of New Mexico Press.
Homer, Michael W.
1994 Similarity of Priesthood in Masonry: The Relationship between Freemasonry and Mormonism. *Dialogue* 27:1–113.
Horowitz, Roger
2006 *Putting Meat on the American Table: Taste, Technology, Transformation.* Baltimore: Johns Hopkins University Press.
Horsman, Reginald
1981 *Race and Manifest Destiny: The Origins of American Racial Anglo-Saxonism.* Cambridge, Mass.: Harvard University Press.
Humphreys, Margaret
1992 *Yellow Fever and the South.* Baltimore: Johns Hopkins University Press.
2001 *Malaria: Poverty, Race, and Public Health in the United States.* Baltimore: Johns Hopkins University Press.
Hutchinson, Dale L., and Rebecca Richman
2006 Regional, Social, and Evolutionary Perspectives on Treponemal Infection in the Southeastern United States. *American Journal of Physical Anthropology* 129: 544–558.
Isenberg, Nancy, and Andrew Burstein
2003 Introduction. In *Mortal Remains: Death in Early America,* ed. Nancy Isenberg and Andrew Burstein, pp. 1–13. Philadelphia: University of Pennsylvania Press.
Jacob, Margaret C.
2006 *The Origins of Freemasonry: Facts and Fictions.* Philadelphia: University of Pennsylvania Press.
Jacobson, Matthew Frye
1998 *Whiteness of a Different Color: European Immigrants and the Alchemy of Race.* Cambridge, Mass.: Harvard University Press.
Jeane, D. Gregory
1992 The Upland South Folk Cemetery Complex: Some Suggestions of Origin. In *Cemeteries and Gravemarkers: Voices of American Culture,* ed. Richard E. Meyer, pp. 107–136. Logan: Utah State University Press.
Jefferson, Thomas
1984 *Writings.* The Library of America. New York: Literary Classics of the United States.
Jeffrey, Julie Roy
1998 *Frontier Women: "Civilizing" the West? 1840–1880.* Rev. ed. New York: Hill and Wang.

Jones, Michael Owen

1967 Climate and Disease: The Traveler Describes America. *Bulletin of the History of Medicine* 41:254–266.

Keefe, James F., and Lynn Morrow (eds.)

1988 *A Connecticut Yankee in the Frontier Ozarks: The Writings of Theodore Pease Russell.* Columbia: University of Missouri Press.

Keeney, Elizabeth Barnaby

1989 Unless Powerful Sick: Domestic Medicine in the Old South. In *Science and Medicine in the Old South,* ed. Ronald L. Numbers and Todd L. Savitt, pp. 276–294. Baton Rouge: Louisiana State University Press.

Kelly, Catherine E.

2005 "Well bred country people": Sociability, Social Networks, and the Creation of a Provincial Middle Class, 1820–1860. In *Cultural Change and the Market Revolution in America, 1789–1860,* ed. Scott C. Martin, pp. 111–141. Lanham, Md.: Rowman and Littlefield.

Kelly, M., and M. Micozzi

1984 Rib Lesions in Chronic Pulmonary Tuberculosis. *American Journal of Physical Anthropology* 65:381–387.

Kenney, Scott G. (ed.)

1983 *Wilford Woodruff's Journal.* 10 vols. Midvale, Utah: Signature Books.

Key, Joseph Patrick

2005 "Outcasts upon the world": The Louisiana Purchase and the Quapaws. In *A Whole Country in Commotion: The Louisiana Purchase and the American Southwest,* ed. Patrick G. Williams, S. Charles Bolton, and Jeannie M. Whayne, pp. 91–105. Fayetteville: University of Arkansas Press.

Kiple, Kenneth F., and V. H. King

1981 *Another Dimension to the Black Diaspora.* Cambridge: Cambridge University Press.

Kleinberg, S. J.

1999 *Women in the United States, 1830–1945.* New Brunswick, N.J.: Rutgers University Press.

Knack, Martha C.

2001 *Boundaries Between: The Southern Paiutes, 1775–1995.* Lincoln: University of Nebraska Press.

Knight, Amelia Stewart

1928 [1853] Diary of an Oregon Pioneer of 1853. *Transactions of the Oregon Pioneer Association,* pp. 38–56.

Knight, Edgar W.

1922 *Public Education in the South.* Boston: Ginn.

Komlos, John

1987 The Height and Weight of West Point Cadets: Dietary Change in Antebellum America. *Journal of Economic History* 47:897–927.

1996 Anomalies in Economic History: Reflections on the Antebellum Puzzle. *Journal of Economic History* 56:202–214.

1998 Shrinking in a Growing Economy? The Mystery of Physical Stature during the Industrial Revolution. *Journal of Economic History* 53:779–802.

Krakauer, Jon
2003 *Under the Banner of Heaven: A Story of Violent Faith.* New York: Anchor Books.
Krogman, Wilton Marion, and Mehmet Yasar Iscan
1986 *The Human Skeleton in Forensic Medicine.* 2nd ed. Springfield, Ill.: Charles C. Thomas.
Labaree, Benjamin Woods
1964 *The Boston Tea Party.* New York: Oxford.
Laderman, Gary
1996 *The Sacred Remains: American Attitudes toward Death, 1799–1883.* New Haven, Conn.: Yale University Press.
Lair, Jim
1983 *An Outlander's History of Carroll County, Arkansas.* Marceline, Mo.: Walsworth.
Lair, Jim (ed.)
1991 *Carroll County Families: These Were the First.* Berryville, Ark.: Carroll County Historical and Genealogical Society.
Langford, Ella Molloy
1998 [1921] *History of Johnson County, Arkansas: The First Hundred Years.* 5th ed. Clarksville, Ark.: Johnson County Historical Society.
Lankford, George E.
1977 The Cherokee Sojourn in North Arkansas. *Independence County Chronicle* 18: 2–19.
1999 Shawnee Convergence: Immigrant Indians in the Ozarks. *Arkansas Historical Quarterly* 58:390–413.
Larimer, Ted, and V. L. Mike Mahoney
2003 A Short History of Yell Lodge No. 64 F. & A.M. *Carroll County Historical Quarterly* 48:153.
Larsen, Clark S.
1997 *Bioarchaeology: Interpreting Behavior from the Human Skeleton.* New York: Cambridge University Press.
Larsen, Clark Spencer, Joseph Craig, Leslie E. Sering, Margaret J. Schoeninger, Katherine F. Russell, Dale L. Hutchinson, and Matthew A. Williamson
1995 Cross Homestead: Life and Death on the Midwestern Frontier. In *Bodies of Evidence: Reconstructing History through Skeletal Analysis,* edited by Anne L. Grauer, pp. 139–159. New York: Wiley-Liss.
Leavitt, Judith W. and Ronald L. Numbers (eds.)
1997 *Sickness and Health in America: Readings in the History of Medicine.* Madison: University of Wisconsin Press.
Lee, John D.
2001 [1877] *Mormonism Unveiled.* Reprint. Albuquerque, N.M.: Fierra Blanca Publications.
Levy, JoAnn
1990 *They Saw the Elephant: Women in the California Gold Rush.* Hamden, Conn.: Archon.
Lewis, Mary E.
2007 *The Bioarchaeology of Children: Perspectives from Biological and Forensic Anthropology.* Cambridge: Cambridge University Press.

Linden-Ward, Blanche

1992 Strange but Genteel Pleasure Grounds: Tourist and Leisure Uses of Nineteenth-Century Rural Cemeteries. In *Cemeteries and Gravemarkers: Voices of American Culture*, ed. Richard E. Meyer, pp. 294–328. Logan: Utah State University Press.

Lipson, Dorothy A.

1977 *Freemasonry in Federalist Connecticut, 1789–1835*. Princeton, N.J.: Princeton University Press.

Little, Barbara J., Kim M. Lanphear, and Douglas W. Owsley

1992 Mortuary Display and Status in a Nineteenth-Century Anglo-American Cemetery in Manassas, Virginia. *American Antiquity* 57(3):397–418.

Logan, Roger V., Jr.

1978 *History of the North Arkansas Baptist Association*. Harrison, Ark.

1992 New Light on the Mountain Meadows Caravan. *Utah Historical Quarterly* 60: 224–237.

1998 A Short History of Boone County, Arkansas. In *History of Boone County, Arkansas*, ed. Boone County Historical and Railroad Society, pp. 6–85. Paducah, Ky.: Turner Publishing.

Los Angeles Star

1857*a* The Late Horrible Massacre. 17 October.

1857*b* More Outrages on the Plains!! 24 October.

Lyman, R. Lee

1994 *Vertebrate Taphonomy*. New York: Cambridge University Press.

Mann, R. W., and S. P. Murphy

1990 *Regional Atlas of Bone Disease: A Guide to Pathologic and Normal Variation in the Human Skeleton*. Springfield, Ill.: Charles C. Thomas.

Mathews, John Joseph

1961 *The Osages: Children of the Middle Waters*. Tulsa: University of Oklahoma Press.

Mattes, Merrill J.

1969 *The Great Platte River Road*. Lincoln: Nebraska State Historical Society.

1977 The Gold Rush Mania: Victims and Survivors. *Nebraska Medical Journal* 6:72–77.

May, Dean L.

1980 Mormons. In *Harvard Encyclopedia of American Ethnic Groups*, ed. Stephan Thernstrom, pp. 720–730. Cambridge, Mass.: Harvard University Press, Belknap Press.

McArthur, Priscilla

1986 *Arkansas in the Gold Rush*. Little Rock, Ark.: August House.

McDonald, Forrest, and Ellen Shapiro McDonald

1980 The Ethnic Origins of the American People, 1790. *William and Mary Quarterly* 37:179–199.

McEuen, Douglas

1996 *The Legend of Francis Marion Poteet and the Mountain Meadows Massacre: History of the Poteet Family*. Pleasanton, Tex.: Zabava Printing.

McLoughlin, William G.

1986 *Cherokee Renascence in the New Republic*. Princeton, N.J.: Princeton University Press.

McMillen, Sally
1990 Obstetrics in Antebellum Arkansas: Women and Doctors in a New State. In *Contributions to Arkansas Medical History: History of Medicine Associates Research Award Papers, 1986–1987*, pp. 64–88. Charlotte, N.C.: History of Medicine Associates.
McMurtry, Larry
2005 *Oh What a Slaughter: Massacres in the American West, 1846–1890*. New York: Simon and Schuster.
McNeill, William H.
1992 *The Global Condition: Conquerors, Catastrophes, and Community*. Princeton, N.J.: Princeton University Press.
1998 *Plagues and Peoples*. New York: Anchor Books.
McNeilly, Donald P.
2000 *The Old South Frontier: Cotton Plantations and the Formation of Arkansas Society, 1819–1861*. Fayetteville: University of Arkansas Press.
McWhiney, Grady
1988 *Cracker Culture: Celtic Ways in the Old South*. Tuscaloosa: University of Alabama Press.
Meinig, D. W.
1986 *The Shaping of America: A Geographical Perspective on 500 Years of History*. Vol. 1, *Atlantic America, 1492–1800*. New Haven, Conn.: Yale University Press.
The Shaping of America: A Geographical Perspective on 500 Years of History. Vol. 2, *Continental America, 1800–1867*. New Haven, Conn.: Yale University Press.
Merbs, Charles R.
1992 A New World of Infectious Disease. *Yearbook of Physical Anthropology* 35:3–42.
Merrill, Michael
1977 Cash Is Good to Eat: Self-sufficiency and Exchange in the Rural Economy of the United States. *Radical History Review* 4:42–71.
Merton, Richard K.
1968 Patterns of Influence: Local and Cosmopolitan Influentials. In *Social Theory and Social Structure*, enlarged ed., pp. 441–474. New York: Free Press.
Milner, George R.
2005 Nineteenth-Century Arrow Wounds and Perceptions of Prehistoric Warfare. *American Antiquity* 70:144–156.
Mintz, Sidney W.
1985 *Sweetness and Power: The Place of Sugar in Modern History*. New York: Viking.
Mitchell, Sallie [Sarah Francis] Baker
1940 The Mountain Meadows Massacre—An Episode on the Road to Zion. *American Weekly*, 1 September.
Moffatt, Walter
1951 Medicine and Dentistry in Pioneer Arkansas. *Arkansas Historical Quarterly* 10: 89–94.
1954 Transportation in Arkansas, 1819–1840. *Arkansas Historical Quarterly* 15:187–201.
Moneyhon, Carl H.
1994 *The Impact of the Civil War and Reconstruction on Arkansas: Persistence in the Midst of Ruin*. Baton Rouge: Louisiana State University Press.

Monks, William
1907 *A History of Southern Missouri and Northern Arkansas.* West Plains, Missouri.
Mooney, James
1975 *Historical Sketch of the Cherokee.* Chicago: Aldine.
2005 *Historical Sketch of the Cherokee.* New Brunswick, N.J.: Transaction Publishers.
Moore, R. Laurence
1986 *Religious Outsiders and the Making of Americans.* New York: Oxford University Press.
Moorrees, C. F. A., E. A. Fanning, and E. E. Hunt Jr.
1963a Formation and Resorption of Three Deciduous Teeth in Children. *American Journal of Physical Anthropology* 21:205–213.
1963b Age Variation of Formation Stages for Ten Permanent Teeth. *Journal of Dental Research* 42:1490–1502.
Moritz, A. R.
1954 *The Pathology of Trauma.* 2nd ed. Philadelphia: Lea and Febiger.
Morrow, Lynn
1996 Ozark/Ozarks: Establishing a Regional Term. *White River Valley Historical Quarterly* 36(2):4–11.
Morse, Dan F.
1991 On the Possible Origin of the Quapaws in Northeast Arkansas. In *Arkansas before the Americans,* ed. Hester A. Davis, pp. 40–54. Research Series No. 40. Fayetteville: Arkansas Archeological Survey.
Murphy, Robert
1957 Intergroup Hostility and Social Cohesion. *American Anthropologist* 59:1018–1035.
Myers, Robert A.
1997 Cherokee Pioneers in Arkansas: The St. Francis Years, 1785–1813. *Arkansas Historical Quarterly* 56:127–157.
Nisbett, Richard E., and Dov Cohen
1996 *Culture of Honor: The Psychology of Violence in the South.* Boulder, Colo.: Westview Press.
Niswonger, Thomas (ed.)
1992 *Newton County Family History.* Vol. 1. Jasper, Ark.: Newton County Historical Society.
North, Douglass C.
1961 *The Economic Growth of the United States, 1790–1860.* Englewood Cliffs, N.J.: Prentice-Hall.
Novak, Shannon A., and Derinna Kopp
2003 To Feed a Tree in Zion: Osteological Analysis of the 1857 Mountain Meadows Massacre. *Historical Archaeology* 37:85–108.
Novak, Shannon A., and Lars Rodseth
2006 Remembering Mountain Meadows: Collective Violence and the Manipulation of Social Boundaries. *Journal of Anthropological Research* 62:1–25.
Nunis, Doyce B., Jr.
1959 The Enigma of the Sublette Overland Party, 1845. *Pacific Historical Review* 28: 331–349.

Nuttall, Thomas
1821 *A Journal of Travels into the Arkansas Territory, during the Year 1819*. Philadelphia: T. H. Palmer.
O'Brien, Gerald V.
2003 Indigestible Food, Conquering Hordes, and Waste Materials: Metaphors of Immigrants and the Early Immigration Restriction Debate in the United States. *Metaphor and Symbol* 18:33–47.
O'Dea, Thomas F.
1954 Mormonism and the Avoidance of Sectarian Stagnation: A Study of Church, Sect, and Incipient Nationality. *American Journal of Sociology* 60:285–293.
1957 *The Mormons*. Chicago: University of Chicago Press.
Olch, Peter D.
1985 Treading the Elephant's Tail: Medical Problems on the Overland Trails. *Bulletin of the History of Medicine* 59:196–212.
Ortner, Donald J.
1991 Theoretical and Methodological Issues in Paleopathology. In *Human Paleopathology: Current Syntheses and Future Options*, ed. Donald J. Ortner and Arthur C. Aufderheide, pp. 5–11. Washington, D.C.: Smithsonian Institution Press.
2003 *Identification of Pathological Conditions in the Human Skeleton*. 2nd ed. San Diego, Calif.: Academic Press.
Ortner, Donald J., and W. J. G. Putschar
1981 *Identification of Pathological Conditions in Human Skeletal Remains*. Smithsonian Contributions to Anthropology No. 28. Washington D.C.: Smithsonian Institution Press.
Ortner, Sherry B.
1998 The Hidden Life of Class. *Journal of Anthropological Research* 54:1–17.
Otterbein, Keith F.
1996 Feuding. In *The Encyclopedia of Cultural Anthropology*, vol. 2, ed. David Levinson and Melvin Ember, pp. 492–496. New York: Henry Holt.
2000 Five Feuds: An Analysis of Homicides in Eastern Kentucky in the Late Nineteenth Century. *American Anthropologist* 102:231–243.
Otto, John Solomon
1980 Slavery in the Mountains: Yell County, Arkansas, 1840–1860. *Arkansas Historical Quarterly* 39:35–52.
Owsley, Frank Lawrence
1949 *Plain Folk of the Old South*. Baton Rouge: Louisiana State University Press.
Parker, Basil G.
1902 *The Life and Adventures of Basil G. Parker: An Autobiography*. Plano, Calif.: Fred W. Reed.
Parkman, Francis
1947 The Overland Trail Journal. In *The Journals of Francis Parkman*, vol. 2, edited by Mason Wade. New York: Harper.
Parshall, Ardis
2005 "Pursue, retake & punish": The 1857 Santa Clara Ambush. *Utah Historical Quarterly* 73:64–86.

Parsons, Lucena

1983 [1850] The Journal of Lucena Parsons. In *Covered Wagon Women*, vol. 2, ed. Kenneth L. Holmes. Glendale, Calif.: Arthur H. Clark.

Patterson, K. David

1989 Disease Environments of the Antebellum South. In *Science and Medicine in the Old South*, ed. Ronald L. Numbers and Todd L. Savitt, pp. 152–165. Baton Rouge: Louisiana State University Press.

1992 Yellow Fever Epidemics and Mortality in the United States, 1693–1905. *Social Science and Medicine* 34:855–865.

Peavy, Linda, and Ursula Smith

1994 *Women in Waiting in the Westward Movement: Life on the Home Frontier*. Norman: University of Oklahoma Press.

Penrose, Charles W.

1884 *The Mountain Meadows Massacre: Who Were Guilty of the Crime?* Salt Lake City: Juvenile Instructor Office.

Pessen, Edward

1973 *Riches, Class, and Power before the Civil War*. Lexington, Mass.: D. C. Heath.

Phifer, Edward W.

1962 Slavery in a Microcosm: Burke County, North Carolina. *Journal of Southern History* 28:137–165.

Pickard, Madge E., and R. Carlyle Buley

1945 *The Midwest Pioneer: His Ills, Cures, and Doctors*. Crawfordsville, Ind.: R. E. Banta.

Pindborg, J. J.

1970 *Pathology of the Dental Hard Tissue*. Philadelphia: W. B. Saunders.

Porter, Roy (ed.)

1996 *The Cambridge Illustrated History of Medicine*. Cambridge: Cambridge University Press.

Powell, Mary Lucas

1985 The Analysis of Dental Wear and Caries for Dietary Reconstruction. In *Analysis of Prehistoric Diets*, ed. R. I. Gilbert and J. H. Mielke, pp. 307–338. London: Academic Press.

Powell, Mary Lucas, and Della C. Cook (eds.)

2005 *The Myth of Syphilis: The Natural History of Treponematosis in North America*. Gainesville: University of Florida Press.

Pratt, Mary Louise

1992 *Imperial Eyes: Travel Writing and Transculturation*. London: Routledge.

Prince, Major Henry

1859 Ground of the Mountain Meadow Massacre. Mountain Meadows, 17 May. RG 94, Record and Pension File 751395. National Archives, Washington, D.C.

Putnam, Robert D.

1993 *Making Democracy Work: Civic Traditions in Modern Italy*. Princeton, N.J.: Princeton University Press.

2000 *Bowling Alone: The Collapse and Revival of American Community*. New York: Simon and Schuster.

Quinn, Michael D.

1997 *The Mormon Hierarchy: Extensions of Power*. Salt Lake City, Utah: Signature Books.

Rafferty, Milton

2001 *The Ozarks: Land and Life*. 2nd ed. Fayetteville: University of Arkansas Press.

Rainer, Joseph T.

2005 The "Sharper" Image: Yankee Peddlers, Southern Consumers, and the Market Revolution. In *Cultural Change and the Market Revolution in America, 1789–1860*, ed. Scott C. Martin, pp. 89–110. Lanham, Md.: Rowman and Littlefield.

Ramsey, (Denton) Yetive

1991 Fancher, Thomas Washington and Elizabeth (Sneed). In *Carroll County Families: These Were the First*, ed. Jim Lair, p. 189. Berryville, Ark.: Carroll County Historical and Genealogical Society.

Randolph, Vance

1931 *The Ozarks: An American Survival of Primitive Society*. New York:

Rathbun, Ted A., and Richard H. Steckel

2002 The Health of Slaves and Free Blacks in the East. In *The Backbone of History: Health and Nutrition in the Western Hemisphere*, ed. Richard H. Steckel and Jerome C. Rose, pp. 208–225. Cambridge: Cambridge University Press.

Read, Georgia Willis, and Ruth Gaines (eds.)

1949 *Gold Rush: The Journals, Drawings, and Other Papers of J. Goldborough Bruff*. New York: Columbia University Press.

Redfield, H. V.

2000 [1880] *Homicide, North and South*. Columbus: Ohio State University Press.

Reichs, Kathleen J. (ed.)

1998 *Forensic Osteology: Advances in the Identification of Human Remains*. Springfield, Ill.: Charles C. Thomas.

Reid, John Phillip

1997a *Policing the Elephant: Crime, Punishment, and Social Behavior on the Overland Trail*. San Marino, Calif.: Huntington Library.

1997b *Law for the Elephant: Property and Social Behavior on the Overland Trail*. San Marino, Calif.: Huntington Library.

Reiss, Benjamin

2001 *Showman and the Slave: Race, Death, and Memory in Barnum's America*. Cambridge, Mass.: Harvard University Press.

Reynolds, John Hugh (ed.)

1906 Marquette's Reception by the Quapaws, 1673. *Publications of the Arkansas Historical Association* 1:500–502.

Richards, Leonard L.

2007 *The California Gold Rush and the Coming of the Civil War*. New York: Knopf.

Rieck, Richard L.

1991 A Geography of Death on the Oregon-California Trail, 1840–1860. *Overland Journal* 9:13–21.

Roberts, Brian

2000 *American Alchemy: The California Gold Rush and Middle-Class Culture*. Chapel Hill: University of North Carolina Press.

Roberts, Charlotte A., and Jane E. Buikstra

2003 *The Bioarchaeology of Tuberculosis: A Global View on a Reemerging Disease*. Gainesville: University Press of Florida.

Roberts, Charlotte A., Dave Lucy, and Keith Manchester

1994 Inflammatory Lesions of Ribs: An Analysis of the Terry Collection. *American Journal of Physical Anthropology* 95:169–182.

Roberts, Charlotte A., and Keith Manchester

2005 *The Archaeology of Disease*. 3rd ed. Ithaca, N.Y.: Cornell University Press.

Rodseth, Lars, and Shannon A. Novak

2000 Social Modes of Men: An Ecological Model of Male Human Relationships. *Human Nature* 11:335–366.

Rodseth, Lars, and Jennifer Olsen

2000 Mystics against the Market: American Religions and the Autocritique of Capitalism. *Critique of Anthropology* 20:265–288.

Rodseth, Lars, and Richard W. Wrangham

2004 Human Kinship: A Continuation of Politics by Other Means? In *Kinship and Behavior in Primates*, ed. Bernard Chapais and Carol Berman, pp. 389–419. New York: Oxford University Press.

Rogers, W. H.

1860 Statement of Mr. Wm. H. Rogers. *Valley Tam* 2(16), 29 February.

Rose, Jerome C., and Philip Hartnady

1991 Interpretation of Infectious Skeletal Lesions from a Historic Afro-American Cemetery. In *Human Paleopathology: Current Synthesis and Future Options*, ed. Donald J. Ortner and Arthur C. Aufderheide, pp. 119–127. Washington, D.C.: Smithsonian Institution Press.

Rosenberg, Charles E.

1960 The Cause of Cholera: Aspects of Etiological Thought in Nineteenth Century America. *Bulletin of the History of Medicine* 34:331–354.

1986 Introduction to the New Edition. In *Gunn's Domestic Medicine*, 1830. Knoxville: University of Tennessee Press.

1992 *Explaining Epidemics and Other Studies in the History of Medicine*. Cambridge: Cambridge University Press.

1997a Banishing Risk: Continuity and Change in Moral Management of Disease. In *Morality and Health*, ed. Allan M. Brandt and Paul Rozin, pp. 35–51. New York: Routledge.

1997b *No Other Gods: On Science and American Social Thought*. Baltimore: Johns Hopkins University Press.

Rothman, Sheila M.

1995 *Living in the Shadow of Death: Tuberculosis and the Social Experience of Illness in American History*. Baltimore: Johns Hopkins University Press.

Ruff, Christopher B.

1992 Biomechanical Analyses of Archaeological Human Skeletal Samples. In *Skeletal Biology of Past Peoples: Research Methods*, ed. S. R. Saunders and M. A. Katzenberg, pp. 37–58. New York: Wiley-Liss.

2000 Biomechanical Analyses of Archaeological Human Skeletons. In *Biological Anthropology of the Human Skeleton*, ed. M. A. Katzenberg and S. R. Saunders, pp. 71–102. New York: Wiley-Liss.

Rupke, Nicolaas A.

1996 Humboldtian Medicine. *Medical History* 40:193–310.

Rust, Val D.
2004 *Radical Origins: Early Mormon Converts and Their Colonial Ancestors.* Urbana: University of Illinois Press.

Sahlins, Marshall
1972 *Stone Age Economics.* Chicago: Aldine-Atherton.

Said, Edward
1978 *Orientalism.* New York: Pantheon.

Santos, Anna Luisa, and Charlotte A. Roberts
2001 A Picture of Tuberculosis in Young Portuguese People in the Early 20th Century: A Multidisciplinary Study of the Skeletal and Historical Evidence. *American Journal of Physical Anthropology* 115:38–49.

Sauer, Carl O.
1920 *The Geography of the Ozark Highland of Missouri.* Chicago: University of Chicago Press. Reprint. New York: Greenwood Press, 1968.

Saum, Lewis O.
1975 Death in Pre–Civil War America. In *Death in America,* ed. David E. Stannard, pp. 30–48. Philadelphia: University of Pennsylvania Press.
1980 *The Popular Mood of Pre–Civil War America, 1830–1860.* Westport, Conn.: Greenwood Press.

Savitt, Todd L.
1978 *Medicine and Slavery: The Diseases and Health Care of Blacks in Antebellum Virginia.* Urbana: University of Illinois Press.
1997 Black Health on the Plantation: Masters, Slaves, and Physicians. In *Sickness and Health in America: Readings in the History of Medicine and Public Health,* 3rd ed., ed. Judith Walzer Leavitt and Ronald L. Numbers, pp. 354–368. Madison: University of Wisconsin Press.

Schantz, Mark S.
1997 Religious Tracts, Evangelical Reform, and the Market Revolution in Antebellum America. *Journal of the Early Republic* 17:425–466.

Schlissel, Lillian
1992 *Women's Diaries of the Westward Journey.* New York: Schocken Books.

Schneider, David M.
1984 *A Critique of the Study of Kinship.* Ann Arbor: University of Michigan Press.

Schoolcraft, Henry R.
1996 *Rude Pursuits and Rugged Peaks: Schoolcraft's Ozark Journal, 1818–1819.* Edited by Milton D. Rafferty. Fayetteville: University of Arkansas Press. Originally published as *Journal of a Tour into the Interior of Missouri and Arkansaw.* London: Sir Richard Phillips, 1821.

Schweiger, Beth Barton
2004 Max Weber in Mount Airy, or, Revivals and Social Theory in the Early South. In *Religion in the American South: Protestants and Others in History and Culture,* ed. Beth Barton Schweiger and Donald G. Mathews, pp. 31–66. Chapel Hill: University of North Carolina Press.

Scott, Douglas D., P. Willey, and Melissa A. Connor
1998 *They Died with Custer: Soldiers' Bones from the Battle of the Little Bighorn.* Norman: University of Oklahoma Press.

Seefeldt, W. Douglas

2001 Constructing Western Pasts: Place and Public Memory in the Twentieth-Century American West. Ph.D. dissertation, Department of History, Arizona State University.

Sellers, Charles

1991 *The Market Revolution: Jacksonian America, 1815–1846*. New York: Oxford University Press.

Sessions, Gene A.

1982 *Mormon Thunder: A Documentary History of Jedediah Morgan Grant*. Urbana: University of Illinois Press.

Sheehan, Bernard W.

1973 *Seeds of Extinction: Jeffersonian Philanthropy and the American Indian*. Chapel Hill: University of North Carolina Press.

Shryock, Richard H.

1930 Medical Practice in the Old South. *South Atlantic Quarterly* 29:160–178.

Shweder, Richard A., Nancy C. Much, Manamohan Mahapatra, and Lawrence Park

1997 The "Big Three" of Morality (Autonomy, Community, Divinity) and the "Big Three" Explanations of Suffering. In *Morality and Health*, ed. Allan M. Brandt and Paul Rozin, pp. 119–169. New York: Routledge.

Sledzik, Paul S., and Peer H. Moore-Jansen

1991 Dental Disease in 19th Century Military Skeletal Samples. In *Advances in Dental Anthropology*, ed. C. Larsen and M. Kelley, pp. 215–224. New York: Wiley-Liss.

Slotkin, Richard

1985 *The Fatal Environment: The Myth of the Frontier in the Age of Industrialization, 1800–1890*. New York: Atheneum.

Smith, Anthony D.

2003 *Chosen Peoples: Sacred Sources of National Identity*. Oxford: Oxford University Press.

Smith, Chris

2000 The Dilemma of Blame. *Salt Lake Tribune*, 14 March, p. A1.

Smith-Rosenberg, Carroll

1978 The Female World of Love and Ritual: Relations between Women in Nineteenth-Century America. In *The American Family in Social-Historical Perspective*, ed. Michael Gordon, pp. 334–358. New York: St. Martin's Press.

1979 Beauty, the Beast, and the Militant Woman: A Case Study in Sex Roles and Social Stress in Jacksonian America. In *A Heritage of Her Own*, ed. Nancy F. Cott and Elizabeth H. Pleck, pp. 197–221. New York: Simon and Schuster.

1985 *Disorderly Conduct: Visions of Gender in Victorian America*. New York: Oxford University Press.

Sofaer, Joanna R.

2006 *The Body as Material Culture: A Theoretical Osteoarchaeology*. Cambridge: Cambridge University Press.

Stanley, Amy Dru

1996 Home Life and the Morality of the Market. In *The Market Revolution in America: Social, Political, and Religious Expressions, 1800–1860*, ed. Melvyn Stokes and Stephen Conway, pp. 74–96. Charlottesville: University Press of Virginia.

Stansbury, Howard

1853 *Exploration and Survey of the Valley of the Great Salt Lake of Utah*. Washington, D.C.

Stanton, W.

1960 *The Leopard's Spots: Scientific Attitudes towards Race in America, 1815–1859*. Chicago: University of Chicago Press.

Steckel, Richard H.

1988 The Health and Mortality of Women and Children, 1850–1860. *Journal of Economic History* 48:333–345.

1995 Stature and the Standard of Living. *Journal of Economic Literature* 33:1904–1940.

Steckel, Richard H., and Jerome C. Rose

2002 Conclusion. In *The Backbone of History: Health and Nutrition in the Western Hemisphere*, ed. Richard H. Steckel and Jerome C. Rose, pp. 583–589. Cambridge: Cambridge University Press.

Steinbock, R. T.

1976 *Paleopathological Diagnosis and Interpretation: Bone Diseases in Ancient Human Populations*. Springfield, Ill.: Charles C. Thomas.

Stenhouse, Mrs. T. B. H. [Fanny]

1873 *"Tell It All": The Story of a Life's Experience in Mormonism, an Autobiography*. Hartford, Conn.: A. D. Worthington.

Stephan, Scott M.

2001 Faith and Family in the Old South. Ph.D. dissertation, Indiana University.

Stern, Julia

2003 The Politics of Tears: Death in the Early American Novel. In *Mortal Remains: Death in Early America*, ed. Nancy Isenberg and Andrew Burstein, pp. 108–119. Philadelphia: University of Pennsylvania Press.

Stiles, Charles W.

1903 *Report upon the Prevalence and Geographic Distribution of Hookworm Disease (Uncinariasis* or *Ancylostomiasis) in the United States*. Bulletin No. 10. Hygienic Laboratory, Public Health and Marine Hospital Service of the United States, Treasury Department. Washington, D.C.: U.S. Government Printing Office.

Stocking, George W., Jr.

1968 *Race, Culture, and Evolution: Essays in the History of Anthropology*. Chicago: University of Chicago Press.

1987 *Victorian Anthropology*. New York: Free Press.

Stocks, Hugh

n.d. *The Book of Mormon, 1830–1879: A Publishing History*. Draper, Utah: Greg Kofford Books.

Stowe, Steven M.

2004 *Doctoring the South: Southern Physicians and Everyday Medicine in the Mid-Nineteenth Century*. Chapel Hill: University of North Carolina Press.

Sutter, Richard C.

1995 Dental Pathologies among Inmates of the Monroe County Poorhouse. In

Bodies of Evidence: Reconstructing History through Skeletal Analysis, ed. Anne L. Grauer, pp. 37–48. New York: Wiley-Liss.

Tabbert, Mark A.

2005 *American Freemasonry: Three Centuries of Building Communities*. Lexington, Mass.: National Heritage Museum.

Tanner, Jerald, and Sandra Tanner

1987 [1964] *Mormonism: Shadow or Reality?* Salt Lake City: Utah Lighthouse Ministry.

Taylor, Orville W.

1958 *Negro Slavery in Arkansas*. Durham, N.C.: Duke University Press.

Temple, William Bedford

1850a Letter dated 11 May to wife and children. Mss #1508, File: Temple 1850 Letter. Oregon Historical Society. Transcribed by Will Bagley, 21 July 2004.

1850b Letter dated 2 June to Wife and little ones. Mss #1508, File: Temple 1850 Letter. Oregon Historical Society. Transcribed by Will Bagley, 21 July 2004.

Terry, Elizabeth Baker

1938 Memoir. In "Survivor of a Massacre: Mrs. Betty Terry of Harrison Vividly Recalls Massacre of Westbound Arkansas Caravan in Utah More Than 80 Years Ago," by Clyde R. Greenshaw. *Arkansas Gazette*, 4 September, Sunday Magazine Section, p. 6.

Thoden van Velzen, H. U. E., and W. van Wetering

1960 Residence, Power Groups, and Intra-societal Aggression. *International Archives of Ethnography* 49:169–200.

Thompson, Kenneth

1976 Wilderness and Health in the Nineteenth Century. *Journal of Historical Geography* 2:145–161.

Thornton, Mark

1995 Alcohol Consumption and the Standard of Living in Antebellum America. *Atlantic Economic Journal* 23:156.

Thurston, Malinda Cameron Scott

1877 Depositions in support of H.R. 3945, 18 December 1877. Record Group 123, Indian Depredation Claim 8479, Thurston v. the United States and the Ute Indians. National Archives.

1911 Malinda Thurston, Joel Scott, George T. Scott, Statements, 2 May 1911. Record Group 123, Indian Depredation Claim 8479, Thurston v. the United States and the Ute Indians. National Archives.

Tigner-Wise, Lori F.

1989 Skeletal Analysis of a Mormon Pioneer Population from Salt Lake Valley, Utah. Master's thesis, University of Wyoming, Laramie.

Topping, Gary

1999 Overland Emigration, the California Trail, and the Hastings Cutoff. In *Excavation of the Donner-Reed Wagons: Historic Archaeology along the Hastings Cutoff*, ed. B. R. Hawkins and D. B. Madsen, pp. 9–29. Salt Lake City: University of Utah Press.

Trouillot, Michel-Rolph

1995 *Silencing the Past: Power and the Production of History*. Boston: Beacon Press.

Unruh, John D., Jr.
1979 *The Plains Across: The Overland Emigrants and the Trans-Mississippi West, 1840–1860*. Urbana: University of Illinois Press.
U.S. Congress
1830 Richard H. Wilde of Georgia, 19 May. *Congressional Debates*. 21st Cong., 1st sess., p. 1083. Washington, D.C.
Valenčius, Conevery Bolton
2002 *The Health of the Country: How American Settlers Understood Themselves and Their Land*. New York: Basic Books.
Veblen, Thorstein
1899 *The Theory of the Leisure Class: An Economic Study of Institutions*. New York: Vanguard.
Verdery, Katherine
1999 *The Political Lives of Dead Bodies: Reburial and Postsocialist Change*. New York: Columbia University Press.
Walker, Margaret F.
1998 A Woman's Work Is Never Done: or, the Dirt on Men and Their Laundry. *Overland Journal* 16:4–13.
Walker, Ronald W., Richard E. Turley Jr., and Glen M. Leonard
2008 *Massacre at Mountain Meadows*. New York: Oxford University Press.
Wallace, Anthony F. C.
1956 Revitalization Movements. *American Anthropologist* 58:264–281.
Waller, Altina L.
1988 *Feud: Hatfields, McCoys, and Social Change in Appalachia, 1860–1900*. Chapel Hill: University of North Carolina Press.
Walz, Robert Bradshaw
1958 Migration into Arkansas, 1834–1880. Ph.D. dissertation, University of Texas.
Wapler, U., E. Crubézy, and M. Schultz
2004 Is Cribra Orbitalia Synonymous with Anemia? Analysis and Interpretation of Cranial Pathology in Sudan. *American Journal of Physical Anthropology* 123: 333–339.
Warner, John Harley
1989 The Idea of Southern Medical Distinctiveness: Medical Knowledge and Practice in the Old South. In *Science and Medicine in the Old South*, ed. Ronald L. Numbers and Todd L. Savitt, pp. 179–205. Baton Rouge: Louisiana State University Press.
1997 From Specificity to Universalism in Medical Therapeutics: Transformation in the 19th-Century United States. In Sickness *and Health in America: Readings in the History of Medicine and Public Health*, ed. Judith Walzer Leavitt and Ronald L. Numbers, pp. 87–101. Madison: University of Wisconsin Press.
Washburn, Cephas
1869 *Reminiscences of the Indians*. Richmond, Va.: Presbyterian Committee of Publication. Reprint. New York: Johnson Reprint Corp., 1971.
Watts, Sheldon
1999 *Epidemics and History: Disease, Power, and Imperialism*. New Haven, Conn.: Yale University Press.

Webb, James

2004 *Born Fighting: How the Scots-Irish Shaped America.* New York: Broadway Books.

Webster, Noah

1799 *A Brief History of Epidemic and Pestilential Disease.* 2 vols. Hartford, Conn.: Hudson and Goodwin.

Wells, Jonathan Daniel

2004 *The Origins of the Southern Middle Class, 1800–1860.* Chapel Hill: University of North Carolina Press.

Wells, Robert V.

2000 *Facing the "King of Terrors": Death and Society in an American Community, 1750–1990.* Cambridge: Cambridge University Press.

West, Elliott

1989 *Growing Up with the Country: Childhood on the Far Western Frontier.* Albuquerque: University of New Mexico Press.

Whayne, Jeannie M.

2002 The Turbulent Path to Statehood: Arkansas Territory, 1803–1836. In *Arkansas: A Narrative History,* ed. Jeannie M. Whayne, Thomas A. DeBlack, George Sabo III, and Morris S. Arnold, pp. 75–108. Fayetteville: University of Arkansas Press.

2005 A Shifting Middle Ground: Arkansas's Frontier Exchange Economy and the Louisiana Purchase. In *A Whole Country in Commotion: The Louisiana Purchase and the American Southwest,* ed. Patrick G. Williams, S. Charles Bolton, and Jeannie M. Whayne, pp. 59–75. Fayetteville: University of Arkansas Press.

Whitney, Orson F.

1892 *History of Utah.* Salt Lake City: George Q. Cannon and Sons.

Willey, P., and Douglas D. Scott

1991 "The bullets buzzed like bees": Gunshot Wounds in Skeletons from the Battle of the Little Bighorn. *International Journal of Osteoarchaeology* 6:15–27.

Williams, D. Fred

1980 The Bear State Image: Arkansas in the Nineteenth Century. *Arkansas Historical Quarterly* 39(2):99–111.

Williams, John Alexander

2002 *Appalachia: A History.* Chapel Hill: University of North Carolina Press.

Wilson, John S.

1860 Health Department. *Godey's Lady's Book,* February.

Wilson, Peter J.

1988 *The Domestication of the Human Species.* New Haven, Conn.: Yale University Press.

Wise, William

1976 *Massacre at Mountain meadows: An American Legend and a Monumental Crime.* 2nd ed. New York: Thomas Crowell.

Wolf, Eric R.

1982 *Europe and the People without History.* Berkeley: University of California Press.

Wood, Charles L.

2004 *The Mormon Conspiracy.* Chula Vista, Calif.: Black Forest Books.

Wood, J. W., G. R. Milner, H. C. Harpending, and K. M. Weiss
1992 The Osteological Paradox: Problems of Inferring Prehistoric Health from Skeletal Samples. *Current Anthropology* 33:343–358.
Worley, Ted R. (ed.)
1952 Letters from an Early Settler. *Arkansas Historical Quarterly* 11:327–329.
Wray, Matt
2006 *Not Quite White: White Trash and the Boundaries of Whiteness*. Durham, N.C.: Duke University Press.
Wright, Lori E., and Cassady J. Yoder
2003 Recent Progress in Bioarchaeology: Approaches to the Osteological Paradox. *Journal of Archaeological Research* 11:43–70.
Wyatt, William N.
1930 *Wyatt's Travel Diary, 1836*. Chicago: privately printed.
Wyatt-Brown, Bertram
1982 *Southern Honor: Ethics and Behavior in the Old South*. New York: Oxford University Press.
The Shaping of Southern Culture: Honor, Grace, and War, 1760s–1880s. Chapel Hill: University of North Carolina Press.
Yasuba, Yasukichi
1962 *Birth Rates of the White Population of the United States, 1800–1860: An Economic Study*. Baltimore: Johns Hopkins University Press.

INDEX